Four Girls at
Cottage City

THE SCHOMBURG LIBRARY OF
NINETEENTH-CENTURY BLACK WOMEN WRITERS

General Editor, Henry Louis Gates, Jr.

Titles are listed chronologically; collections that include works published over a span of years are listed according to the publication date of their initial work.

Four Girls at Cottage City

EMMA D. KELLEY-HAWKINS

With an Introduction by
DEBORAH E. McDOWELL

❧ ❧ ❧

❧ ❧ ❧

OXFORD UNIVERSITY PRESS
New York   Oxford

Oxford University Press

Oxford   New York   Toronto
Delhi   Bombay   Calcutta   Madras   Karachi
Petaling Jaya   Singapore   Hong Kong   Tokyo
Nairobi   Dar es Salaam   Cape Town
Melbourne   Auckland

and associated companies in
Berlin   Ibadan

Library of Congress Cataloging-in-Publication Data

Kelley, Emma Dunham.
Four girls at Cottage City/Emma Dunham Kelley; with an
introduction by Deborah E. McDowell.
p. cm.—(The Schomburg library of nineteenth-century black
women writers)
I. Title.   II. Series.
PS2159.K13F6   1988   813'.4—dc19   87-21470
ISBN 0-19-505242-0
ISBN 0-19-505267-6 (set)
ISBN 0-19-506787-8 (PBK.)

2 4 6 8 10 9 7 5 3 1

Printed in the United States of America

The
Schomburg Library
of
Nineteenth-Century
Black Women Writers
is
Dedicated
in Memory
of
PAULINE AUGUSTA COLEMAN GATES

1916–1987

PUBLISHER'S NOTE

FOREWORD
In Her Own Write

Henry Louis Gates, Jr.

One muffled strain in the Silent South, a jarring chord and a
vague and uncomprehended cadenza has been and still is the
Negro. And of that muffled chord, the one mute and voiceless note has been the sadly expectant Black Woman, ...

The "other side" has not been represented by one who "lives
there." And not many can more sensibly realize and more
accurately tell the weight and the fret of the "long dull pain"
than the open-eyed but hitherto voiceless Black Woman of
America.

. . . as our Caucasian barristers are not to blame if they
cannot *quite* put themselves in the dark man's place, neither
should the dark man be wholly expected fully and adequately
to reproduce the exact Voice of the Black Woman.

——ANNA JULIA COOPER, *A Voice From the South* (1892)

The birth of the Afro-American literary tradition occurred
in 1773, when Phillis Wheatley published a book of poetry.
Despite the fact that her book garnered for her a remarkable
amount of attention, Wheatley's journey to the printer had
been a most arduous one. Sometime in 1772, a young African girl walked demurely into a room in Boston to undergo
an oral examination, the results of which would determine
the direction of her life and work. Perhaps she was shocked
upon entering the appointed room. For there, perhaps gath-

ered in a semicircle, sat eighteen of Boston's most notable citizens. Among them were John Erving, a prominent Boston merchant; the Reverend Charles Chauncy, pastor of the Tenth Congregational Church; and John Hancock, who would later gain fame for his signature on the Declaration of Independence. At the center of this group was His Excellency, Thomas Hutchinson, governor of Massachusetts, with Andrew Oliver, his lieutenant governor, close by his side.

Why had this august group been assembled? Why had it seen fit to summon this young African girl, scarcely eighteen years old, before it? This group of "the most respectable Characters in *Boston*," as it would later define itself, had assembled to question closely the African adolescent on the slender sheaf of poems that she claimed to have "written by herself." We can only speculate on the nature of the questions posed to the fledgling poet. Perhaps they asked her to identify and explain—for all to hear—exactly who were the Greek and Latin gods and poets alluded to so frequently in her work. Perhaps they asked her to conjugate a verb in Latin or even to translate randomly selected passages from the Latin, which she and her master, John Wheatley, claimed that she "had made some Progress in." Or perhaps they asked her to recite from memory key passages from the texts of John Milton and Alexander Pope, the two poets by whom the African claimed to be most directly influenced. We do not know.

We do know, however, that the African poet's responses were more than sufficient to prompt the eighteen august gentlemen to compose, sign, and publish a two-paragraph "Attestation," an open letter "To the Publick" that prefaces Phillis Wheatley's book and that reads in part:

> We whose Names are under-written, do assure the World, that the Poems specified in the following Page, were (as we

verily believe) written by Phillis, a young Negro Girl, who was but a few Years since, brought an uncultivated Barbarian from *Africa*, and has ever since been, and now is, under the Disadvantage of serving as a Slave in a Family in this Town. She has been examined by some of the best Judges, and is thought qualified to write them.

So important was this document in securing a publisher for Wheatley's poems that it forms the signal element in the prefatory matter preceding her *Poems on Various Subjects, Religious and Moral*, published in London in 1773.

Without the published "Attestation," Wheatley's publisher claimed, few would believe that an African could possibly have written poetry all by herself. As the eighteen put the matter clearly in their letter, "Numbers would be ready to suspect they were not really the Writings of Phillis." Wheatley and her master, John Wheatley, had attempted to publish a similar volume in 1772 in Boston, but Boston publishers had been incredulous. One year later, "Attestation" in hand, Phillis Wheatley and her master's son, Nathaniel Wheatley, sailed for England, where they completed arrangements for the publication of a volume of her poems with the aid of the Countess of Huntington and the Earl of Dartmouth.

This curious anecdote, surely one of the oddest oral examinations on record, is only a tiny part of a larger, and even more curious, episode in the Enlightenment. Since the beginning of the sixteenth century, Europeans had wondered aloud whether or not the African "species of men," as they were most commonly called, *could* ever create formal literature, could ever master "the arts and sciences." If they could, the argument ran, then the African variety of humanity was fundamentally related to the European variety. If not, then it seemed clear that the African was destined by nature to be a slave. This was the burden shouldered by Phillis Wheatley when she successfully defended herself and the authorship of her book against counterclaims and doubts.

Indeed, with her successful defense, Wheatley launched two traditions at once—the black American literary tradition *and* the black woman's literary tradition. If it is extraordinary that not just one but both of these traditions were founded simultaneously by a black woman—certainly an event unique in the history of literature—it is also ironic that this important fact of common, coterminous literary origins seems to have escaped most scholars.

That the progenitor of the black literary tradition was a woman means, in the most strictly literal sense, that all subsequent black writers have evolved in a matrilinear line of descent, and that each, consciously or unconsciously, has extended and revised a canon whose foundation was the poetry of a black woman. Early black writers seem to have been keenly aware of Wheatley's founding role, even if most of her white reviewers were more concerned with the implications of her race than her gender. Jupiter Hammon, for example, whose 1760 broadside "An Evening Thought. Salvation by Christ, With Penitential Cries" was the first individual poem published by a black American, acknowledged Wheatley's influence by selecting her as the subject of his second broadside, "An Address to Miss Phillis Wheatly [*sic*], Ethiopian Poetess, in Boston," which was published at Hartford in 1778. And George Moses Horton, the second Afro-American to publish a book of poetry in English (1829), brought out in 1838 an edition of his *Poems By A Slave* bound together with Wheatley's work. Indeed, for fifty-six years, between 1773 and 1829, when Horton published *The Hope of Liberty*, Wheatley was the *only* black person to have published a book of imaginative literature in English. So central was this black woman's role in the shaping of the Afro-American literary tradition that, as one historian has maintained, the history of the reception of Phillis Wheatley's poetry *is* the history of Afro-American literary criticism. Well into the nineteenth century, Wheatley and the black literary tradition were the same entity.

But Wheatley is not the only black woman writer who stands as a pioneering figure in Afro-American literature. Just as Wheatley gave birth to the genre of black poetry, Ann Plato was the first Afro-American to publish a book of essays (1841) and Harriet E. Wilson was the first black person to publish a novel in the United States (1859).

Despite this pioneering role of black women in the tradition, however, many of their contributions before this century have been all but lost or unrecognized. As Hortense Spillers observed as recently as 1983,

> With the exception of a handful of autobiographical narratives from the nineteenth century, the black woman's realities are virtually suppressed until the period of the Harlem Renaissance and later. Essentially the black woman as artist, as intellectual spokesperson for her own cultural apprenticeship, has not existed before, for anyone. At the source of [their] own symbol-making task, [the community of black women writers] confronts, therefore, a tradition of work that is quite recent, its continuities, broken and sporadic.

Until now, it has been extraordinarily difficult to establish the formal connections between early black women's writing and that of the present, precisely because our knowledge of their work has been broken and sporadic. Phillis Wheatley, for example, while certainly the most reprinted and discussed poet in the tradition, is also one of the least understood. Ann Plato's seminal work, *Essays* (which includes biographies and poems), has not been reprinted since it was published a cen-

tury and a half ago. And Harriet Wilson's *Our Nig,* her
compelling novel of a black woman's expanding consciousness in a racist Northern antebellum environment, never received even *one* review or comment at a time when virtually
all works written by black people were heralded by abolition-
ists as salient arguments against the existence of human slavery. Many of the books reprinted in this set experienced a
similar fate, the most dreadful fate for an author: that of
being ignored then relegated to the obscurity of the rare book
section of a university library. We can only wonder how
many other texts in the black woman's tradition have been
lost to this generation of readers or remain unclassified or
uncatalogued and, hence, unread.

This was not always so, however. Black women writers
dominated the final decade of the nineteenth century, perhaps
spurred to publish by an 1886 essay entitled "The Coming
American Novelist," which was published in *Lippincott's
Monthly Magazine* and written by "A Lady From Philadel-
phia." This pseudonymous essay argued that the "Great
American Novel" would be written by a black person. Her
argument is so curious that it deserves to be repeated:

> When we come to formulate our demands of the Coming
> American Novelist, we will agree that he must be native-
> born. His ancestors may come from where they will, but we
> must give him a birthplace and have the raising of him. Still,
> the longer his family has been here the better he will represent
> us. Suppose he should have no country but ours, no traditions
> but those he has learned here, no longings apart from us, no
> future except in our future—the orphan of the world, he
> finds with us his home. And with all this, suppose he refuses
> to be fused into that grand conglomerate we call the "Amer-
> ican type." With us, he is not of us. He is original, he has
> humor, he is tender, he is passive and fiery, he has been

taught what we call justice, and he has his own opinion about it. He has suffered everything a poet, a dramatist, a novelist need suffer before he comes to have his lips anointed. And with it all he is in one sense a spectator, a little out of the race. How would these conditions go towards forming an original development? In a word, suppose the coming novelist is of African origin? When one comes to consider the subject, there is no improbability in it. One thing is certain,—our great novel will not be written by the typical American.

An atypical American, indeed. Not only would the great American novel be written by an African-American, it would be written by an African-American *woman:*

Yet farther: I have used the generic masculine pronoun because it is convenient; but Fate keeps revenge in store. It was a woman who, taking the wrongs of the African as her theme, wrote the novel that awakened the world to their reality, and why should not the coming novelist be a woman as well as an African? She—the woman of that race—has some claims on Fate which are not yet paid up.

It is these claims on fate that we seek to pay by publishing The Schomburg Library of Nineteenth-Century Black Women Writers.

This theme would be repeated by several black women authors, most notably by Anna Julia Cooper, a prototypical black feminist whose 1892 *A Voice From the South* can be considered to be one of the original texts of the black feminist movement. It was Cooper who first analyzed the fallacy of referring to "the Black man" when speaking of black people and who argued that just as white men cannot speak through the consciousness of black men, neither can black *men* "fully and adequately . . . reproduce the exact Voice of the Black Woman." Gender and race, she argues, cannot be conflated, except in the instance of a black woman's voice, and it is this voice which must be uttered and to which we must listen. As Cooper puts the matter so compellingly:

> It is not the intelligent woman vs. the ignorant woman; nor the white woman vs. the black, the brown, and the red,—it is not even the cause of woman vs. man. Nay, 'tis woman's strongest vindication for speaking that *the world needs to hear her voice*. It would be subversive of every human interest that the cry of one-half the human family be stifled. Woman in stepping from the pedestal of statue-like inactivity in the domestic shrine, and daring to think and move and speak,— to undertake to help shape, mold, and direct the thought of her age, is merely completing the circle of the world's vision. Hers is every interest that has lacked an interpreter and a defender. Her cause is linked with that of every agony that has been dumb—every wrong that needs a voice.
>
> It is no fault of man's that he has not been able to see truth from her standpoint. It does credit both to his head and heart that no greater mistakes have been committed or even wrongs perpetrated while she sat making tatting and snipping paper flowers. Man's own innate chivalry and the mutual interdependence of their interests have insured his treating her cause, in the main at least, as his own. And he is pardonably surprised and even a little chagrined, perhaps, to find his legislation not considered "perfectly lovely" in every respect. But in any case his work is only impoverished by her remaining dumb. The world has had to limp along with the wobbling gait and one-sided hesitancy of a man with one eye. Suddenly the bandage is removed from the other eye and the whole body is filled with light. It sees a circle where before it saw a segment. The darkened eye restored, every member rejoices with it.

The myopic sight of the darkened eye can only be restored when the full range of the black woman's voice, with its own special timbres and shadings, remains mute no longer.

Similarly, Victoria Earle Matthews, an author of short
stories and essays, and a cofounder in 1896 of the National
Association of Colored Women, wrote in her stunning essay,
"The Value of Race Literature" (1895), that "when the literature of our race is developed, it will of necessity be different in all essential points of greatness, true heroism and
real Christianity from what we may at the present time, for
convenience, call American literature." Matthews argued that
this great tradition of Afro-American literature would be the
textual outlet "for the unnaturally suppressed inner lives which
our people have been compelled to lead." Once these "unnaturally suppressed inner lives" of black people are un-
veiled, no "grander diffusion of mental light" will shine more
brightly, she concludes, than that of the articulate Afro-
American woman:

And now comes the question, What part shall we women play
in the Race Literature of the future? . . . within the compass
of one small journal ["Woman's Era"] we have struck out a
new line of departure—a journal, a record of Race interests
gathered from all parts of the United States, carefully selected,
moistened, winnowed and garnered by the ablest intellects of
educated colored women, shrinking at no lofty theme, shirk-
ing no serious duty, aiming at every possible excellence, and
determined to do their part in the future uplifting of the
race.

If twenty women, by their concentrated efforts in one
literary movement, can meet with such success as has engen-
dered, planned out, and so successfully consummated this
convention, what much more glorious results, what wider
spread success, what grander diffusion of mental light will
not come forth at the bidding of the enlarged hosts of women
writers, already called into being by the stimulus of your
efforts?

And here let me speak one word for my journalistic sisters

who have already entered the broad arena of journalism. Before the "Woman's Era" had come into existence, no one except themselves can appreciate the bitter experience and sore disappointments under which they have at all times been compelled to pursue their chosen vocations.

If their brothers of the press have had their difficulties to contend with, I am here as a sister journalist to state, from the fullness of knowledge, that their task has been an easy one compared with that of the colored woman in journalism.

Woman's part in Race Literature, as in Race building, is the most important part and has been so in all ages. . . . All through the most remote epochs she has done her share in literature. . . .

One of the most important aspects of this set is the republication of the salient texts from 1890 to 1910, which literary historians could well call "The Black Woman's Era." In addition to Mary Helen Washington's definitive edition of Cooper's *A Voice From the South*, we have reprinted two novels by Amelia Johnson, Frances Harper's *Iola Leroy*, two novels by Emma Dunham Kelley, Alice Dunbar-Nelson's two impressive collections of short stories, and Pauline Hopkins's three serialized novels as well as her monumental novel, *Contending Forces*—all published between 1890 and 1910. Indeed, black women published more works of fiction in these two decades than black men had published in the previous half century. Nevertheless, this great achievement has been ignored.

Moreover, the writings of nineteenth-century Afro-American women in general have remained buried in obscurity, accessible only in research libraries or in overpriced and poorly edited reprints. Many of these books have never been reprinted at all; in some instances only one or two copies are extant. In these works of fiction, poetry, autobiography, biography, essays, and journalism resides the mind of the nineteenth-century Afro-American woman. Until these works are made readily available to teachers and their students, a significant segment of the black tradition will remain silent.

Oxford University Press, in collaboration with the Schomburg Center for Research in Black Culture, is publishing thirty volumes of these compelling works, each of which contains an introduction by an expert in the field. The set includes such rare texts as Johnson's *The Hazeley Family* and *Clarence and Corinne*, Plato's *Essays*, the most complete edition of Phillis Wheatley's poems and letters, Emma Dunham Kelley's pioneering novel *Megda*, several previously unpublished stories and a novel by Alice Dunbar-Nelson, and the first collected volumes of Pauline Hopkins's three serialized novels and Frances Harper's poetry. We also present four volumes of poetry by such women as Mary Eliza Tucker Lambert, Adah Menken, Josephine Heard, and Maggie Johnson. Numerous slave and spiritual narratives, a newly discovered novel—*Four Girls at Cottage City*—by Emma Dunham Kelley (-Hawkins), and the first American edition of *Wonderful Adventures of Mrs. Seacole in Many Lands* are also among the texts included.

In addition to resurrecting the works of black women authors, it is our hope that this set will facilitate the resurrection of the Afro-American woman's literary tradition itself by unearthing its nineteenth-century roots. In the works of Nella Larsen and Jessie Fauset, Zora Neale Hurston and Ann Petry, Lorraine Hansberry and Gwendolyn Brooks, Paule Marshall and Toni Cade Bambara, Audre Lorde and Rita Dove, Toni Morrison and Alice Walker, Gloria Naylor and Jamaica Kincaid, these roots have branched luxuriantly. The eighteenth- and nineteenth-century authors whose works are presented in this set founded and nurtured the black women's literary tradition, which must be revived, explicated, analyzed, and debated before we can understand more completely the formal shaping of this tradition within a tradition, a coded literary universe through which, regrettably, we are only just beginning to navigate our way. As Anna Cooper said nearly one hundred years ago, we have been blinded by the loss of sight in one eye and have therefore been unable to detect the full *shape* of the Afro-American literary tradition.

Literary works configure into a tradition not because of some mystical collective unconscious determined by the biology of race or gender, but because writers read other writers and *ground* their representations of experience in models of language provided largely by other writers to whom they feel akin. It is through this mode of literary revision, amply evident in the *texts* themselves—in formal echoes, recast metaphors, even in parody—that a "tradition" emerges and defines itself.

This is formal bonding, and it is only through formal bonding that we can know a literary tradition. The collective publication of these works by black women now, for the first time, makes it possible for scholars and critics, male and female, black and white, to *demonstrate* that black women writers read, and revised, other black women writers. To demonstrate this set of formal literary relations is to demonstrate that sexuality, race, and gender are both the condition and the basis of *tradition*—but tradition as found in discrete acts of language use.

A word is in order about the history of this set. For the past decade, I have taught a course, first at Yale and then at Cornell, entitled "Black Women and Their Fictions," a course that I inherited from Toni Morrison, who developed it in the mid-1970s for Yale's Program in Afro-American Studies. Although the course was inspired by the remarkable accomplishments of black women novelists since 1970, I gradually extended its beginning date to the late nineteenth century, studying Frances Harper's *Iola Leroy* and Anna Julia Cooper's *A Voice From the South,* both published in 1892. With the discovery of Harriet E. Wilson's seminal novel, *Our Nig* (1859), and Jean Yellin's authentication of Harriet Jacobs's brilliant slave narrative, *Incidents in the Life of a Slave Girl* (1861), a survey course spanning over a century and a quarter emerged.

But the discovery of *Our Nig,* as well as the interest in nineteenth-century black women's writing that this discovery generated, convinced me that even the most curious and diligent scholars knew very little of the extensive history of the creative writings of Afro-American women before 1900. Indeed, most scholars of Afro-American literature had never even read most of the books published by black women, simply because these books—of poetry, novels, short stories, essays, and autobiography—were mostly accessible only in rare book sections of university libraries. For reasons unclear to me even today, few of these marvelous renderings of the Afro-American woman's consciousness were reprinted in the late 1960s and early 1970s, when so many other texts of the Afro-American literary tradition were resurrected from the dark and silent graveyard of the out-of-print and were reissued in facsimile editions aimed at the hungry readership for canonical texts in the nascent field of black studies.

So, with the help of several superb research assistants—including David Curtis, Nicola Shilliam, Wendy Jones, Sam Otter, Janadas Devan, Suvir Kaul, Cynthia Bond, Elizabeth Alexander, and Adele Alexander—and with the expert advice of scholars such as William Robinson, William Andrews, Mary Helen Washington, Maryemma Graham, Jean Yellin, Houston A. Baker, Jr., Richard Yarborough, Hazel Carby, Joan R. Sherman, Frances Foster, and William French, dozens of bibliographies were used to compile a list of books written or narrated by black women mostly before 1910. Without the assistance provided through this shared experience of scholarship, the scholar's true legacy, this project could not have been conceived. As the list grew, I was struck by how very many of these titles that I, for example, had never even heard of, let alone read, such as Ann Plato's *Essays,* Louisa Picquet's slave narrative, or Amelia Johnson's two novels, *Clarence and Corinne* and *The Hazeley Family.* Through our research with the Black Periodical Fiction and Poetry Project (funded by NEH and the Ford Foundation), I also realized that several novels by black women, including three works of fiction by Pauline Hopkins, had been serialized in black periodicals, but had never been collected and published as books. Nor had the several books of poetry published by black women, such as the prolific Frances E. W. Harper, been collected and edited. When I discovered still another "lost" novel by an Afro-American woman (*Four Girls at Cottage City,* published in 1898 by Emma Dunham Kelley-Hawkins), I decided to attempt to edit a collection of reprints of these works and to publish them as a "library" of black women's writings, in part so that I could read them myself.

Convincing university and trade publishers to undertake this project proved to be a difficult task. Despite the commercial success of *Our Nig* and of the several reprint series of women's works (such as Virago, the Beacon Black Women Writers Series, and Rutgers' American Women Writers Series), several presses rejected the project as "too large," "too limited," or as "commercially unviable." Only two publishers recognized the viability and the import of the project and, of these, Oxford's commitment to publish the titles simultaneously as a set made the press's offer irresistible.

While attempting to locate original copies of these exceedingly rare books, I discovered that most of the texts were housed at the Schomburg Center for Research in Black Culture, a branch of The New York Public Library, under the direction of Howard Dodson. Dodson's infectious enthusiasm for the project and his generous collaboration, as well as that of his stellar staff (especially Diana Lachatanere, Sharon Howard, Ellis Haizip, Richard Newman, and Betty Gubert), led to a joint publishing initiative that produced this set as part of the Schomburg's major fund-raising campaign. Without Dodson's foresight and generosity of spirit, the set would not have materialized. Without William P. Sisler's masterful editorship at Oxford and his staff's careful attention to detail, the set would have remained just another grand idea that tends to languish in a scholar's file cabinet.

I would also like to thank Dr. Michael Winston and Dr. Thomas C. Battle, Vice-President of Academic Affairs and the Director of the Moorland-Spingarn Research Center (respectively) at Howard University, for their unending encouragement, support, and collaboration in this project, and Esme E. Bhan at Howard for her meticulous research and bibliographical skills. In addition, I would like to acknowledge the aid of the staff at the libraries of Duke University, Cornell University (especially Tom Weissinger and Donald Eddy), the Boston Public Library, the Western Reserve Historical Society, the Library of Congress, and Yale University. Linda Robbins, Marion Osmun, Sarah Flanagan, and Gerard Case, all members of the staff at Oxford, were extraordinarily effective at coordinating, editing, and producing the various segments of each text in the set. Candy Ruck, Nina de Tar, and Phillis Molock expertly typed reams of correspondence and manuscripts connected to the project.

I would also like to express my gratitude to my colleagues who edited and introduced the individual titles in the set. Without their attention to detail, their willingness to meet strict deadlines, and their sheer enthusiasm for this project, the set could not have been published. But finally and ultimately, I would hope that the publication of the set would help to generate even more scholarly interest in the black women authors whose work is presented here. Struggling against the seemingly insurmountable barriers of racism *and* sexism, while often raising families and fulfilling full-time professional obligations, these women managed nevertheless to record their thoughts and feelings and to *testify* to all who dare read them that the will to harness the power of collective endurance and survival is the will to write.

The Schomburg Library of Nineteenth-Century Black Women Writers is dedicated in memory of Pauline Augusta Coleman Gates, who died in the spring of 1987. It was she who inspired in me the love of learning and the love of literature. I have encountered in the books of this set no will more determined, no courage more noble, no mind more sublime, no self more celebratory of the achievements of all Afro-American women, and indeed of life itself, than her own.

A NOTE FROM
THE SCHOMBURG CENTER

Howard Dodson

The Schomburg Center for Research in Black Culture, The New York Public Library, is pleased to join with Dr. Henry Louis Gates and Oxford University Press in presenting The Schomburg Library of Nineteenth-Century Black Women Writers. This thirty-volume set includes the work of a generation of black women whose writing has only been available previously in rare book collections. The materials reprinted in twenty-four of the thirty volumes are drawn from the unique holdings of the Schomburg Center.

A research unit of The New York Public Library, the Schomburg Center has been in the forefront of those institutions dedicated to collecting, preserving, and providing access to the records of the black past. In the course of its two generations of acquisition and conservation activity, the Center has amassed collections totaling more than 5 million items. They include over 100,000 bound volumes, 85,000 reels and sets of microforms, 300 manuscript collections containing some 3.5 million items, 300,000 photographs and extensive holdings of prints, sound recordings, film and videotape, newspapers, artworks, artifacts, and other book and nonbook materials. Together they vividly document the history and cultural heritages of people of African descent worldwide.

Though established some sixty-two years ago, the Center's book collections date from the sixteenth century. Its oldest item, an Ethiopian Coptic Tunic, dates from the eighth or ninth century. Rare materials, however, are most available for the nineteenth-century African-American experience. It is from these holdings that the majority of the titles selected for inclusion in this set are drawn.

The nineteenth century was a formative period in African-American literary and cultural history. Prior to the Civil War, the majority of black Americans living in the United States were held in bondage. Law and practice forbade teaching them to read or write. Even after the war, many of the impediments to learning and literary productivity remained. Nevertheless, black men and women of the nineteenth century persevered in both areas. Moreover, more African-Americans than we yet realize turned their observations, feelings, social viewpoints, and creative impulses into published works. In time, this nineteenth-century printed record included poetry, short stories, histories, novels, autobiographies, social criticism, and theology, as well as economic and philosophical treatises. Unfortunately, much of this body of literature remained, until very recently, relatively inaccessible to twentieth-century scholars, teachers, creative artists, and others interested in black life. Prior to the late 1960s, most Americans (black as well as white) had never heard of these nineteenth-century authors, much less read their works.

The civil rights and black power movements created unprecedented interest in the thought, behavior, and achievements of black people. Publishers responded by revising traditional texts, introducing the American public to a new generation of African-American writers, publishing a variety of thematic anthologies, and reprinting a plethora of "classic texts" in African-American history, literature, and art. The reprints usually appeared as individual titles or in a series of bound volumes or microform formats.

The Schomburg Center, which has a long history of supporting publishing that deals with the history and culture of Africans in diaspora, became an active participant in many of the reprint revivals of the 1960s. Since hard copies of original printed works are the preferred formats for producing facsimile reproductions, publishers frequently turned to the Schomburg Center for copies of these original titles. In addition to providing such material, Schomburg Center staff members offered advice and consultation, wrote introductions, and occasionally entered into formal copublishing arrangements in some projects.

Most of the nineteenth-century titles reprinted during the 1960s, however, were by and about black men. A few black women were included in the longer series, but works by lesser known black women were generally overlooked. The Schomburg Library of Nineteenth-Century Black Women Writers is both a corrective to these previous omissions and an important contribution to Afro-American literary history in its own right. Through this collection of volumes, the thoughts, perspectives, and creative abilities of nineteenth-century African-American women, as captured in books and pamphlets published in large part before 1910, are again being made available to the general public. The Schomburg Center is pleased to be a part of this historic endeavor.

I would like to thank Professor Gates for initiating this project. Thanks are due both to him and Mr. William P. Sisler of Oxford University Press for giving the Schomburg Center an opportunity to play such a prominent role in the set. Thanks are also due to my colleagues at The New York Public Library and the Schomburg Center, especially Dr. Vartan Gregorian, Richard De Gennaro, Paul Fasana, Betsy

Pinover, Richard Newman, Diana Lachatanere, Glenderlyn Johnson, and Harold Anderson for their assistance and support. I can think of no better way of demonstrating than in this set the role the Schomburg Center plays in assuring that the black heritage will be available for future generations.

INTRODUCTION

Deborah E. McDowell

The Schomburg Library of Nineteenth-Century Black Women Writers is recognizably among the most significant publication ventures in Afro-American literary history. The collection will fill in many gaps, correct many distortions and inaccuracies, and precipitate a number of fundamental questions that will surely advance scholarship in the field. Among the most obvious questions are: What is "black" about these thirty volumes, and how do they alter existing assumptions and generalizations about Afro-American literature of the nineteenth century? More specifically, how do they alter existing assumptions about nineteenth-century literature by *black women?* What formal and thematic features, what narrative strategies give these books a black woman's signature? What have these books to say about the lives of black women in the nineteenth century that adds to what we know? These are questions that readers of Emma Dunham Kelley (-Hawkins's) *Four Girls at Cottage City* might readily ask, and the search for answers begins properly with a reconstruction of the historical moment in which the novel appeared.

Published in 1898, *Four Girls at Cottage City* appeared at the close of one of the most intense and productive decades in the history of Afro-American women writers and intellectuals, the decade that Frances E. W. Harper named the "Woman's Era." Maria Stewart, widely considered the first American-born woman—black or white—to give a public address, had inspired audiences as early as the 1830s with her fiery speeches. Her challenge to the "land of freedom" to "do away with tyranny and oppression" was issued by many blacks of the era. Heard perhaps less often was Stewart's particular appeals on behalf of black women. Her piercing question—"How long shall the fair daughters of Africa be compelled to bury their minds and talents beneath a load of iron pots and kettles?"—was raised with renewed vigor and urgency in the 1890s. At that time, such black women as Frances E. W. Harper, Anna Julia Cooper, Ida B. Wells-Barnett, and Pauline Hopkins recorded and protested against the era's most volatile and oppressive social issues confronting black Americans: the rising tide of lynching (understood as a terrorist weapon of social control) and the tightening strictures of Jim Crow. Most of these women were founding members of the National Association of Colored Women, a federation of club women who organized to combat racial oppression in these, its most virulent forms. Much of their organizing was done on the pages of the *Woman's Era,* the official journal of the Woman's Era Club in Boston.

Although published in Boston in the midst of this fervid climate in which black female writers, intellectuals, and activists assumed uncompromising and determined stands against racism, *Four Girls at Cottage City* took a kind of retreat, making its setting—a fictionalized Oak Bluffs on Martha's Vineyard [1]—rich with suggestion. In other words, the novel appeared during the same historical moment that produced Ida B. Wells-Barnett's "Southern Horrors: Lynch Law in All Its Forms" (1892); Anna Julia Cooper's *A Voice From the South* (1892) in which she insisted on the higher education of women; Frances E. W. Harper's *Iola Leroy* (1892), the story of a refined mulatto's commitment to racial uplift; and Pauline Hopkins's *Contending Forces* (1900) in which she urged black writers to "faithfully portray the inmost thoughts and feelings of the Negro."

In this lineup, Kelley's novel seems naive and frivolous in its depiction of four carefree girls "in their pretty summer dresses" off for vacation at a Massachusetts resort. Vera, Jessie, Allie, and Garnet seem sprung from some halcyon days of yore. More importantly for considerations of Afro-American women's fiction, they are not what Alice Walker calls "black black women" (or those unprotected by class and light-skinned privilege) in her essay "If the Present Looks Like the Past, What Does the Future Look Like?"[2] Rather, two are "white skin[ned]" with "golden hair" and blue eyes, and though the other two have "rich complexions and dark eyes," they still have "rosy cheeks" and "rosy mouths." Their most severe confrontation with racial injustice is having to sit in "nigger heaven" when they go to the theater.

But to set Emma Dunham Kelley strictly apart from her black female contemporaries and to argue that she retreated from the reformist spirit of her age is to oversimplify and misrepresent the matter. In choosing to create heroines who are physically indistinguishable from white women, Kelley was no different from Frances Harper and Pauline Hopkins, both of whom wrote novels featuring heroines who could pass for white. Further, although *Four Girls at Cottage City* seems, on the surface, oblivious to the horrors of black life in the nineteenth century, it is no less a product of the Woman's Era. It simply chooses a different "mission." However foreign it might seem to the sensibilities of modern readers, that mission was as urgent in Kelley's day as organizing against lynching, rape, Jim Crow, and black disenfranchisement: the mission of spiritual uplift, alternately termed, spiritual feminism or domestic feminism. In fact, one of the most popular arguments of the nineteenth century held that only the elevation of the spirit would obliterate racism and other "earthly" injustices.

In *Four Girls at Cottage City* Kelley combines conventions from spiritual autobiography with those from the sentimental novel to create a work that shows more thematic affinities with what Nina Baym has labeled "woman's fiction" than with the novels of Kelley's black female contemporaries.[3] As in the novels by white women that Baym examines in her study *Woman's Fiction*, Kelley's focus was interior and domestic; her aim, like theirs, was to show readers how they should live. As Baym notes, "these women authors envisioned themselves as lay ministers, their books as evangelical sermons that might spur conversion" (p. 44). That Kelley believes equally in the book as sermon is clear from the endless discussions the characters have about religion throughout the novel. In one such discussion, a character argues that, in writing novels, Dickens "was as well-employed as in preaching the gospel." These gospels, in fictional form, addressed what William Andrews calls the central question in spiritual autobiography in the Christian tradition: "the fate of the individual soul." In his introduction to *Sisters of the Spirit*, Andrews explains that the genre "chronicles the soul's journey not only from damnation to salvation, but also to a realization of one's true place and destiny in the divine scheme of things".[4]

Kelley announces her evangelical intentions early in the novel. When the girls stop at the first cottage that advertises rooms for rent, they are directed to an upper room "before a pair of very steep, very narrow stairs," which Vera stumbles down. Jokingly, she prophesies that, because of the cottage owner's treacherous steps, her place in the afterlife would be "in the lower regions." Leaving this cottage, the girls find more suitable lodging at Trinity Park. The cottage is right opposite the tabernacle. The spatial relationship between the

cottage and the church signifies the "twinness" and insepara-
bility of religiosity and domesticity, the sacred and the secular.

When the four girls journey, "happy light-hearted, careless
and gay," to Cottage City, little do they know that their
summer vacation will lead to a lifetime vocation: the struggle
for salvation and the commitment to Christian service. Although scriptural passages and hymns abound in the novel,
the hymn most often repeated and requested is "Nearer My
God to Thee." While the girls begin their journey as a close-
knit group of friends—fitting Carole Smith-Rosenberg's description of relations between women in her classic essay "The
Female World of Love and Ritual: Relations Between Women
in Nineteenth Century America"—they become "sisters of the
spirit" and accept "the Savior" as their one true friend.[5]

True to the generic conventions of sentimental fiction, "our
girls," as the narrator refers to them, have guides along their
spiritual journey: Charlotte Hood (an example of what Elizabeth Ammons terms the mother-savior)[6] and her ailing son,
Robin. Both the mother-savior and the child are dominant
character types in the sentimental novel with a spiritual focus.
The role children played in nineteenth-century fiction—Harriet Beecher Stowe's Little Eva in *Uncle Tom's Cabin* is a
prototypical example—has been well documented. Believed
to be innocent and uncorrupted, children, it was reasoned,
were eminently well suited to assist in moral instruction. In
addition to children, women, largely because they were ex-
cluded from male domains, were believed to be morally
superior to men and thus better spiritual leaders. In "Wom-
en's Political Future," for example, Frances E. W. Harper
echoed the age's widespread sentiments: "the world has need
of all the spiritual aid that women can give for the social
advancement and moral development of the human race."[7]

It is, Harper added, "the women of a country who help to mold its character and to influence if not determine its destiny." *Four Girls* shares this ideology that arrogates to children and women (especially mothers) unique salvific powers.

Although all four girls are in need of spiritual assistance, Vera, who is described by turns as skeptical and haughty, a "flame of fire" and an "icicle cold [and] proud," stands most in need. Robin is the "taper that would light the path that Vera's young feet were to tread on their way to the 'better country,'" the "light that would guide her out of the night of doubt and uncertainty into the blessed day of light and glory." Though bedridden and paralyzed, Robin, together with his mother, teaches the girls a lesson in the virtues and transformative powers of suffering. Further, both teach the girls that gaining the kingdom of heaven is "long and weary work."

Appropriate to Kelley's evangelistic mission, Vera first sees Charlotte Hood in church and reads a "sermon" in her "pale radiant face" "lifted to heaven" and showing signs of "deep sorrow . . . passed through bravely." In one of the many coincidences and examples of awkward plotting in the novel, the girls meet the "sermonic" face at her cottage where she supports herself and her ailing son on her meager earnings as a laundress. The girls remark that Charlotte and Robin have suffered a cruel and unjust fate, but Charlotte interrupts in "thrilling tones" to declare her fate the workings of an "all-wise and . . . all-merciful God."

From this point, which is the novel's structural center, Charlotte Hood controls the point of view, telling her life story—a sermonic set piece—as inspiration and testimony. Her story conforms to the standard morphology of conversion: conviction of sin, inner doubt and struggle, repentance, salvation, and inner peace. Each day, from Robin's sickroom, Charlotte gives the girls the next installment of her life of suffering and her struggle for repentance and salvation. Despite her minister's urgings that she turn to God to assuage her suffering, the minister and his male orthodoxy and moralisms ultimately fail to console and lead her along the path to salvation. Rather, she is saved by the experience of reading a woman's novel.[8] Here, the most interesting and suggestive features of *Four Girls at Cottage City* emerge, and the feminist elements of its spiritual mission are most apparent.

Having lost her daughter, Margie, her "little white lamb," and after losing her mother and two sisters in close succession, Charlotte sinks into the depths of despair. Falling into a deep sleep, she has the dream that "save[s] [her] soul from everlasting death." She likens her three-day journey in the dream to the scenes described in Elizabeth Stuart Phelps's *Beyond the Gates* (1883), one of four religious novels that included the best-selling *The Gates Ajar* (1868), *The Gates Between* (1887), and *Within the Gates* (1901). *Beyond the Gates* offers an account of the afterlife with distinctly feminist suggestions.

In *The Life and Works of Elizabeth Stuart Phelps* (1983), Lori Kelley explains that in her novels Phelps successfully ministered to the needs of female Christians dissatisfied with the offerings of male orthodoxy and achieved, thereby, a "quasi-clerical status."[9] Importantly, the religion she preached bypassed the formal church and its hierarchies. In the heaven created in these novels, Lori Kelley continues, women "receive the public acclaim and approval so long denied them in the male-dominated society of earth."

Emma Dunham Kelley incorporates this feminist dimension of Phelps's novel of the afterlife into *Four Girls at Cottage City*. As God's medium, Charlotte assumes a quasi-clerical status in the novel. God moves her heart so that she, "through His guidance," will move the girls to accept "the Savior for [their] friend." Charlotte recounts the Judgment Day of her dream in which she is summoned to the throne of God, a figure decribed in terms that parallel earlier descriptions of Charlotte herself: Hers is a "pale radiant face" with blue eyes; his is a "fair face" with "eyes [of] deep blue." In the dream, God the Judge becomes God the gentle, loving, somewhat maternal parent who takes Charlotte on a tour to see other souls "working their way to Heaven." Although Charlotte's earthly minister figures in the dream, wearing an expression of "proud triumph," he is finally given no place near the throne. It is not he who stands at God's "right hand," but Hester, a "poor old woman" who is given a jewel from God's crown.

Just as Hester serves as inspiration and example to Charlotte in the dream, Charlotte becomes inspiration and example to Vera and the girls at Cottage City. She teaches them that their "beautiful little resort" on earth has an even more blissful counterpart in heaven, imaged in the dream as a "beautiful country! All light, and joy and music . . . green hills, pleasant valleys . . . men and women" all "lov[ing] one another with equal love."

This "heaven," which might be viewed as a feminist utopia, peopled by men and women who love each other as equals, could not be easily replicated on earth due largely to male dominance and the influence of masculine values. Together with the other literary "evangelists" of the nineteenth century, however, Emma Dunham Kelley imagined an antidote, an alternative earth that might be saved by maternal values. This world relegated men to the peripheries of women's daily lives.

There is no better example than the relationship between Mother and Father, the keepers of the cottage where the girls spend their vacation. When the girls arrive, Mother leads them to their room up a pair of "Christian stairs." The girls quickly surmise that she is the "ruling spirit" of the house, the "velvet hand in an iron glove." There are repeated references to her holding Father "determinedly back" and to his "retir[ing] obediently." When they visit the girls' room, Mother blocks Father's entry, forcing him to stand outside the doorway, in the shadows of what is clearly represented as a "woman's room."

Although the girls spend much of their time with their two gentlemen callers, Fred and Erfort, Jessie complains that the men are too much underfoot. "When we came down here, I thought we four girls were going around together and have a good time. There is no fun when there's a parcel of men around." As is typical in sentimental novels, the heroines eventually do fulfill their traditionally expected roles as wives and mothers. In fact, the novel ends with a scene that features Vera in such roles. But despite that conventional narrative ending, marriage is depicted here, as in so many novels by women, as "breaking the link . . . in the golden chain" of female communities, to borrow a passage from Kelley's first novel, *Megda* (1891).

These matrifocal communities, which valued relationships and connection, would be the era's answer to the corruption of masculine ideals and values of conquest and competition. But contemporary critics are not amiss in arguing that women, because their sphere of influence and power was delimited to home and hearth, had no real power to effect lasting social change, a criticism that might well be leveled against *Four Girls at Cottage City*. Certainly, the reader leaves the novel wondering what, if any, power spiritual feminism holds for transforming society. The novel alludes to racial injustice (in the description of "nigger heaven") and to class inequities (in Jessie's criticism of a woman whose poodle is better provided for than Charlotte and her son). It even offers a model solution to at least the inequities of class by having the girls sacrifice personal pleasures and plans in order to finance the operation that will correct Robin's spinal injury.

For the most part, however, the narrative foregoes the dramatic possibilities that the material realities of race and class suggest, subsuming them under the larger spiritual vision that collapses all social distinctions in the interest of Christian egalitarianism. But the reader cannot easily ignore the implications of Kelley's decision to cast a white-skinned woman as mother-savior. This decision might be read by some as Kelley's capitulation to the era's race-prejudiced theology, which saw blackness as synonymous with evil and equated whiteness with grace. Kelley's intention is clearly not to embroil herself in theological controversy or to demonstrate how the lessons of spiritual journeying can be applied in the here-and-now for the betterment of humankind.

A contemporary feminist might hope that a novel in a series devoted to black women writers would attempt to formulate just such an application, to dramatize the relationship between spiritual elevation and social responsibility with respect to the conditions of Afro-Americans. But to note the novel's neutrality on racial concerns and the politics of theology that it reflects is not to argue that all literature by blacks must take up the racial banner in protest against injustice. Nor is it to pit Emma Dunham Kelley against other black women writers of her day in the interest of creating some literary hierarchy based on political ideology. It is, rather, much more fruitful to see her as one precursor of the spiritual feminism that is currently resonating throughout contemporary Afro-American women's fiction, as seen in such works as Ntozake Shange's *for colored girls who have considered suicide when the rainbow is enough* (1977), Toni Cade Bambara's *The Salt Eaters* (1980), and Alice Walker's *Meridian* (1976) and *The Color Purple* (1982). Continuing the tradition of which *Four Girls at Cottage City* is a part, these contemporary black women writers see God as maternal, as a spiritual force within the female self, a force detached from the institutional, hierarchical, male-dominated church. But taking up where Kelley left off, their concern with female spirtuality is firmly rooted in the material realities of black women's lives. Such retentions and transformations, such continuities and discontinuities are the stuff of literary tradition. How good it is that *Four Girls* is having a second life in the Schomburg set, enabling scholars and teachers to trace another link in the "golden chain" of Afro-American women's fiction.

NOTES

1. In 1907, Cottage City was renamed Oak Bluffs. For a description of the town's history, see Chris Stoddard, *A Centennial History of Cottage City* (Oak Bluffs, Mass.: Oak Bluffs Historical Commission, 1980).

2. In Alice Walker, *In Search of Our Mothers' Gardens: Womanist Prose* (New York: Harcourt Brace Jovanovich, 1983), pp. 290–312.

3. Nina Baym, *Woman's Fiction: A Guide to Novels by and about*

Women in America, 1820–1870 (Ithaca: Cornell University Press, 1978).

4. William Andrews, *Sisters of the Spirit: Three Black Women's Autobiographies of the Nineteenth Century* (Bloomington: Indiana University Press, 1986), pp. 10–11.

5. Carole Smith-Rosenberg, "The Female World of Love and Ritual: Relations Between Women in Nineteenth Century America." *Signs* 1 (Autumn 1975):1–29.

6. See Elizabeth Ammons, "Stowe's Dream of the Mother-Savior: *Uncle Tom's Cabin* and American Women Writers Before the 1920s," in *New Essays on Uncle Tom's Cabin,* ed. Eric J. Sundquist (Cambridge: Cambridge University Press, 1986), pp. 155–95.

7. In Bert James Loewenberg and Ruth Bogin, eds., *Black Women in Nineteenth-Century American Life* (University Park: Pennsylvania State University Press, 1976), pp. 244–45.

8. Here, and elsewhere in the narrative, male ministers are shown to be ineffectual. In a discussion about the church's opposition to the "evils" of theater-going, Erfort, one of the girls' gentlemen callers, pulls from his breast pocket a pamphlet entitled "The Common Sense View of the Theatre." Justifying theater-going by tracing it to its religious origins, the author of the pamphlet then places the blame for empty church pews not on the existence of theaters, but on the ineffectiveness of ministers.

9. Lori Kelley, *The Life and Works of Elizabeth Stuart Phelps, Victorian Feminist Writer* (Troy, N.Y.: Whitson Publishing, 1983).

Four Girls

At Cottage City

— BY —

EMMA D. KELLEY-HAWKINS

AUTHOR OF "MEGDA."

———◆———

BOSTON:
JAMES H. EARLE, PUBLISHER
178 WASHINGTON STREET
1898

TO

DEAR AUNT LOTTIE

WHOM I HAVE OFTEN AND
TRULY CALLED MY

'Second Mother'

I DEDICATE THIS BOOK.
THE REWARD,
"WELL DONE, THOU GOOD AND
FAITHFUL SERVANT,"
WILL SURELY ONE DAY
BE HERS.

The Author.

PREFACE.

If you who read this book, should meet with my four girls who spent three such delightful weeks at that beautiful resort, Cottage City, ask them "if such and such a thing of which I write" did actually happen. They would answer for the most part "yes" and give you a smile with the answer. The cottage at which they stopped is easily found, but the dear old people who made it so pleasant for them, are gone—never to return. "Mother" and "Grandpa" clasp hands in a better country than this. The story of Charlotte Hood is but little changed, although it was not related to our young people and is known to but one of them. Yet it is only one of the many sad stories that may truthfully be told of lives that are lost and homes made desolate on the shores of bleak Cape Cod. How many aching hearts have been lulled to eternal sleep by the solemn music of the old Atlantic. If any discontented one, after reading the life of Charlotte Hood, will say to herself, "I am thankful it is as well with me as it is," the Mission of this Book will have been fulfilled.

THE AUTHOR.

CONTENTS.

Four Girls at Cottage City.

CHAPTER I.

"What a shame it should rain this day, of all days, Net! Yesterday was a perfectly delightful day, and now—just look here!" and Jessie Dare drew back the window curtain and looked over her shoulder at her sister, who was lying snugly down between the sheets with the calmest of all calm faces, which was, to say the least, very exasperating to the troubled Jessie.

"Well, never mind, Jess; we can't help the weather. Come back to bed—we needn't get up yet," and Garnet turned comfortably over and prepared herself for a few minutes more of that sleep which was one of her greatest luxuries, and which came as easily to her as it does to a kitten.

"Come back to bed and run the risk of losing our train? Not much, Miss Dare. You just vacate that bed just about as quick as you can do it; if you can't do it alone, I'll furnish assistance," and like a flash Jessie ran around to the other side of the bed, and before Garnet had had hardly time enough to open her great dark eyes and make a feeble protest against such treatment, Jessie had her out on the floor, and was issuing forth her commands in true military style.

Garnet paid little attention to them, however, but went around in her quiet, calm way, well knowing that she would be the first to announce herself ready, although Jessie was already partly dressed.

And so she was. Jessie had so much running around to do (her tongue keeping remarkably good time with her feet) flying to the window every now and then to peer with anxious little face out into the gray, misty, rainy morning, losing her brush or ribbon, or pin, and calling on Garnet to help her find it, until at last Garnet stood ready to go down to the dining room, while Jessie had a good five minutes' more work before her. Garnet good-naturedly rendered assistance to her careless, but lovable little sister, and the two girls descended the stairs and entered the dining room together.

Mrs. Dare looked up with a smile. "It is too bad you have not a better day for your journey, my dears," she said, sympathizingly. " Do you think the other girls will venture out ? "

As if in answer to her question, the door-bell rang. Jessie ran down stairs and opened the door. A slender, blue-eyed girl stood on the steps, holding a huge umbrella over her head, which was little protection from the driving sheets of water. Jessie greeted her with a laugh in which joy and fear were most comically intermingled.

"Oh, Allie Hunt! If you don't look too comical for anything — just like a toad under a cabbage leaf. Come right in out of all this rain!"

She drew Allie, who had looked a trifle indignant at being compared to a toad, into the hall and shut the door; then she went on: "You don't mean to tell me, Allie Hunt, that you have come to say you are not going? because if you have, you can save yourself the trouble of saying it — I won't listen to it."

Allie laughed her low, lady-like laugh, (everybody *did* laugh at Jessie's little sayings.) "I didn't come to say any such thing, Miss Jessie, I only came to see if the rest were going."

"Well, you just believe the rest are going. We wouldn't stay away for this little rain."

"I thought it was a pretty big rain while I was coming down here; but I can stand it if the rest can. Have you heard from Vera? She may not come."

How Jessie laughed! "Vera Earle not come? That shows you do not know her as well as I. She will come if she is not sick in bed."

"Well, then, I may as well go back and get ready."

"Yes, and you be sure and get to the depot in time."

" Oh, yes, sure."

" An hour after found the three girls standing in
the ladies' waiting room of P—— depot, looking
with anxious eyes ·out into the driving rain.   In
spite of Jessie's repeated assurances that she knew
Vera would come, her sparkling little face was just
the least bit shadowed with the cloud of nervous
fear that she *might* not come after all—it did rain so.

A low exclamation from Garnet caused her to
turn quickly ; the next moment she was running
across the wide room, regardless of the many eyes
watching her, and holding out both hands to a tall,
gray-eyed girl who was just coming from the side
entrance.   Jessie's girlish voice rang out sweet and
joyous."

" Oh, you darling—you *have* come.   I *knew* you
would ; what made you so late ?   We had almost
given you up."   And Jessie clasped her hands
around her tall friend's arm and hurried her forward
to the other two girls.

Then began such a chattering and laughing as
would have done any one's heart good to hear.
The two gentlemen, Vera's brother, and Garnet's
and Jessie's brother-in-law, procured the tickets,
attended to the baggage and then hovered around
the "outskirts," so to speak, listening to the gay
chatter, with superior smiles on their faces, until the
whistle of the approaching train resounded, when
all was bustle and confusion.

" Good-bye, Philip ! " " Good-bye, Jessie ! "
" Good-bye, Herb ! " " Good-bye, Vera ! " " Good-
bye, Good-bye, Good-bye ! Be sure and send
postals just as soon as you arrive."

" Dear me, Vera, do tell me if there is a smooch
on my face," exclaimed Jessie, impatiently, as the
four girls entered the car and stopped at two seats
near the door. " That great lummax of a man
brushed his dirty old gossamer right against my
cheek."

Vera turned with her hand on the half-turned
seat. " Nothing there but roses, Jess," she said,
and over went the seat.

" You'll spoil the child Vera," said Garnet,
settling her plump little form comfortably upon the
seat facing Allie and Jessie, and making room for
Vera beside her.

" Child ! " pouted Jessie. " What do you call
yourself, Granny ? "

" I am three years your senior," replied Garnet,
calmly. " And therefore feel responsible for your
behavior while away from home."

" H'm. You be responsible for your own
behavior and I'll look out for mine. Hey, Allie ? "

Vera laughed outright. Allie smiled her sweet,
pretty smile and threw Jessie's gossamer up into
the rack with her own.

" My sakes ! " exclaimed Jessie. " I have just
this moment thought of it, Allie ! We are going

off with two sedate school-marms.   We'll have to
behave or we'll have curtain-lectures read to us
every night."

" Girls who are seniors in the High School
should never OBLIGE any one to deliver curtain-
lectures to them."

This was in Vera's clear, proud tones.   Jessie
acknowledged the reproof with the pretty respect
she always showed to Vera.   She had a girlish,
but, nevertheless, very deep and loving admiration
for Vera, and Vera loved the impulsive young girl
with all the strength of her strong heart.   She was
only five years her senior, but she .felt fifty at
times.

" Now look here, girls," said Garnet, in her
matter-of-fact voice.   " Suppose we give our
tickets up to one, and let her keep them until we
need them.   What do you say ? "

" Depends upon whom that one will be.   If it is
my sister Garnet Maria, Jessie says ' No, thanks ; '
but if it is Vera—" said Jessie.

" Yes, let Vera keep them," said Allie, passing
her's over.

" I didn't have the least idea of offering myself
as banker for the party," said Garnet.   " I'm careless about such things and know it.   Others are
careless and *don't* know it; or if they know it,
wont acknowledge it."   (" That's me," murmured
Jessie, making up a face.)   " Besides my reticule is

about full and I've no outside pocket." ("Have you an inside one with fifteen *cents* in it?" asked Jessie, innocently.) Garnet passed over this slangy question as being unworthy of notice. "Vera, yours has a nice long pocket with a clasp. Do you dare to take the responsibility?" "Yes, and I'll add to the responsibility by keeping your purses for you if you would like to have me. We'll call it the bank," said Vera, opening her reticule to show how much room there was in it.

In flew Jessie's dainty little purse before the words were hardly spoken. The silver clasp struck against a bottle.

"Got a 'shothecary pop' in there?" asked Jessie, bending over and peering in.

Vera dashed a fine spray of violet water into the pretty, laughing face. Jessie sprang back, a little startled, then leaned forward again, shut her eyes and puckered up her rosy little mouth.

"What you might call a 'mute appeal,'" said Vera, with a laugh, and dashed a second spray into Jessie's face. Then she put the bottle back into her reticule and closed it with a decided little snap. "No more this time, Jasmine. Perhaps you'll need a shower of it before we get to Cottage City. It looks as if it might be decidedly rough on the water."

Jessie pushed her white tennis cap on the back of her dark head, and nestled down in the corner of the seat. "I hope *I* shan't be sick," she murmured. Then she commenced to laugh. "But I bet a cookie Net will. She ate the biggest breakfast you ever saw. I kept telling her to stop, but she seemed to think she must either eat or die—one of the two."

Vera and Allie laughed. It was an old joke among them that if Garnet could eat and sleep she was perfectly happy.

"I think I shall eat whenever I am hungry—sea-sick or not sea-sick," returned Garnet, not in the least displeased. "And that makes me think."

She leaned forward suddenly and pulled a bag out from somewhere. She put her hand into it, drew out a fruit cracker, opened her book, and commenced to take comfort. "Help yourselves, girls," she said, taking her first bite ; and then the girls', that so far as *she* was concerned, conversation had stopped for an hour.

Jessie gave her cap a savage little pull that brought it over one ear, and nestled still farther down in her seat. "Thank goodness that I'm not blessed with such an enormous appetite," she said, spitefully. "Give Net a bag of fruit crackers and a book, and she'll munch and read away forever and the day afterward."

No one spoke. Allie smiled a little and Vera gave a little reproving shake of her head. The rain came dashing against the window, the train

sped along through the gray, wet, cheerless country.
In a little while Vera had drawn "Tale of Two
Cities" from her travelling bag and was lost to
everything around her.   Allie sat with "Judge
Burnham's Daughters" open in her lap, but her blue
eyes were looking out into the dim, rain-lashed
country.   She was thinking of her father and
wondering how he would get along without her.
Jessie made two or three attempts at conversation,
but Garnet and Vera never even heard her and
Allie only answered with an absent smile.   After
a few moments of this, Jessie sprang out of her
seat and crossed the aisle with something that
sounded like "dull old party."   Half an hour later,
when the conductor came through for tickets, she
was sound asleep with her head against the window
and her white cap resting on one ear.   The conductor looked at her and then answered the smile
on the girls' faces with one that was very pleasant.
"There is a tired little girl so soon," he said, and
passed on.

"Let us be thankful that Jess did not hear that,"
said Garnet, closing her book and putting away
the bag of crackers (or what was left of them).

"We won't tell her," said Vera, looking across
at the girlish figure with a smile.   Then she rose,
stepped across the aisle and laid her fair face lightly
against Jessie's rosy one.   The big black eyes
opened lazily, then smiled up into the gray ones.

"We've come back to the land of the living, little girl. Will you join us?" said Vera.

Jessie caught her cap just as it was disappearing over the back of the seat. "I am not sure that it is safe to," she said.

Nevertheless she followed Vera back to Garnet and Allie. Vera looked at her watch. "What time is it?" asked Allie.

"9 : 30," replied Vera.

"We'll get to New Bedford in about twenty minutes," said Garnet.

"Where's the 'bank'?" asked Jessie, rather loudly.

Vera made a frantic clutch at her reticule, while Garnet gave Jessie's foot a warning touch with her own. Jessie looked at her questioningly, and Garnet rolled her large eyes around until they rested on a big, rough looking man two seats in front of them, on the opposite side of the car. Vera and Allie followed the rolling eyes with their own, and unsuspicious Jessie blurted out: "What of it?"

Then Garnet leaned forward, and the three heads, one black, one brown and one golden, gathered close around the curly one.

That man has been looking over here for the last half hour. He may be all right, but we had better not say too much about the 'bank.'"

Garnet's low tones were full of deep, mysterious caution. She sat back in her seat and looked

carelessly out of the window, as if to convince the
" suspicious looking character" that what she had
said had no reference to him at all. The other
girls gave each other a solemn look and sank
slowly back into their respective places, but Vera's
small hand took a firmer clutch of the handle to the
"bank," and her face betokened desperate determination.

"He'll have to step over your dead body to get
it; won't he, Vera ? " giggled Jessie, and Garnet
frowned at her for her indiscretion.

"New Bedford ! " shouted the brakeman. " Boat
ready for Cottage City on the left."

Our four girls scrambled to their feet and commenced a frantic gathering together of their
"belongings." They buttoned up their gossamers,
pulled the hoods over their heads, tucked their
books under their arms, clutched their reticules,
and hastened out. The " desperate character"
had disappeared.

Vera and Allie, who had never taken the trip
before, followed close upon the heels of Garnet and
Jessie. The blinding mist flew into their faces and
the wind blew their gossamers wildly about them,
but, fortunately, they had but a short distance to go
and were soon on the boat, pushing their way
among the wet, chattering crowd.

Vera stopped irresolutely before the cosily
appointed saloon. " Shall we go in ? " she asked.

Jessie sprang lightly up the stairs. "I am answered," said Vera, laughing, and followed.

"I *do* wish it didn't rain; then we might sit on deck," sighed Garnet, as she laid her bundles on one of the side seats and drew up a camp stool in front of them.

For an hour they sat there, laughing and talking, though quietly, then Vera stood up and drew her light brown peasant cape about her. "I am going on deck for a few moments, at any rate. Does any one else want to come?"

"Let's all go," cried Jessie.

The rain still came down in torrents; the wind blew a gale. Nothing could be seen, before, behind or on either side. The girls tied their hats on with their veils, and clung to the posts and to each other.

"My! But it more than blows; eh, Er?" cried a merry voice near them, and a young man, with his coat collar turned up and his head very much on one side, (probably with an idea of keeping his hat on,) went past them with a rush, followed by a slender young man with his hands in the pockets of his "Prince Albert."

"Fred Travers!" exclaimed Jessie, speaking the name very loud in her excitement.

The young man who had spoken, turned his head, stared a moment, and then came forward, hat in hand.

"Jessie! Is it really you? And Garnet? I am delighted."

"Who *ever* thought of seeing you here," cried Jessie, shaking hands.

"My friends, Miss Earle and Miss Hunt," said Garnet, in her low, quiet tones. "My cousin, Mr. Travers, ladies."

Vera and Allie acknowledged the introduction as best they could under the circumstances. Fastidious Vera, with one arm around a post, indeed attempted a bow, and was blown completely around the post for her pains. If it had been anyone else Jessie would have gone into convulsions, as it was she sprang to Vera's assistance, but Cousin Fred was before her and offered his arm as substitute for the post.

"He of the Prince Albert" was all this time seen to flutter suspiciously near and cast imploring glances at Fred. Fred, taking pity upon him, led the girls to some seats in a sheltered corner and asked their permission to bring his friend to them to be introduced. The favor was graciously granted, and in a moment more "My friend Mr. Richards" was bowing gravely before them.

Fred Travers was a tall, finely-formed young man, with light-brown curly hair, merry dark blue eyes, and a very pretty light (very *light*) mustache and side-tabs. Vera, looking at him, smiled to herself as she thought, "One might think 'Miss

Mowcher' had been at work there putting up a scaffolding for a pair of whiskers." The young man's face was handsome, but it was a good face as well; a pleasant face and a frank face. He had besides, perfect teeth, even, white and good shaped.

Erfort Richards was his exact opposite in every particular. He was of medium height, but slender, with a smooth dark face, a handsome pair of dark eyes, a small mouth with thin sensitive lips, and a straight, handsome nose. His forehead was broad and very white, and he wore his thick, dark hair brushed carelessly back. His hands were brown and slender, but the fingers looked firm and strong as steel. His face was full of poetry — dark, wistful, and melancholy. He looked like a great thinker; yes, and a great dreamer too. He took his seat near Garnet and spoke but little. When Jessie made the others laugh at her bright sayings, a faint, flickering light passed over his dark face, touching the sensitive lips and just lighting the deep eyes for a moment. It could scarcely have been called a smile, rather the shadow of one.

" How long do you intend to stay at the city?" asked Fred.

All eyes turned towards Vera. " Three weeks," she answered.

" What is your Hotel?"

Terrible question! All eyes turned to Vera again, and there was a dead pause. The fact was, that the girls did not really know where they were going—certainly not to any hotel. They were going to trust to luck in finding a good place at the lowest possible price, for our girls were far from being rich girls. But, of course, it would never do to let these gentlemen know their situation. What would they think of them! "And Vera is so terribly honest," groaned Jessie in spirit.

But Vera was proud as well as honest. She met Fred's question with a fair, unruffled face and calm gray eyes. "We have no Hotel. We are intending to stop at a private cottage," she answered steadily, and Jessie murmered to herself: "Praise the Lord! If the inquisitive thing wont ask at *whose* cottage."

But Vera's heart was beating fast, despite her calm face, at this very same thought "I must confess that this wind is a little too much for me," she said shivering. "Suppose we go inside."

Accordingly inside they went, Fred saying on the way : "We are going to put up at the Wesley."

On account of the stormy passage the boat did not reach Cottage City until nearly 2 o'clock.

"Let me see to your trunks," said Fred.

"No, thank you, Fred," said Garnet, with an earnestness that rather surprised him. "We will not trouble you to do that. We are not quite ready to go up just now," and she smiled very pleasantly as she said it, as though she were anticipating some secret pleasure in staying down there.

Fred looked around—saw the wet, dismal wharf, the hurrying, impatient people making for their various destinations as fast as their feet could carry them, and then looked at our four girls with an open look of astonishment on his face. But he was too much a gentleman to stay where it was very obvious he was not wanted.

"I don't believe those girls know where they are going," he said, speaking his thoughts aloud in his perplexity.

"It surely isn't for us to ask them," said Erfort gravely, slipping his arm through Fred's and hurrying him along.

CHAPTER II.

"Now girls, what shall we do first," asked Garnet, briskly.

"I should think you'd know what *you* want to do first," said Jessie.

"What is that?" asked Garnet innocently.

"Find a restaurant," replied Jessie with a feeble laugh. (Jessie had felt the motion of the boat a little too plainly to feel just well.)

Garnet turned and looked at her little sister very gravely for a moment. "I will dear, when I have found a bed to put you into," she said.

"It is very plain to me," said Vera, "what we must do. Follow me." Then she turned to an express man standing near. "We will leave our baggage here for a short time," she said, a trifle haughtily, (but Vera always spoke in that way to strangers). "We will probably be back or send for them in about an hour."

"How much of Cottage City do we own, Vera?" asked Jessie, very pale now, but still having life enough to jest. "I should think we owned the whole of Circuit avenue — shops and all, with a little of Ocean avenue thrown in."

"Well, no matter if everyone *docsn't* know where we are going," said Vera, grandly.

"My gracious, if they do I wish they would kindly tell us, for I'd like to go there," replied Jessie.

This made the girls laugh, and despite wet skirts and dripping umbrellas, the walk up Circuit avenue did not seem so very long. They turned into one of the shorter avenues and "took stock," as Jessie called it, of the cottages. Only one bore the placard "Rooms to Let," and before this one they halted.

"It doesn't look as though it had many rooms, anyway," said Vera, "but we may as well try."

She tapped on the door and it was immediately opened by a pleasant-faced, middle-aged woman.

"Come right in out of the rain," she said at once, and the girls were only too glad to accept the invitation.

"We saw by your card that you have rooms to let," said Vera, sitting very upright on a hard little lounge, and holding her wet umbrella out as if she were popping corn with it. "We are in search of rooms—either two small ones or one large one with two beds. Do you think you can accommodate us?"

"I think so," replied the lady. "Excuse me for one moment, and I will see," and she left the room.

"Anybody'd think she kept a hotel," said Jessie, in a stage whisper.

"Jessie!" said Garnet, warningly.

In a moment the lady came back. "This way, please," she said.

Vera went first, and stopped short before a pair of very steep, very narrow stairs. She looked up at them and then at the lady with such a perfectly astonished face, that Jessie, bringing up the rear, giggled hysterically. This recalled Vera to herself.

"Excuse me; shall we go—go up?" she asked.

The lady bowed, a little stiffly, and Vera, fearing that she had offended her, started to run lightly up the stairs. Alas! She stubbed her toe on the second one, tried to save herself by clutching at the place where the bannisters should have been, and fell sprawling, hitting Garnet who came immediately behind her, with her feet as she did so. Garnet dropped easily and quietly onto her knees. When the girls had picked themselves up the lady had vanished.

Vera stalked majestically up the stairs, the rest following. In the middle of a low, small room, which two narrow, dyspeptic looking beds almost entirely filled, Vera stood still and looked scornfully about her.

Jessie threw herself on one of the beds and laughed until she cried. Garnet and Allie sank wearily down on the other and looked at Vera. Vera watched the writhing Jessie for a moment and then a laughing light crept into her gray eyes and

around her red lips. The girls took courage at
this and smiled in sympathy. Vera was going to
assume the character in which they all loved her
the best. When she chose she could keep all
about her in perfect gales of laughter. Jessie's
light at these times paled like the light of the moon
before the sun.

Vera made a low bow towards the door, as
though dismissing some person, and laid her
" belongings " on the floor. " We'll bide here a
bit, my maids," she said drolly, " before presenting
our declination of the room to our friend in the
lower regions. May the saints forgive me, but I'm
very much thinking that her place in the after-life
will be in the lower regions, if she has those kind
of stairs put up for innocent people to break their
necks upon. I wonder," she added gravely, " if
she really means to give us to understand that this
room is at our command? *Is* she as mad as that? "

" This is the room she evidently means for us to
take," said Garnet. " No clothes-press, but — can
you complain ? " and she pointed to the hooks and
nails that were driven into the beams and walls.

" If I were to open my eyes in the morning onto one of my dresses hanging on one of those
hooks," said Vera, " I would imagine it was myself suspended by the neck and would wonder
when I could have done the deed. No. Let those
of us who like the surroundings, stay. I go. Let

me put the question : All those in favor of stopping at this station raise the right hand."

Not a hand went up.

"Contrary minds, the same sign."

Up went all the hands, Jessie raising both of hers.

"We will go," said Vera.

"And the sooner the better," added Jessie.

"You tell her, Vera," said Garnet.

"Yes, I'll smooth it over," answered Vera.

And she did ; expressing herself in such a pretty, lady-like manner that the lady was not at all offended, and wished them all success, as she followed them to the door.

"Jessie," said Vera, where was it you and your mother stayed the time you came here three or four years ago ? "

"Sure enough ! " exclaimed Jessie, " How stupid in us Garnet, not to have thought of it. Let me see." She stood still in the middle of the street, her umbrella over her shoulder, and puckered her forehead into a dozen little wrinkles. " Oh, dear, dear, dear, where was it ? "

"Don't stand in the middle of the street, Jess," said Garnet. " People will think you have struck an attitude for their especial benefit."

"Let them think," retorted Jessie. " Why couldn't you have kept still, Net Dare, for another minute ? I was just thinking of it."

"Was it Trinity Park?" asked Allie, absently.

"Right you are, Al!" exclaimed Jessie, elegantly. "Whatever made you think of it?"

"I happened to look up and see the name," nodding her head towards a sign-post.

"Well, of all things!" exclaimed Jessie. "Here we are, and I verily believe that is the self-same house before us — the one on the corner. There used to be the *darlingest* old lady and gentleman there when mother and I were down that summer! Let us try, anyway; it *looks* like the house."

"Rooms to let, anyway," said Vera. "There's a card in the window."

There were two front doors, both opening onto a wide piazza with a low railing around it. One of the front rooms projected out some little distance ahead of the other. As the girls went up the neat walk and ascended the steps, the green blind-door of one of the parlors opened, and a tall, white-haired gentleman stood on the step. His broad shoulders were bent with age, and the hand that held back the door, trembled; but the smile that lighted the worn face and shone in the dim blue eyes, was a bright and cheery one.

"Are you in search of rooms, young ladies?" he asked, and his voice was very quavering.

"Yes, sir," answered Vera. "Have you any to dispose of?"

"I think mother has," he replied. "Come right in, out of the rain. Mother is up stairs; but sit down, please, and I'll call her," and he walked slowly and unsteadily out of the room.

"'Mother' is evidently the ruling spirit," whispered Vera, sitting down with Garnet on a low, comfortable lounge.

"I like here," said Garnet, decidedly. "And I do hope 'Mother' can accommodate us."

"I wish she'd hurry up," said Jessie. "My feet are wet."

"He looked like a nice old gentleman, didn't he?" observed Allie.

"'Sh," said Vera, warningly. "Here they come."

Steps were heard, slowly approaching the door. It opened, and "Mother" stood on the threshold.

Four fair, girlish faces, were turned expectantly toward the spot where she stood; four pair of bright, girlish eyes, were lifted to her face; and four warm, impulsive, girlish hearts, were at once laid at the trembling feet of "Mother." But even while the girls looked at, and loved at once, the pale, refined, gentle old face, framed with its soft waves of silvery hair, they couldn't help noticing, that while one slender hand patted nervously the pale blue cap that had evidently been put on hurriedly, the other rested on the arm of, and held determinedly back, her husband.

———————

"Mr. Atherton tells me you are in search of rooms," she began, and when the girls heard her voice, they wondered how they could have thought Mr. Atherton's was quavering; it was strong, compared with "Mother's."

"I have some rooms that are very good. Would you want two single ones or one large one?"

"We would prefer one large one, if you have it," replied Vera.

"Well, I have. Will you walk up stairs?"

"Mother" led the way up a pair of "christian stairs," as Vera called them, and opened the door of a room, the sight of which elicited little cries of delight from the girls. "Mother" heard the cries with a pleased smile.

"Yes, I think you will like this room," she said, with childish pleasure.

"Like it!" said Vera. "It is perfectly lovely."

It was a good-sized, square room. A double door, half glass, opened on to a cunning little balcony. On one side of the room there was a window with inside blinds. Two beds were in the room, a rocking-chair, two common chairs, a table, and a washstand. To the girls great delight there were two good-sized closets.

"We will go right down to the wharf and have our trunks sent up," said Vera.

"Yes, you and Net do that and Allie and I will send postals home," said Jessie.

"Wait just a minute and I'll write a line to mother, and you can drop it in for me," said Vera.

When the girls went out they found the rain had stopped to a considerable extent, but the streets were very wet and muddy, and their walk down to the wharf was anything but a pleasant one. When they returned to the cottage they found their room empty — Allie and Jessie had not come back.

"Just like that lazy little Jess," said Garnet. "She means to stay away until the room is ready."

"Here are some sheets and pillow cases," said Vera. "Suppose we begin on the beds?"

"All right. You take that one and I'll take this."

Vera stood in the middle of the room and shook a pillow into its case. "I consider it a great streak of luck — our getting such a good room," she said. Then she stopped with the pillow in mid-air, and a look of horror on her face.

"Come right up. The girls are at home — I hear them talking. Yes, here they are," and Jessie threw open the door and walked into the room followed by Allie and — oh, horror of horrors! Cousin Fred and Mr. Richards! Vera sank on the bed she was making, holding her pillow in her lap as though it were a baby. Garnet, after bestowing a look on Jessie that was meant to annihilate her, sank on her bed also, and glared wildly on the unwelcome visitors. Mr. Richards saw their mistake in accepting Jessie's invitation to "come up and see their room," and drew hastily back into the passage, but Cousin Fred came right in and looked about him with delighted eyes.

"What a splendid room," he cried, admiringly. "Just as pleasant as it can be. Beats ours all to hollow, Er," and he sat himself down comfortably on the foot of Garnet's bed.

Vera had assumed her "dignified manner." She was all proud reserve in a moment; yet the reserve was just touched with a sweetness that made her very charming. She rose quietly from the bed.

"Wont you come in, Mr. Richards?" and she placed a chair for him as she spoke. "I think, Mr. Travers, you will find this seat more comfortable," offering him a chair, also. "You must excuse our disorder, but we have scarcely had time to settle."

"Oh, I told them they would find everything topsy-turvey," said Jessie, easily, throwing her gossamer over the foot-board, and her hat on the bed. "Haven't you two lazy girls got the beds made yet?"

"I feel that I have committed an unpardonable offense," said Mr. Richards, gravely. I regret our thoughtlessness exceedingly.

"Oh, it is all right," said Garnet, feebly.

Fred, who had looked a little blank at what his friend had said, brightened up at this. "Of course it is all right. You don't care for your cousin."

Vera might have reminded him that *she* could claim relationship with neither him or his friend, and Mr. Richards might have done the same with regard to the girls, but they thought it best to say nothing.

The gentlemen stayed about half an hour. Fred would have stayed until dark, had not Mr. Richards, insisted upon their going.

"I suppose you will take in most of the band concerts, won't you?" asked Fred, as they rose to go.

"Well, we hope to, but we do not know whether we will venture out to-night or not," replied Garnet.

"It will be decidedly damp," said Fred. "We shall hope to see you to-morrow."

"We shall be glad to have you call."

"Perhaps the weather will permit our entertaining on the piazza," said Vera, smiling.

"That would be very pleasant," said Mr. Richards.

Jessie showed the gentlemen out. It was the punishment that Vera inflicted upon her for showing them *in*. When she came back, quiet little Garnet turned on her with her black eyes blazing. "Jessie Dare, you don't know *any*thing. You are worse than any baby."

There were two pairs of black eyes blazing now. "I'm not to blame for taking after my sister," retorted Jessie. Then she added, vehemently: "For pity's sake, don't begin to jaw, Net, but let us have something to eat, I'm starving."

Garnet's eyes lost their fire, and she grew calm. Jessie chuckled wickedly. "I thought the eating dodge would quiet her," she whispered to Allie.

Vera and Garnet finished the bed-making, and then the bags of sandwiches and crackers were produced. Vera and Garnet sat on one bed, Jessie and Allie on the other, and "fell to."

In the midst of the feast, there came a low knock on the door. "Who now?" said Vera, putting the hand that held the sandwich, back of her, and going to open the door. "Mother" stood in the passage, with "Grandpa" peering over her shoulder.

"Excuse me, please, but is there anything more that you want? If there is, tell me, and I'll bring it to you."

"Oh, no, thank you," said Vera, gently. "We have everything needful."

"Will you have another quilt? The nights are quite chilly just now. Mr. Atherton will get you one if you would like it."

"Oh, yes, yes," quavered "Grandpa," over "Mother's" shoulder. "I'll get you one."

"Oh, but really, we do not need another," said Vera, earnestly. "You have made us quite comfortable."

"Well, I'm glad to hear it. Now you must make yourselves right to home — just as if you belonged here," went on "Mother," and the girls smiled and nodded their heads, and *tried* not to think of the sandwiches.

"Mr. Atherton and me both like young people, and you're welcome to any room in the house."

"Thank you; thank you," chorused the girls.

"Yes," smilingly assented "Mother," looking more childishly pleased than ever, "when you get tired of staying up here, go down in either of the parlors. I've got a bed in one, but that needn't make any difference."

"No, no, that needn't make any difference," echoed "Grandpa," coming out from behind "Mother" a little way; but the slender, aged hand quickly forced him back again, and he retired obediently.

"We haven't anyone here just now, and perhaps we shan't have for a week or two, but you can't tell. When they come they generally come all together; but you shall have your first choice of the rooms, anyway, no matter how many come."

Just here, Vera almost upset the girls' gravity, by moving her head, so that the door came between it and the old people, and taking a good bite out of her sandwich. The mouthful disposed of, she showed her face to them again, smiling sweet, and full of gentle interest. Still, "Mother's" small talk rippled on, uninterruptedly, like the gentle murmuring of a brook, over its mossy bed, and at stated intervals, Vera's head disappeared behind the door, and she continued her surreptitious lunch. It made Jessie feel almost murderous, as for Garnet, who can describe *her* agony !

At last the gentle murmuring grew fainter and fainter and finally died away all together. Vera's head came from behind the door and Vera's smile was the last the two good old people saw as they moved away — " Mother's " hand still resting on the arm of, and gently propelling onward, "Grandpa."

" Oh, Vera, you wretch ! " cried Jessie. " How *could* you ? "

" Couldn't help it, Jess. I am but human. "

" They are a dear old couple, " said Jessie, taking a bite that surely made up for half a dozen held back, " but most terribly long-winded. " And Garnet did not even reprove her.

At 6 o'clock the girls once more donned their hats and waterproofs. They had put a towel on the back of the rocker and caught it up in one corner with a bright bow of ribbon. They had spread another towel on the table and put their books and work-boxes on it. They had hung their clothes up in the closets and arranged their bottles, brushes, combs and sponges on the washstand, and on the narrow ledge that ran along either side of the room under the eaves. Vera and Garnet had spread

their bright red shawls on the foot of each bed, and
the room looked very cosy and homelike. Then
they had sat in the dim twilight and talked, and
sung snatches of low song, until the electric light, in
the park opposite their room, had flared up suddenly
and brightly and warned them that it was high
time to be looking out for their "resteraunt."
They did not need a lamp, for they opened the door
and the electric light flooded their room with its
moon-like brightness. They locked the other door
and went quietly down the stairs and out of the side
entrance, which "Mother" had informed them
would belong exclusively to them.

The rain had ceased, but the air was full of a
damp, drizzling mist. Just before them on the
corner they saw a sign "Bridgett's Dining-Rooms."
Jessie read it aloud, pronouncing "Bridgett's" with
the emphasis on the first syllable. None of the
others knew but what it was right.

"Well, let us go in and see 'Bridgett,'" said
Vera. "Perhaps she can give us a plate of baked
beans."

The very mention of this "home-dish" made
Jessie and Allie murmur words of delight, but
Garnet could only express her consent with a
groan. It spoke volumes though.

"And now," said Vera, an hour later, as they
walked slowly up Circuit avenue and looked into
the lighted windows, "let us go to the concert."

There were very few promenaders when they
reached the park. The girls found a seat under
one of the trees, spread their gossamers upon it,
put up their umbrellas and sat there, patiently waiting for the band to begin. By and by a little boy
came around with programmes and gave them each
one. The people commenced to come by ones,
and twos and threes, some bringing their camp-
chairs with them, other leaning against the trees or
walking slowly up and down. Little twinkling
lights of red and green and yellow, like fairy lamps,
commenced to move quickly to and fro, meeting
and passing other twinkling lights of red and green
and yellow.

"The bicyclists are beginning to turn out," said
Garnet. "I thought we would see them."

The musicans took their places, the leader stood
before them with his baton raised, a pause — up
went the baton, down it came again, now on the
right, now on the left — then a burst of glad music,
and our girls felt that they were really at Cottage
City. Promenaders walked to and fro, laughing
and talking, despite the drizzling mist, more fairy
lamps twinkled on the avenue. Two or three little
boys with baskets on their arms, went from chair
to chair. "Corn-bars; nice corn-bars, straw-
berry, vanilla, coffee and chocolate. Have
some, ladies?" Our girls thought they would.
By the time they were eaten, "home" was

proposed. On the way back they stopped at a
drug-store and invested in a pound of candy, each
girl buying a quarter. Garnet bought chocolate-
creams; Vera, nougats; Jessie, chocolate-almonds;
and Allie, caramels.

"We'll save them for to-morrow," said Jessie,
putting one slyly into her mouth.

"Yes, we'll want something to do all day," replied Vera.

"Aren't we going to morning services?" asked
Allie, timidly.

"Well, yes, we might as well," said Garnet.
"The tabernacle is right opposite the cottage."

"Yes, we'll go," said Vera. We wont sit very
far down, and if we get tired we can get up and go
out."

"I'll go on that condition," said Jessie.

They entered the house noiselessly for fear of
disturbing the old people, but as they reached the
top of the stairs, "Mother" came out of her room
with a flannel night-dress on and a light in her
hand. Jessie could be heard to faintly groan — she
thought they were out there for half the night; then
her spirits grew lighter as she thought of the package in her hands. If she grew *too* tired — but
"Mother" did not keep them in the passage long.

"I forgot to give you a lamp," she whispered, as
tho' some one lay asleep very near them, but the
girls saw "Grandpa" peering from his room at

them over " Mother's " shoulder.   " Mother " put
her hand out and held him back.

" Take this one.   I am undressed and Mr.
Atherton can undress in the dark.   Did you have
a good supper? "

" Yes'm ; very good," answered Vera.

" Where did you go?   They have some real good
baked-beans every Saturday night at ' Bridgett's '—
on the corner here."   " Mother " put the emphasis
on the last syllable, and the girls nudged each
other softly at their mistake.

" That is where we went," said Garnet.

" Yes ; it's a real good place," said " Mother."
" I hope you will sleep well.   Good-night."

" Good-night," answered the girls.

" My ! " said Jessie.   " There isn't much to
' Mother ' when she is in *dishabilly*, is there ! "

Vera laughed merrily as she set the lamp on the
table.   " No, there isn't," she said.   Then she
turned a face half laughing, half serious towards
them.   " Girls, how long do you suppose ' Mother '
has been holding ' Grandpa ' back with that little
slender hand of hers? "

" I bet she didn't do it when he popped the question," said Jessie, with more force than elegance.

" I guess she commenced holding him back
when the question as to who should rule was first
brought up," said Garnet, disappearing into one of
the closets to hang her dress up.

"'Grandpa' seems to yield to it pretty well," said Allie, from the other closet.

"Yes, 'Mother's' victory seems to have been complete," said Vera, sitting down on the bed and beginning to unbutton her boots. "Who would imagine such a will-power in a delicate body like her. And such a hand as *she* has! Truly it is a 'velvet hand in an iron *glove*.'"

"Poor 'Grandpa' looks as though he realized it fully," said Jessie.

"Speaking of delicate bodies with iron wills," said Allie. "Don't you think that in nine cases out of ten you will find they go together?"

"Yes, I do," said Vera, decidedly. "You can never judge by appearances. Those who look as though they were born to rule are generally the ones who *are* ruled. You will very often find the spirit of a mouse concealed in the frame of a large woman, while your little, slender, wiry one is as courageous as a lion. I wonder how it is? And the rule holds good with the other sex, only timidity in a man is a hundred times more contemptible than in a big woman. The woman's sex excuses her to an extent, but what is more despicable than a cowardly man — especially if he is a big one? *Garnet!* what are you doing in that closet so long?"

"Listening to your learned discourse for one thing, and —" here she appeared in the doorway

bearing something in her hands, "getting the
alcohol lamp out to make some cocoa, for another."

"Garnet, you are my dearly-beloved sister,"
said Jessie, enthusiastically. "I choose the biggest
cup."

"Where shall I set it?" asked Garnet, standing
still in her white night dress, and looking around.

"Put it on here," said Vera, drawing forward a
chair. "It is steady."

"Now you three, make some spills out of that
paper on the floor," said Garnet, pouring some
alcohol in the basin of the lamp. "We haven't
any matches to spare; and for pity's sake close
that blind, some one; I don't care about the young
gent next door having a view of me just now."

"Sure death to him if he did," said Jessie, obeying the command.

Garnet, on her knees, gave her undivided attention to the burning alcohol, the other three girls
crouched on the floor around her and watched the
process with deep interest, each one holding a spill
in her hand.

"My, but it shmells goot," said Jessie, skinning
her little nose up, until it well-nigh disappeared
from view.

"Well, we haven't *goot* our cups ready," said
Vera; and Jessie, with a gasp, fell over on the floor
as if the miserable little pun, had stricken her
lifeless.

"Don't, Vera," groaned Garnet. "I want some appetite left for the cocoa."

"Never fear but what you will have some, my dear," returned Vera. "It will take more than a pun to spoil that."

"I'll give you the first taste, Vera," said Garnet. "You deserve something. Pass your cup."

"I will. A c(o)uple of them, if you say so."

": Drink it quick, dear," said Garnet, soothingly. "It *may* have the desired effect. Ready, Allie? Now, Jess! Have some, Garnet? Yes, I will, thank you."

I think you would have laughed if you had seen those four girls (young ladies, rather), sitting on the floor in their night dresses, their knees drawn up to their chins, and the cups of steaming cocoa in their hands.

Vera held her's up above her head. "I drink to our adopted grand-parents," she said, in a low, clear voice.

Jessie spoiled the effect by saying, reproachfully: "Oh, why didn't you do it before? I've drunk all mine. Give me some more, Net."

"Are you intending to make any more toasts, Vera?" asked Garnet, gravely. "Because, if you are, I'll put some more water on."

"I have done my did," said Vera, rather vaguely, and Jessie choked so that her cocoa was spilled all over her night dress, and Garnet had to slap

her back, saying as she did so: "Get into bed,
every one of you.   Some of the alcohol must have
gotten into Vera's cocoa, and it's gone to her
head."

Vera held her cup out coaxingly.   "Just a drop
more?" she pleaded.

"Not one," answered Garnet, sternly.   "Come,
put yourselves into that bed."   And Vera obeyed,
murmuring faintly.   "It's too *bed* of you, Garnet."

"What's that?" giggled Jessie, lifting her head
from her pillow.   "Say it again, Ve."

"She'll do no such thing," said Garnet, hopping
into bed beside Vera.   "Go to sleep, Jess."

"Say it again, Vera," urged Jessie.

"Can't, I'm dead," said Vera, in an exhausted
tone.   And Jessie was obliged to lie down and
content herself with laughing at something she had
not heard.

"Wont some one get up and open the blind-
door, so that the electric light will shine in?"
asked Allie.   "I would, only I am on the back
side."

Garnet was out of bed in a moment.   "Thanks,"
murmured Allie.

Fifteen minutes later, the silvery, moon-like
radiance rested softly upon the four girlish faces
lying calm and untroubled on their white pillows.
It touched, and lingered lovingly upon Jessie's
small, childish face, and showed the smile, still

lingering on the red lips. It lighted Allie's pale, quiet one, beside it. It seemed to hover pityingly over Vera's pillow, softening the proud lines of the white face, resting upon it, and turning to silver the golden hair. It seemed to change the expression of Vera's face entirely, making it one of almost childish trust and restfulness. An expression her face never wore in her waking moments. Anyone seeing it, well might think, "That will be the look it will wear in death."

The light, falling on Garnet's face, betrayed none of the girl's inward thoughts. The expression seen upon it, was simply one of a contented mind and perfect bodily health. *Was* there nothing more?

CHAPTER III.

The next morning the girls were awakened by the sun shining brightly into their room.

"Oh, what a lovely morning," cried Jessie, jumping out of bed and going to the door that led out on the balcony. "Girls, do come and look. It is perfectly lovely."

And indeed it was. There was a large tree before the house, whose branches almost rested on the roof. Between the leaves, could be seen the Methodist tabernacle, with its sloping red roof, old fashioned pulpit and rows of white, empty seats The lovely green grass in the park, fairly shone with the rain drops that still lingered upon it, and the leaves of the trees also glistened with them. The birds were singing, and from one of the cottages near, came the sound of a piano and the clear, full tones of a woman's voice, singing. Some children were walking through the park, and the the sound of their voices was music, too.

While the girls stood with their arms around each other, enjoying the perfect beauty of the scene, the loud notes of a bell startled them. They came from the church near by. Garnet looked at her watch that lay upon the table.

"Eight o'clock. That bell is for morning prayers; don't you remember, Jess?"

"Yes! they have only a very few minutes for them, though."

"Ten," said Garnet, beginning to dress.

Vera turned from the door with a softened look in her gray eyes. Somehow or other the whole scene of this glorious Sabbath morning, impressed her solemnly, and the sound of the bell calling all to prayers, added to the solemnity.

"I think I would like to attend an early service like that," she said, softly.

"Well, we will to-morrow morning, if we can get up early enough," said Garnet.

"I would like it too," said Allie.

"Umph! I don't know as I care about getting in with a lot of shouting Methodists," said Jessie, holding her head down and letting the glorious mass of hair fall over her face.

"Just look at that child's hair," said Vera, standing with her brushes poised above her head, while she gazed admiringly. "Do let me arrange it for you, will you, Jess?"

"With the greatest of pleasure," said Jessie, with alacrity, sitting down on her trunk.

"Doesn't anyone go to the church but shouting Methodists?" asked Allie.

"Yes, of course they do," answered Garnet. "Jess was only joking. Anyone goes who wants to."

"I suppose we are all going to the meeting in the tabernacle, aren't we?" asked Vera, putting a pin into Jessie's head a little more deeply than she meant to.

"Ow! That's my scalp you are boring into, Vera," squealed Jessie,

Vera made haste to pull out the offending pin. "Excuse me, Jess, but you hair is so thick it seems impossible for a pin to go through it."

"Well, it can, just the same," murmured Jessie, in an injured tone.

"I am going to meeting for one," said Garnet.

"So am I," said Vera.

"And I," said Allie.

"Well, then I suppose I must," said Jessie.

"You know you want to, Jessica," said Vera, lovingly, giving the glossy braids a final pat.

"Much obliged to you, ma'am, for doing my hair," said Jessie, getting off the trunk and making a low bow. "It feels splendiferous."

"It feels as it looks then," said Garnet. "I wish I could do something with my mop."

"I wonder if we will see the young men at church," said Jessie.

"Such a thing cannot concern a child like you, at any rate," said Garnet, at which reproof Jessie could only reply, lamely: "Hh! Child your own self."

"The first thing we had better do," said Vera, "will be to get some breakfast. 'Mother' said last night that we could use one of the tables in the kitchen and some of her dishes. Suppose you and I go over to the 'Central House' and get the breakfast, Net?"

"Very well; and Jess and Allie can clean up the room while we are gone."

Vera and Garnet made their way to the hotel in question; just through the Casino and across the avenue. Vera carried the pot of beans; Garnet, the brown-bread. When they returned to the cottage they found the table set, and Jessie and Allie waiting impatiently.

"Wonders will never cease," said Garnet. "We scarcely hoped to find you two young ladies down stairs. Now I'll make the cocoa."

"What are we going to have to top off with?" asked Jessie.

"Well, we ought to have thought and bought some fruit last night," said Vera, putting the pot of beans in the center of the table, while Garnet went out into the back kitchen to make the cocoa.

"We can have the rest of the crackers if we feel as if we really need anything, after we have attacked that bean-pot," said Allie.

Their first breakfast proved to be a most pleasant meal. The girls were hungry, and beans, brown-bread and cocoa never seemed to taste so good before, even though the table was not set "in style," and the table cloth was a piece of stiff, brown paper.

"Which would you rather do, Al and Jess," said Garnet, as they rose from the table, "wash the dishes or make the beds?"

"Let us take turns," said Vera. "We'll wash dishes this morning, and they can to-morrow morning."

"A good idea," said Garnet. "Now get to work, for there is no time to spare."

"Yes, its almost church-time," said Vera.

"Oh, bother church!" muttered Jessie.

"Jessie!" said Garnet, reprovingly.

"To tell the truth I don't care particularly about going myself," said Vera, putting the plates together. "But I suppose we might as well go; it will help kill time at all events."

"Yes," said Garnet. "and if we grow tired we can leave quietly."

When the girls were ready they looked each other over critically to see that everything was all right. A fairer sight could scarcely be asked for than they in their pretty summer dresses. Vera was dressed all in soft black, that made her white skin and golden hair look perfectly lovely. Allie wore a pretty, cool looking dress of white and nile-green. Garnet and Jessie wore cream, which was most becoming to their rich complexions and dark eyes.

They took their places near the entrance. When the hymn "Nearer My God to Thee" was sung, their voices joined in the harmony, and very sweet they sounded too. Yet, while they sang, their eyes roved carelessly from one part of the tabernacle to another, and when they saw the tall, bent form of " Grandpa " walk slowly up the aisle to one of the front seats, they nudged one-another and smiled.

> " Though like a wanderer,
> The sun gone down ;
> Darkness come over me,
> My rest a stone. "

The grand melody floated up to the dark dome of the tabernacle, but our girls' hearts beat calmly and regularly in their bosoms. Allie alone felt a name-less longing. What was it?

> " Yet in my dreams I'd be,
> Nearer my God to Thee. "

Vera's gray eyes, roving carelessly around, fell upon a pale face lifted to Heaven, and she stopped her singing to gaze in wonder. The blue eyes, that looked as though they knew well what it was to be filled with bitter tears, were full of a soft, radiant light now. The pale lips were slightly parted and quivering a little.

> " Nearer, my God to Thee,
> Nearer to Thee. "

The face was fairly luminous now and the next moment it was hidden from sight in two small, neatly-gloved hands, as the voice of the minister fell on the sudden silence.

"Oh, God, who takest away the sins of the world "—

Garnet softly touched Vera on the arm to remind her, and the golden head bowed itself immediately, but not one word of the beautiful prayer did Vera hear. Whose was that pale, radiant face? What deep sorrow had come into her life? The story of it was written in the luminous eyes, the quivering lips, the pale, peaceful face.

"What a heartlessly long sermon!" said Jessie, as they passed out from the cool duskiness of the tabernacle to the warm, bright sunlight. "I do think that minister ought to be arrested for cruelty to animals."

"What are you looking so sober about, Vera?" asked Garnet. "Are you thinking of the sermon?"

"There was but one sermon for me this morning," replied Vera.

"Conscience!" groaned Jessie. "How many would you have?"

"I don't mean the sermon the minister preached."

The girls turned and looked at her wonderingly.

"I found my sermon in a face this morning," was Vera's answer to the question so plainly asked.

"Why, good-morning, ladies," said a cheery voice, and "Cousin Fred" and Erfort Richards sauntered up.

"A miraculous discovery made, gentlemen, by our friend Vera," said Jessie.

"What is that?" asked Erfort, calmly taking the bunch of lace flounces, that served as a parasol, from Jessie's hand and using it for a cane.

"Why, she found a sermon in a face this morning."

"Cousin Fred" stepped quietly up to Vera. "Explain the mystery, Jess," he said.

"Oh, let Vera do that," replied Jessie.

"Does it seem such an impossible thing—finding a sermon in a face?" asked Vera. "Well, did any of you notice a lady, a small, slight lady with a pale face."

"Oh, did she have on a lovely white lace dress and a hat just one bed of pansies?" interrupted Jessie, turning around with an animated face.

The flickering smile passed over Erfort's face at the question, just touching the lips and lighting the dark eyes for a moment, and then vanished.

"No," replied Vera, "the truth is I didn't notice her dress, but she had large, blue eyes, and she seemed to be so interested in the sermon, and while they were singing "Nearer My God to Thee," I could not keep my eyes off her face — it was fairly radiant. That woman has suffered — I know she has, but whatever her sufferings have been, she has passed through them bravely and is feeling perfectly at rest."

" Why, Vera ! "

Jessie had stood still and was staring at Vera with all her eyes.   Fred looked ill at ease and was eyeing Vera askance. Was she one of these religious girls? He had liked her very much the day before, but if she was going to be religious it would spoil all the fun.   Erfort seemed to be intensely admiring the fantastic pattern of Jessie's parasol handle.

" What's the matter, Jasmine? " asked Vera.

" Well, that is just what I want to know," returned Jessie.   " What are you so solemn about? "

" I am not solemn," replied Vera.   " That is, I do not think I am ; and yet, that face as I watched it, made me feel strangely.   It somehow made me feel as though I would like to meet with the lady and talk with her."

" Perhaps you will meet with her," said Erfort, quietly.

" Oh, I hope so," replied Vera, warmly.

" Advertise for her," said Jessie, tilting her head back and looking at Vera over her shoulder with laughing eyes.   " I'll do the composing.   Ahem ! ' Wanted : — Knowledge of the whereabouts of a small, slight lady, with a pale face, luminous blue eyes, and a general aspect of one who has fought the battle of life bravely and is now patiently waiting to have her name erased from the great roll-call. The person who will give the desired information will be liberally rewarded.' "   Jessie held out a little hand. " Ten cents, please, Vera," she said ; but Vera did not smile.

"But I mean it, Jess. I would really like to know who she is."

" I noticed her," said Allie's quiet voice.

" Cæsar's Ghost ! " exclaimed Jessie, in horrified tones.

" Jessie ! " came from Garnet, in reproving tones.

Fred laughed. "You'll get yourself in trouble, Jess," he said, glad to have a chance of changing the tone of the conversation.

" Hh ; is·that so ? " retorted Jessie, but she said no more, and walked along by Erfort.

" Won't you come in ? " asked Vera, as they reached the cottage. " ' Grandpa' and ' Mother' have given us permission to use the front parlor, so we can entertain our friends in there."

Fred seated himself comfortably on the steps and just as he opened his mouth to say, " Oh, yes, thank you, we'll stay," Erfort said, "Thank you, but by the time we get back to the hotel, it will be our dinner-hour, and I suppose it is the same with you, ladies. If you are willing, we will call around this afternoon. Come, Fred."

Jessie skipped into the house, twirled herself around on one foot, made a sweeping courtesy to the door, and said in her most ceremonious tones. "Ah, yes, Mr. Richards, it *is* our dinner-hour. Come, ladies, we will repair to the dining-room of

Hotel d' Atherton and — lunch off fruit crackers and chocolate creams."

And with a laugh, the four girls ran lightly up the stairs to their room.

CHAPTER IV.

It is the afternoon of the next day, and again it is a pouring down rain storm. The girls are in their room. Vera is sitting in one of the rocking chairs, with a volume of Tennyson on her lap. Garnet occupies the other rocker, with a little volume called "Sea Music," in her hand. Allie is lying on one of the beds, with one hand under her cheek, and her blue eyes looking steadily at " nothing." Jessie is sitting on the foot of the other bed, one of her feet under her, the other swinging rather violently back and forth, between the bed and the floor ; her elbow is resting on the foot-board, her cheek is in her hand and her large black eyes are roving restlessly around the room. The exhaustless bag of fruit-crackers, holds its conspicuous place on the table, between Vera and Garnet, and every once in a while, first one little white hand and then the other, of the two readers, wander absently to it, disappear for an instant, and then withdraw itself, (and a cracker). They munch, and read, and rock, and are happy.

Poor Jessie! She is very human, and can bear it no longer. The swinging foot goes the least bit higher in its upward motion, and when it comes down, it brings Garnet's book with it; then Jessie throws herself backwards on the bed, partly to laugh and partly to escape the angry light of Garnet's dark eyes.

"You are certainly growing more lady-like every day," is Garnet's sarcastic comment, as she stoops to pick up her book.

"Oh, bother!" retorts Jessie. "Why don't the crowd wake up then? I never saw such a dull set! You two girls would be perfectly happy on an island, all by yourselves, if you only had a book of sentimental poetry and a bag of fruit crackers. *I* call it downright selfish in you. I don't know what *you* call it."

"Oh, Jasmine, don't speak lightly of Tennyson. I am reading the 'Lady of Shalott' for the eighth time, and it grows more beautiful every time I read it," said Vera.

"Ugh! His poetry is too ancient for me," replied Jessie.

"Ah, that is just the beauty of it. And he expresses himself so prettily. There is only one fault I can find with him."

"What is that?" asked Garnet.

"He makes his women too weak."

"Physically, intellectually, or morally?"

"Oh, morally. His description of them as they are *physically*, suits me exactly. Tall, slender, fair and proud! But weak — too weak."

"They had one rare qualification. They knew how to suffer in silence," said Garnet, thoughtfully.

"The fate of all true and pure women," answered Vera.

"*You* always make me think of Guinevere, Vera," said Garnet, lovingly. "I am going to call you that."

Vera raised both white hands in horror. "I beseech you not to, Garnet. Call me anything but that. Why, she was his weakest heroine."

"She proved herself to be strong at the last, though, Vera. And see what she suffered. Poor woman! She was a very woman in her suffering."

"Yes, the queen was indeed lost in the woman, in more sense than one. She deserved all the suffering she had to endure and she had no one to thank but herself."

"What's this all about, anyway," asked Jessie, who was sitting up on her elbow by this time, and listening to the conversation with interest, as was Allie. "Tell me all about it, Vera, I hate to read, but I like to listen to stories," and she drew her mouth down and rolled her eyes around, like the baby that she was.

"Well, I'll tell it to you," said Vera, closing her book and leaning her head back against her chair.

Garnet closed her book, rested her elbow upon it, leaned her head upon her hand, and prepared to listen. Allie and Jessie fixed their eyes upon

Vera, and so with the rain falling heavily on the
roof, and the wind moaning low among the branches
of the great tree, Vera told over, the beautiful story
of "Queen Guinevere," and as Garnet watched
the intensity of feeling expressed in the fair face,
she thought: "She *does* make an ideal 'Queen
Guinevere,' whatever she may say."

STORY OF "GUINEVERE."

"I will begin with 'The coming of Arthur.'
The first four lines are these:

> "'Leodogran, the King of Cameliard,
> Had one fair daughter, and none other child;
> And she was fairest of all flesh on earth,
> Guinevere, and in her, his one delight.'"

"Before Arthur came to the isle of Cameliard a
great many petty kings had ruled, and were always
waging war upon each other, wasting all the land.
Aurelius lived before Arthur came, and he fought
and died; then came King Uther, and *he* fought
and died. But neither of these kings could make
the kingdom one. But when King Arthur came,
he made a realm and reigned. All recognized
him as their head and king. But the island had
become such a waste that wild beasts rooted in the
fields and even wallowed in the gardens of the
king. And sometimes a wolf would devour a
child. King Leodogran had heard of Arthur newly

crowned, and he sent for him to come and fight the
the beasts, altho' some said that Arthur was not
Uther's son. So, Arthur came. And when he
passed the castle walls, Guinevere saw him, but
she did not know he was a king, for he did not
wear any sign of his kinglihood, but was dressed as
a simple knight. But Arthur saw and knew her,
and fell in love with her on the spot. But he
passed on, and pitched his tents beside the forest.
And he drove out the heathen, and slew the beasts,
and filled the forest, and made broad pathways for
the hunter and the knight, and then he went back,
for while he was there, some of the great lords and
barons were jealous of him, and they colleagued
with some of the smaller kings to bring doubts as
to his really being Uther's son, and his right to rule
them. They said he did not resemble Uther, and
they declared he was not Uther's son, but Anton's.
But Arthur thought of nothing but Guinevere. He
loved her with all the strength of his being, and he
was a very strong and noble man. But he went to
fight a great battle with these jealous barons and
kings, and first it seemed as though they were
going to win the fight, and then as tho' he was to
be the victor. But Arthur seemed to be possessed
with superhuman strength, and threw all the kings,
and the victory was his. He was so overjoyed that
he laughed aloud, and he said to his favorite warrior, whom he loved and honored most : "

" ' Thou dost not doubt me king,
So well thine arm hath wrought for me to-day.' "

" And the warrior replied : "

" ' Sir, and my liege, the fire of God decends
    upon thee in the battle field :
I know thee for my king.' "

" Then they swore on the field of death a deathless love, and Arthur said : "

" ' Man's word is God in man :
Let chance what will, I trust thee to the death ! ' "

" And this warrior was ' Sir Launcelot.' Then
Arthur asked Leodogran to give Guinevere to him
to be his bride, and Leodogran liked and admired
him, but he was doubtful as to his birth, for some
declared he was son of Gorloïs, or else the child of
Anton, and no king. Or else base born, so
Leodogran didn't know what to do. He sent out
knights to learn the history of Arthur's life. He
consulted with everyone whom he thought would
know, but he received but little satisfaction. He
sent for the ' Queen of Orkney,' for she was
Gorloïs' daughter, and asked her if she were not
Arthur's own sister, but she either could not or
would not tell him. At last he sent word to Arthur
that he might have Guinevere for his queen.
When Arthur received this word he bade Sir
Launcelot to ride forth and bring the queen, and
he watched him leave the gates. This was in the

latter part of April, and in May he returned with Guinevere. They were married, and at the shrine they swore a deathless love, and Arthur said : "

" ' Behold, thy doom is mine.
Let chance what will, I love thee to the death.' ' "

" And the queen replied with drooping eyes : "

" ' King and my lord, I love thee to the death.' ' "

" After his marriage, Arthur fought and won twelve great battles, and made a realm and reigned. One of the maidens of the queen's court was named Enid, and was wife to Geraint. She loved the queen and the queen loved her, and often the queen would deck Enid with her own white hands, and she would be the lovliest lady at the court — next to the queen herself. But now arose whispers of the guilty love of the queen for Sir Launcelot, and, although there was no proof of the truth of this, yet Geraint was fearful lest his young wife's honor should be sullied through her great love for the queen. So he went to the king, and, under pretext of desiring to go to his princedom to save it from bandit earls and assassins, he asked permission to take his wife and go hence, and the king, after musing awhile, allowed them to depart." (Here Vera stopped to say, " The poem of Geraint and Enid is beautiful, but I cannot do it justice. It must be read carefully to be appreciated.") Sir Launcelot was ordered by the king to go and search for the last and largest of the eight diamonds that was to be put into the center of the crown that was to be presented to the queen. On the morning of his departure the queen was sick, and Arthur asked her if she felt too sick to look upon Sir Launcelot before he went away. She lifted her eyes then and Sir Launcelot read in their depths:

" ' Stay with me, I am sick ; my love is more than many diamonds.' " And he yielded and told the king that the wound he had received a long time ago was not yet healed, and the king looked first at him and then at her and went his way, and then the queen and Sir Launcelot talked together and the queen was in a bitter mood so that he left her and went away angry. He went to the 'Castle of Astolat' where dwelt "

" ' Elaine, the fair ; Elaine, the lovable,
Elaine, the lily maid of Astolat,' "

" With her father and two brothers. And when he reached the castle gate the old dumb keeper let him in. And Elaine's father and two brothers greeted Sir Launcelot kindly and hospitably. And Elaine when she looked into his face read there the guilty love he had for his queen, but she loved him, although his face was seamed with an old sword cut and he was twice her years, yet "

" ' She lifted up her eyes
And loved him with a love that was her death.' "

" In the morning he departed with her brother, and while he was standing at the castle gate stroking his horse's mane, Elaine came down the tower stairs and stood before him. She asked him to wear her ' favor ' to the tourney. But he told her that he had never worn a lady's favor. She begged him to wear her's, and he said he would and asked her what it was. She told him it was a red sleeve, broidered with pearls, and she brought it, and while he bound it on his helmet he said : "

" ' I never yet have done so much
For any maiden living.' "

" And the words filled her with great delight. And he gave his shield to her and asked her to keep it until he came again. And Launcelot went to battle and it reached the queen's ears how he wore a red sleeve, broidered with pearls ; and the queen threw herself down on her couch and writhed in agony and called him ' traitor,' for she thought he loved someone else ; and in a little while she heard that it was the ' Maid of Astolat.' And the queen moved about her castle, pale and proud. But the poor little ' Lily Maid of Astolat,' unconscious of how her name was being bandied about at court, stayed in her turret window beside the shield, and watched for Launcelot's return. But he did not come for he had been wounded in battle, and Elaine told her father she must seek for him, and he gave her a guide saying : "

"'Being so very wilful, you must go.'"

"And as she went, the words kept singing in her heart, only the last one was changed:"

"'Being so very wilful you must die.'"

"She found Sir Launcelot in a cave wounded and sick, but her red silk sleeve still fluttered from his helmet, only it was tattered and torn, and half the pearls had been shot off. She nursed him every day, and every night she went to stay with her kin in the city. Launcelot was not always gentle with her, but sometimes gruff, but she bore it very meekly — she loved him so. And Launcelot thought to himself that if he had only met her before she might have made the world beautiful to to him, but now — "

"'The shakles of an old love straightened him.
His honor rooted in dishoner stood.
And faith unfaithful kept him falsely true.'"

"When Launcelot was better the three returned to Astolat, and Elaine dressed herself in her most becoming attire, and came and stood before Launcelot. She hoped he would tell her that he loved her, but he only bade her tell him what he could give her to repay her for her kindness to him, and he said:"

"'Delay no longer, speak your wish,
Seeing I must go to-day.'"

"Then poor Elaine forgot everything but her love, and she cried passionately : "

"'I have gone mad.   I love you ; let me die.'"

"'Ah, sister,' answered Launcelot, 'what is this !'   And innocently extending her white arms —'Your love,' she said, 'your love — to be your wife.'"

"But Launcelot told her he would never marry, for had he been going to he would have wedded earlier in life.   Then she implored him to take her with him, that she might ever see his face, but this he could not do.   He told her it was not love she felt for him, but 'love's first flash in youth,' and he told her he would always be her friend and knight, but more than that he could not.   But she only grew deathly pale, and saying :

"'Of all this will I nothing,'"

she fell, and they carried her swooning to the tower."   "And her father said : "

"'Aye, a flash
I fear me that will strike my blossom dead.
Too courteous are you fair Sir Launcelot, I pray you
     use some rough discourtesy
To blunt or break her passion.'"

"So, Sir Launcelot stayed over till the next morning, and Elaine heard his horse's hoofs upon the stones, and she flung open her casement and looked down and she saw that her sleeve was gone

from his helmet. And she knew that he knew
she was looking at him, but he did not glance up.
'This was the one discourtesy that he used.'

"So he went away, and Elaine sat in her tower
alone, and her father came to her and said: 'Have
comfort,' and her brothers came and said: 'Peace
to thee, sweet sister,' and she greeted them calmly.
And she made a song and called it 'The Song of
Love and Death.'   And when Elaine knew she
was going to die, she sent for her father and
and brothers, and told them she wanted to write
Sir Launcelot a letter, and that after she was dead
they must make her body ready for the grave and
lay it upon a barge, with the letter in her dead
hands, and let their dumb old keeper steer her
down the river to the gates of the queen's palace,
and then bear her into the hall and set her down
among them, and after her long voyage she would
rest.   And they promised to do as she asked. And
so she died.   And her two brothers laid her upon
the barge, and set a lily in her hand, and spread a
silken coverlet over her, and kissed her quiet brow
and said with tears:"

"'Sister, farewell forever.   Farewell, sweet sister.'
Then rose the dumb old servitor, and the dead
Steere'd by the dumb went upward with the flood—
In her right hand the lily, in her left
The letter—all her bright hair streaming down—
And all the coverlid was cloth of gold

Drawn to her waist, and she herself in white,
All but her face, and that clear-featured face
Was lovely, for she did not seem as dead,
But fast asleep and lay as tho' she smiled.' "

" That day, Sir Launcelot craved an audience of Guinevere, to give to her at last, the costly diamond, and she granted it to him; and when she appeared before him, pale and proud, he knelt before her.   And the queen was angry with him, and took her diamonds from her neck and arms, and telling him first to give them to the maid he loved, and then crying that she should not have them, she flung them from her through the casement into the water below, and it was then that the barge, bearing Elaine, passed under the window, and when they had brought her in, they gave the letter she held in her hand to Sir Launcelot, and this was it: "

" ' Most noble lord, Sir Launcelot of the Lake,
I, sometimes called the Maid of Astolat,
Come, for you left me taking no farewell,
Hither, to take my last farewell of you.
I loved you, and my love had no return,
And, therefore, my true love has been my death.
And, therefore, to our Lady Guinevere,
And to all other ladies, I make moan.
Pray for my soul, and yield me burial.
Pray for my soul, thou too, Sir Launcelot,
As thou art a knight, peerless.' "

"Sir Launcelot read it aloud, beside the dead Elaine, and before all the lords and dames, and king and queen, and he told them all her story. Then was the queen happy, for she knew he loved only her, still. And Arthur ordered Elaine's body to be put into a costly tomb, and for the story of her voyage to be blazoned on it, in letters of blue and gold. Then Sir Launcelot drew apart, and when the queen passed him, she said : ' Launcelot, forgive me ; mine was jealousy in love.' He answered : ' That is love's curse ; pass on, my queen, forgiven.' And Arthur came and put his arm about Sir Launcelot's neck, and sympathized with and consoled him in his trouble. He did not know how Launcelot was wronging him. And Launcelot was conscience-smitten and went away and mourned bitterly. After a while it became known to Arthur how he was being deceived, and his anger and sorrow were deep. Then the queen fled the Court, and took refuge in a convent at Almesbury, and had no one with her save a little maid—a novice. And this is how Arthur learned of her sin. Sir Modred hated Sir Launcelot, and he watched him and the queen, and one morning, when the royal party had been a-maying and had returned, Sir Modred climbed to the top of the garden wall, to spy some secret scandal if he might. Sir Launcelot came by, and seeing him, and understanding why he was there, took him by the heel, as one would pluck a caterpillar, and cast him down. Then he helped him to rise, but the prince went away with vengeance in his heart. Sir Launcelot told the queen, but at first she only laughed, then she grew afraid. They used to meet in the tower, and she begged him to fly to his own land, but he would not. At last, one day they agreed upon a night of parting. It came, and they met in the tower for the last time. But while they were bidding each other an affectionate farewell, Modred brought his men to the foot of the tower and cried out: 'Traitor, come out; ye are trapt at last!' And Launcelot rushed out and leapt on him, and hurled him headlong; and he fell, stunned, and his men took and bore him off and all was still. Then Sir Launcelot and Guinevere bade each other a long farewell. He begged her to go with him to his castle beyond the seas, but she would not. He said his was the shame; but she said, no, it was her's, for she was a wife and he was unwedded; so they parted. He went to his own land and she to the convent in Almesbury—fled all night upon the horse he had sat her upon. She told the sisters at the convent that her enemies pursued her, and they believed her and took her in. They never knew her name, for she talked only with the little maid. And one night she was listening to this little maid, who pleased her with her babbling talk, when there came a rumor wildly blown

about, that King Arthur was waging war on Sir
Launcelot.   Then she thought 'With what a hate
the people and the king must hate me.'   And she
bowed her head upon her hands, and the little
maid who did not like the silence said: 'Late, so
late! What hour, I wonder, now.' And when the
queen did not answer, she began to sing a little air
that the nuns had taught her.   'Late, so late.'
And when the queen heard this, she lifted her
head and asked her to sing the whole of it to her,
and she did, and this is the song:"

> " ' Late, late, so late! and dark the night and chill!
> Late, late, so late! but we can enter still.
>   Too late, too late! ye cannot enter now.
> No light had we; for that we do repent;
> And learning this, the bridegroom will relent.
>   Too late, too late! ye cannot enter now.
> No light; so late! and dark and chill the night!
> O, let us in, that we may find the light!
>   Too late, too late? ye cannot enter now.
> Have we not heard the bridegroom is so sweet?
> O, let us in, tho' late, to kiss his feet!
>   No, no, too late! ye cannot enter now.' "

"And after she had sung it she commenced to
talk with the queen about the news they had heard.
And she told the queen how the king thought Sir
Launcelot had the queen in his castle, and that
was why he had gone to fight him, and the little
maid spoke in loving words of the king — so good,

so kind and noble as he was — until the queen moaned to herself: ' Will the child kill me with her innocent talk?' And in listening to the little maid, she seemed to go back to the time when Arthur had sent Launcelot for her, and of the pleasant talk they had had together on their journey, and when she had first seen the king how she had thought him ' high, self-contained and passionless.' But while she brooded thus, there rang a cry through the convent: ' The King!' And while she sat and trembled, armed feet came through the long gallery from the outer doors. Guinevere threw herself on the floor and hid her face in her white arms, and when the king came thro' he saw and stopped before her. Then came silence, and then she heard his voice"—

> " ' Liest thou here so low, the child of one
> I honored? happy dead before thy shame!
> Well it is that no child is born of thee :
> For think not, tho' thou woulds't not love thy lord,
> Thy lord hast wholly lost his love for thee ?
> I am not made of so slight elements ;
> Yet must I leave thee, woman, to thy shame.' "

" He paused, and in the pause she crept an inch nearer, and laid her hands about his feet. And he said : "

> " ' Yet think not I have come to urge thy crimes,
> I did not come to curse thee, Guinevere ;

I, whose vast pity almost makes me die
To see thee lying there ; thy golden head,
My pride in happier summers, at my feet.
And all is passed, the sin is sinn'd, and I,
Lo ! I forgive thee, as Eternal God
Forgives : do thou for thine own soul the rest.
But how to take last leave of all I loved ? ' "

" Then Arthur goes on to give expression to his
deep sorrow, and his last words were : "

" ' But hither shall I never come again,
Never lie by thy side, see thee no more.
Farewell !
And while she grovelled at his feet,
She felt the King's breath wander o'er her neck.
And in the darkness, o'er the fallen head,
Perceived the moving of his hands that blest.' "

" Then the queen struggled to her feet and made
her way to the casement, that she might look once
more upon his face, and she saw him on horseback
at the door, and the sad nuns stood near him with a
light, and she heard him tell them to guard and
foster her evermore.　His helmet was lowered
so she would not see his face which was like an
angels.　Then he rode away, and Guinevere
stretched out her arms and cried : ' Oh, Arthur ! '
Then she knew how great for him her love was
and she moaned : "

" ' Is there none
Will tell the king I love him tho' so late ? ' "

"Then the little maid and the nuns came in and
stood around her, weeping ; and she told them that
hereafter she would make her home with them,
doing all the good she could."

" ' They took her to themselves, and she
Still hoping, fearing, is it yet too late ?
Dwelt with them, till in time their Abbess died.
Then she, for her good deeds and her pure life,
And for the power of ministration in her,
And likewise for the high rank she had borne,
Was chosen Abbess there, an Abbess lived
For three brief years, and there an Abbess passed
To where beyond these voices there is peace.' "

CHAPTER V.

A long drawn sigh from the three girls, as Vera finished, and then silence. Tender-hearted, impulsive Jessie was crying, but so softly that the others did not hear her.

"What a sad, sad story," said Allie, gently.

"Yes, it is sad," replied Vera, "but I don't pity Guinevere one bit."

"Oh, Vera," said Garnet, reproachfully.

"Well, I don't. Nor any other woman who proves herself so faithless. Such a grand man as King Arthur was!"

"He was too grand," said Garnet, with unusual bitterness. "I can imagine just how he looked down on the poor, fallen queen, who lay at his feet with her golden hair sweeping the dust. 'I, whose vast pity almost makes me die.' Ugh! If I were a man I would say: 'Pity be snooked.'"

"Well, Garnet Dare, I would like to know who is using elegant expressions now!" cried Jessie, taking her handkerchief down from her eyes. "But what became of King Arthur, Vera?"

"Oh, he fought and won many battles, and at last he was severely wounded, and — and — well, I can't just tell you where he went, but while he lay wounded on some beach, talking to one of his knights, a barge sailed slowly up to him, in which were seated three beautiful queens. They took Arthur into the barge and he sailed away with them to some beautiful, warm country." ("Oh, he died, then, did he?" interrupted Jessie, wickedly). Allie laughed softly and even Garnet smiled, but Vera replied, innocently: "No, he didn't die. There was one of the three beautiful women taller and more lovely than the others, who smoothed his forehead and—"

"Hh! I bet a dollar bill he up and married her before he'd known her a month. Just like a man," said Jessie, with infinite contempt.

"Oh, Jasmine; what do you know about men?" asked Vera, with a laugh.

"Hh! all I want to."

"You know what Josiah Allen's wife, Samantha, says about the men," said Garnet. "Or more particularly about her's. 'Josiah looked good to me. Men are nice creeturs, but you don't want to see too meny of them to once; likeways with wimmen.'"

"Well, Samantha gets about right about our not wanting to see 'too many of them to once,'" said Jessie. "I've never seen any man yet who looked good to *me*."

"That's strange," said Vera, in mock surprise. "Such an antiquated fossil as you are."

"Superfluity of words, my dear," reproved Jess, grandly. "A fossil is necessarily antiquated." Then she buried her head in the counterpane, to escape the cracker that Vera threw at her.

"Doesn't Mr Richards look good to you, Jess?" asked Allie, innocently. "I think he is real nice looking."

"Oh, he's nice looking enough," said Jessie, carelessly, "but he's stiffer than a ram-rod."

"Say, girls," said Vera, suddenly, "do you think it is wicked to go to the theatre?"

Up sprang Jessie on the bed, and gazed at Vera with big, shining eyes. "What!" she exclaimed. "What did you say, Vera Earle?"

"I asked you," repeated Vera, "if you thought it was wicked to go to the theatre."

"Well, not much," replied Jessie, emphasizing her words with a pound of her little fist on the footboard. "But I would think it mighty wicked if I *couldn't* go."

"Jessie, will you *please* stop using that word?" asked Garnet.

"What word?" Knowing all the time what it was.

"Mighty. You know it is not only unladylike, but actually wrong."

"Yes, that's so," with unexpected meekness. "I won't use it again."

"But *do* you think it is all right to go?" asked Vera.

"Jessie has already answered for herself," said Garnet. "*I* certainly think there is not the least bit of harm in going to a theatre, unless the play is immoral. That, of course, would be apt to have a dangerous effect on one's mind, just as immoral books have. But, as for there being anything wicked in the ordinary theatre, I cannot see the reason."

"You don't think it is wicked, do you, Vera?" asked Jessie, suddenly.

"What a question, Jess," said Garnet, with a low, amused laugh. "When we all four go to one every Saturday afternoon almost as regularly as Saturday afternoon comes."

"Hear Net," said Jessie. "Anybody would think we were female Cæsars."

"Well, we go to the theatre on an average of once a month," retorted Garnet, whether we are female Cæsars or — or male Cæsars," she added, rather lamely.

"Yes, you bet we do," said Jessie, "if we do have to get seats in 'nigger heaven.'"

Garnet looked most indignant. "The idea!" she exclaimed. "I wouldn't say such a thing even in joke, if I were you, Jessie."

"An' sure, I'm *not* saying it in joke. I'm in deadly airnest, be jabbers. But you do not answer me, Vera. Have you changed your mind about going to the theatre? Give me your handkerchiefs, girls, I shall need them if she tells me she does."

"N—o," replied Vera, "I don't know as I think it is *wicked* really, but—"

"N—o—o—o," mimicked Jessie. "What do you mean by your prolongation of the vowel O, Vera Katherine Earle? You appear to be in doubt. Answer me; but don't you dare to tell me you think it is wicked to go to the theatre, or I'll throw the pillow at you," and she raised it threateningly.

Then she turned suddenly to Allie. "What are *you* looking so solemn about, Miss Hunt? Are you going back on the theatre too?"

"Don't look so savage, Jessie," replied Allie, smiling; then she added, softly: "I don't know as I would miss such a great deal if I *did* go back on it. Do you think I would?"

"Well, of course I can't answer for you," replied Jessie, laying down the pillow with a curiously disappointed look on her little face. "But I know *I* wouldn't care to live if I couldn't go to the theatre — *that's* sure."

"Oh, Jasmine!" exclaimed Vera. "Isn't that a little strong?"

"No," replied Jessie, drawing her rosy lips together in a little, straight, determined line. "Not a bit too strong to express my feelings."

"Well," said Vera, "I *have* noticed this one thing, when I have come from the theatre lately

I have felt just a little dissatisfied. At first I laid it to the play — I thought it must be they were not as good as formerly, but I found that that couldn't be the reason, for — you remember the last one we went to, Margaret Mather in 'Joan Of Arc?'" (Both Garnet and Jessie nodded; Jessie very emphatically.) " Well, of course, that was a grand play and it was grand acting, but if you'll believe me, girls, I actually felt that same dissatisfied feeling that I had felt before. Now, what made me?"

No one answered. That Vera, or any one else, could feel in that way after seeing such a grand thing as that play was, was a thing perfectly incomprehensible to Jessie. Garnet's deeper mind could not find a reason. Vera was honestly troubled. She could not answer the question of her own restless heart. Only Allie's pale face flushed; she looked at Vera with eager blue eyes, and once or twice her lips trembled as though she would speak, but it seemed as if she could not and in a moment more it was too late, for a low knock sounded on the chamber door, which all recognized as being " Mother's," and then the door was softly pushed open and the fair, wrinkled face peered in. From force of habit the girls looked past " Mother " and smiled at each other to see the fragile hand holding " Grandpa " back. But he caught a glimpse of the pretty picture in the chamber, and it did his dear old eyes good.

"Come right in, 'Grandma,'" cried all the girls together, "and 'Grandpa,' too." And Vera and Garnet drew their rocking-chairs forward.

"Well, well; thank you, thank you," replied "Mother," in her eager, trembling tones. "I only came up to tell you — now Mr. Atherton, you had better not come in," she broke off to say to "Grandpa," as he was pushing eagerly forward.

"Oh, yes, *do* let him come," pleaded the girls, and "Grandpa" thanked them with a happy smile.

"Well, I declare!" replied "Mother," secretly pleased, but still dictatorial, "then come in and sit down here side of me. As I was saying, children— you don't mind my calling you children, do you?" ("No, no; certainly not," murmured the girls.) "Well, as I saying, I only came up to tell you — oh, last night Mr. Atherton and me heard you singing. It *was* you, wasn't it?" The girls thought for a moment. "I'm pretty sure it was you," went on "Mother," "because it sounded as if it came from this room. First you went w-a-y up and then you came w-a-y down, and kind of quirked your voices once in a while, and you said something about 'neater, on neater' — guess the song must have been about clean habits or something. Wa'n't it you?"

Well it was for the dear old souls that their eyes were dim and the twilight deepening. No one could answer except Allie.

"Yes, 'Grandma,' we were singing and the piece you refer to was 'Juanita,' 'Nita, Nita, Juanita.' We'll sing it for you sometime if you want us to.

"Oh, will you? Well, that will be nice. Me and Mr. Atherton love to hear young people sing. That must be a pretty piece; but do you know 'Nearer My God to Thee?' and 'Jesus, Lover of My Soul?'"

Oh, yes, of course, the girls knew them.

"Well, somehow or other I like them two old pieces better than anything else. Would you just as lief sing one of them now?"

Oh, yes; they would sing them both. The dusky twilight gathered, the rain pattered softly against the glass doors, the wind moaned drearily among the huge branches of the tree, but the beautiful girlish voices rose above both rain and wind: "Nearer, my God to thee, nearer to thee." Vera could see, shining clear and pure through the coming darkness, the pale, illuminated face she had seen and watched in the tabernacle, the pale lips quivering, the blue eyes raised to Heaven. "Jesus lover of my soul." Vera still saw the face. Was the peace that she saw written upon it, the "peace that passeth all understanding?" "While the nearer waters roll, while the tempest still is nigh." "Mother's" wandering hand sought "Grandpa's," folded upon the arm of his chair, drawn close to her side, and there it rested. After the sweet voices ceased, it was very quiet in the room. "Mother" broke the silence.

"Ah, that is a beautiful hymn; a beautiful hymn." And "Grandpa" murmured: "Aye, a beautiful hymn."

"Yes, I think it's pretty," said Jessie, pleasantly, but carelessly.

The tone more than the words, jarred on Vera. Why was it? Only because she had been feeling for a few minutes strangely happy—peaceful, glad.

"Me and Mr. Atherton have morning prayers," went on "Mother." "Wont you join us?"

Jessie made a comical face, which no one saw. The others answered at once: "Oh, thank you; we will be very happy to."

"You might sing those pieces again," said "Grandpa," timidly.

"Yes, we will," answered Garnet, kindly.

"Hadn't we better have a light," queried Jessie, just here.

"Oh, 'Mother,'" whispered "Grandpa," "you didn't tell them."

"Land, I forgot!" replied "Mother." "Them pieces put it all out of my mind. We came up to tell you, children, there are two young gentlemen down stairs, and they wanted me to ask you to come down."

Jessie, on her way to the stand for a match, gave Vera's shoulder an expressive nudge.

" I'll go right down and tell them you're coming."
went on " Mother." " Come, Mr. Atherton ! "

At the door she turned and asked, anxiously :
" You wont forget to-morrow morning, will you? "

" No, we wont forget."

" My conscience ! " exclaimed Jessie, as soon as
" Mother" and " Grandpa " were out of hearing,
" I wonder if those two young men are blessed
with a good stock of patience."

" This is a good test for it if they are," said Vera.

" Wonder if they heard us warbling? " said
Jessie. " Quirking our voices, as ' Mother ' says."

" I can imagine just how the two young men
have spent the last half hour," said Garnet, standing before the glass and brushing her curly hair.
" Fred has walked not *less* than a couple of miles.
I'll wager he has kept up a continual march round
and round the room, with his hands in his pockets
and a most portentious frown on his usual sunny
brow, while Mr. Richards has been sitting calmly
in his chair with his legs crossed, watching his
uneasy friend with a half amused, half superior
smile on his mobile countenance."

" Well, get away from that glass for half a
minute, will you? " said Jessie, giving Garnet a
gentle poke with her comb. " Somebody else
wants to look bewitching as well as yourself."

" Oh, certainly," replied Garnet, in her politest
tones, moving away accommodatingly.

" Now, get huffy," said Jessie, in injured tones.
"You *are* the queerest girl, Net Dare. Nobody
can say anything to you but what you get mad."

" Have I expressed my displeasure at anything?"
asked Garnet, haughtily.

"Yes, you have," snapped Jessie. " If you
didn't in words, you did in actions, and I'd a good
sight rather anyone would give me a good blowing
up and be done with it than to be so plaguey polite
with their ' Ce-r-tainly, Ce-r-tainly,' and Jessie
imitated Garnet to perfection. " I find that people
who are so dreadfully polite can be about as ugly as
they make 'em. And it isn't politeness, anyway, it is
nothing but sarcasm, and you know very well Net
Dare, that sarcasm is indicative of low breeding—"

"Jessie Dare !" interrupted Garnet's low voice
trembling with passion.

"Just wait until I finish, will you?" said Jessie,
breathlessly. " I don't mean low breeding exactly,
but it shows very poor taste. Doesn't it, Vera?"

Vera, who had been first craning her neck to
look in the glass over Jessie's head, and then
dodging under and around her raised arms, hardly
knew what to say to this sudden appeal, so she
" avoided the question."

" I say we had better go down to the parlor
before your cousin wears the carpet entirely out
in his impatient walking."

"It is *certainly* time to go down," remarked

Garnet, meaningly, and Vera could not help thinking, as they went slowly down the stairs, how utterly unlike the two sisters were, and wondered if Garnet conducted herself in *just* the right way towards Jessie.

Their two natures were so entirely opposite. Jessie, quick, passionate and impulsive, yet, oh, so lovable and generous to a fault; Garnet, just as passionate, but possessing a wonderful capability of governing her passion—proud, reserved, not easy to be understood by even her nearest and best friends. Vera often wondered at the wonderful amount of self-control contained in the small body.

CHAPTER VI.

When the girls entered the parlor they found the state of affairs to be just as Garnet had predicted they would be. Fred was walking the floor with his hands in his pockets, and Mr. Richards with his hands ditto, sat in a chair and watched his friend with a smile half amused, half superior. Fred turned around as the door opened and made a low bow.

"Ah, most delighted to see you, *at last*, ladies," he said, not trying to conceal his vexation. "Our aged friends are rather swift, are they not? It would not be a bad idea to suggest a telephone to them, would it?"

"Don't be disrespectful to old age, Fred," said Garnet, reprovingly.

Fred turned and looked at his cousin. "You are not in love with the reverend, are you Net?"

"I am not very far from it," replied Garnet. "They are two very lovable old people, and should be treated with all possible respect, as indeed *all* old people should."

Garnet was quite serious. Fred gave a low whistle and cast an expressive look at Jessie. Jessie laughed.

"Net is on her high horse to-night," she said, carelessly. "I advise you to let her alone, Fred. She is unapproachable when in the present state." Garnet took her seat on the sofa beside Vera, and Vera saw a look of pain on her face, but the small mouth was set in one narrow, stern line. Vera looked at Jessie reproachfully, but Jessie, not dreaming of such a thing as Garnet's feelings being hurt by *her*, answered the look with a smile.

"She is nothing but a child," thought Vera. "She is—"

"Miss Earle, I have some pleasant news for you," said a quiet voice at her elbow. Vera gave a start and looked around.

"Pleasant news?" she repeated, smiling. "Tell it to me at once, please. I do love pleasant news."

"Oh, don't I wish I was pleasant news," said Fred, longingly, from the other side of the room.

Vera laughed and blushed. Mr. Richards looked at Fred gravely for a moment, then turned to Vera.

"Then I am deeply thankful," he said, in a low voice, "of having the power to make you happy. Can you guess what it is?"

Vera's red lips parted in a smile, showing her lovely white teeth. "Oh, do not ask me to guess, Mr. Richards. I forfeit my right of being a Yankee when I try to do that. Please tell me."

"I have found your sermon."

Vera looked perplexed. "My sermon, Mr. Richards? What do you mean?"

"Have you forgotten so soon? I have discovered who the owner of the 'speaking face' is."

Vera's face flushed with pleasure. "You have, really, Mr. Richards, and so early? Oh, how nice that is! Who is she? Where does she live? How did you find it out?" And Vera sat up very straight and clasped her white hands and looked at Mr. Richards with shining eyes.

Jessie came hurrying over, with Fred close behind her. "What's the matter, Vera?" she asked, seating herself in Garnet's lap and putting one arm around Garnet's neck, and Vera noticed even then, how closely and lovingly Garnet held her little sister to her.

"Why, Mr. Richards has really discovered who my 'lady of the tabernacle,' is," she replied. "Will it be possible for us to become acquainted with her?" she asked, turning to Erfort.

"I think so," he replied, gravely. "If you care to."

"If I care to!" repeated Vera. "Certainly I will care to, for she has the loveliest face I ever saw."

"How in the deuce did you find out about her, Er?" asked Fred, his astonishment getting the better of his politeness.

Erfort smiled. "I will explain that later, I will tell you who she is first."

"Oh, do hurry," cried Jessie, impatiently. "Who is she?"

"She is a laundress."

If he had said: "She is a murderess," the effect would have been scarcely more startling. The girls opened their eyes, in surprise.

"A laundress?" repeated Vera, faintly, and Jessie exclaimed: "Well, I never!" while Fred, I am sorry to say, gave vent to the elegant expression: "The divil!" and then begged the ladies' pardon in the same breath. Allie alone seemed unaffected by the startling announcement.

"She is none the less a lady for all that, is she?" she asked, softly. "It certainly cannot make her face any the less lovely in its expression, Vera."

Perhaps for the first time since he had met with her, Erfort Richards looked Allie squarely in the face, and his look was most complimentary, although Allie did not notice it.

Vera pulled herself together at Allie's question. She was ashamed of herself for expressing any surprise or consternation. "Certainly she is none the less a lady," she said, a trifle haughtily. "Her vocation can make no difference to her character. I was only a little surprised, that is all."

It was one of Vera's characteristics to hide her disagreeable feelings, of whatever nature, under an assumed haughtiness of manner. It had always proved a perfect shield from any unpleasant remark. If she had been told that there was danger of people misjudging her — that they might think her proud, and even heartless; not willing to acknowledge herself in the wrong when she knew herself to be, she would have been utterly surprised. And yet there were many — very many — who found it impossible to love her, simply because they did not understand her. She knew herself, but, alas, others did not, except a very few, who had learned her for themselves after years of friendly intercourse, and who loved her through and through for what she was. Strange to say, Mr. Richards thus early understood her perfectly; as well after three days as he would have done after three years. But to poor Fred she was a perfect enigma. First she was a flame of fire — all light, laughter and fun; then she was an icicle — cold, proud, stately as a queen; repelling those about her with a glance, a gesture. He had called her a conundrum to Erfort, the night before, but said he shouldn't " give her up."

" But you haven't told us where she lives," said Garnet.

" She lives in a little cottage back of Circuit avenue," replied Erfort. " Her name is Hood— Charlotte Hood—and she is a widow."

"Any children?" asked Jessie.

" One; a boy."

" I suppose he trots around with the basket,"
said Fred, carelessly.

" No. She goes for the clothes herself and
takes them back again."

" The lazy little beggar!" said Fred. " The
kid, I mean," he explained, " to let his mammy
do all the work. I must say she shows very poor
judgment in bringing her child up, for all of her
angelic expression of countenance."

" We can very easily come to know her," said
Garnet. " Perhaps we can get her to do a little
work for us."

Jessie came very near betraying the whole party
by saying: " It *will* be precious little work we
will be putting out."

" Will you take us to her cottage to-morrow, if it
is pleasant?" asked Vera.

" With pleasure," replied Erfort. Now I will
tell you how I found her out. I went to walk this
morning—although it *was* rather a wild one. I
went down towards the beach, and, while I was
standing under the tower watching the waves, I
noticed a lady coming towards me. That she *was*
a lady, despite the big basket of clothes she carried,
was plainly evident. When she was very near to
where I was standing, an unusually fierce gust of
wind struck her. It knocked the heavy basket up
against her, her foot somehow slipped and before I
could barely start forward to help her she had

fallen to the ground. I assisted her to rise, and was glad to find she had not hurt herself. I had a very short conversation with her, during which she told me about her boy, and — well, that's all."

Fred laughed and rose from his chair. "So you were out mashing the washwoman while I was sleeping the sleep of the just. Business must have been dull if you couldn't find any one better to flirt with, Er, my boy. Come, Jess, I'll teach you that new step I spoke to you about. The old people won't hear us."

"All right," cried Jessie, gleefully, slipping off Garnet's lap, and, while Garnet and Allie watched the "lesson," Vera turned to Erfort with shining eyes.

"No, that was *not* all, Mr. Richards. There was more to it than that."

"Yes?" he said, questioningly; but Vera saw the deep red just showing through his dark cheek, and she went on boldly.

"You helped the poor woman home with her basket."

He did not deny it; he only smiled.

"Why didn't you tell us? It was a generous, manly act."

"Thank you, Miss Earle."

Vera looked at him for a moment — at the dark, tender face, with its thin, sensitive lips and dreamy eyes, and in that moment she saw beneath the sur-

face into the heart.   She held out her white hand
and he grasped it firmly.   No words were spoken
by the lips, but the warm hand-clasp spoke volumes.   It said for each :   "I understand you, and
I respect you;" and then they, too, turned their
attention to the "lesson" in progress.

"One, two, three and a *hop*.   One, two, three
and a *hop*.   *One*, two, three.   *One*, two, three.
One, two, three.   *One*, two, three.   One, two,
three and a *hop*," counted Fred, as he guided Jessie
lightly, but firmly around the room, and Jessie,
with her brilliant little face all flushed and glowing with the heat, and her big black eyes sparkling
with the fun and excitement, now giving a little
gasp of delight at getting the correct step, and now
one of dismay at making a mistake and bringing
one of her little feet down squarely upon Fred's.
Vera laughed softly.   "Jessie's face is full of
lights and shadows, as it were," she thought, and
turned to Erfort to express her thoughts in words.

He was watching Jessie with the peculiar flickering smile he seemed to reserve for her alone.

"Hadn't you better rest awhile Jessie?" asked
Garnet, just then.   "You will get too tired."

"Oh, yes, in-just-one-minute," gasped Jessie.
"I've-al-most-got-it."

"You've gotten it pretty bad, haven't you?"
asked Vera, laughing.   "Come here and sit down
immediately, Jessie Dare ; you look ready to drop !"

Fred gave Jessie a parting whirl, which brought them both near the sofa. She dropped panting between Garnet and Vera, and commenced to fan herself with her handkerchief. Mr. Richards gravely offered her his bicycle cap. She took it with a smiling "You are too kind, Mr. Richards."

"Miss Earle," said Fred, "wouldn't you like to try a waltz with me? I'll whistle."

"Some time I will, but not now," she replied pleasantly. "I want to ask you and Mr. Richards a question."

"I'm your obedient servant," said Fred, drawing an ottoman to her feet and seating himself upon it. "What is your question? I am all attention."

"I want to ask you if you believe in theatre-going," she said, gravely.

"Oh, for pity's sake, don't start that up again," said Jessie, impatiently. "We had it going for about an hour up stairs."

"Well, I have your opinion, now I want the gentlemen's."

Fred had already pretty well expressed himself in his usual way — a low whistle. Vera turned to Mr. Richards. He had drawn a magazine from his pocket, and was turning the leaves rapidly.

"Quite a coincidence," he said, as Vera turned to him. "I was reading only this afternoon an article in here — let me see — who was it by? Some divine or another — ah, here it is. Will one of you ladies be kind enough to read it aloud? It may give you a new idea. It is upon the question of theatre-going," and he passed the book to Vera.

"You read it, Net," said Vera, passing it on to her.

Garnet took the book, which was "Munyon's Monthly Magazine," and read: "'The Common Sense View of the Theatre. By Rev. Madison C. Peters. Extracts from a sermon preached Sunday morning, February 1st, 1891. That they use this world as not abusing it — 1 .Cor. vii: 31. The theatre owes its origin to religion. In Greece, India and China the drama was originally a religious ceremony, and it was intended to promote religion. In the course of time the drama ceased to be a religious ceremony, and became a work of art.'"

"'Every student of church history knows that the modern drama sprang originally from the church. In the dark ages the priests put the whole of theology on the stage, and in this way, the rude and unlettered mob that gathered on Saints' days, were taught in an effective way the truths of religion, so that in the Christian era, the first theatres were the churches, and the first actors the priests.'"

"'But secular competition grew apace, and in 1378, the Dean and Chapter of St. Paul's Cathedral, petitioned Richard II to stop certain dramatic perform inces, which were being gotten up in London, outside the church. Why? Because the Cathedral clergy of St. Paul's had spent so much money on church scenery and costumes inside the Cathedral, they were eager to crush all secular competition.'"

"'In Elizabeth's reign the secular drama had grown so popular that a preacher exclaims : ' Woe is me ! At the play-house it is not possible to get a seat, while at the church vacant seats are plenty.' The clergy did not object to the principle of acting, or because the play was immoral, except when it satirized the drunken and smoking rector. Nor did the clergy object to the play because it hurt the people, but because it pleased them. They groaned when the people shouted.'"

"'God has implanted a dramatic element in most of our natures, recognized and cultivated it in the Bible. It is not something built up outside of ourselves by Thespis and Æschylus and Sophocles and Euripides and Terence and Plautus and Seneca and Congreve and Farquhar and Corneille and Alfieri and Goldsmith and Sheridan and Shakespeare. Man is not responsible for the dramatic element in his soul, but for the perversion of it.'"

"'If vacant seats are so plenty in the church, whose fault is it? The human mind is the same in the pew as in the theatre. The world suffers more from too little dramatic power in the church than from too much outside of it. A preacher asked Garrick, the tradgedian : 'Why is it you are able to produce so much more effect with the recital of your fictions than we do by the delivery of the most important truths?' 'My lord,' said Garrick, 'you speak truths as if they were fictions; we speak fictions as if they were truths.' And, wherever to-day, all Christendom through, there is a man in a pulpit with graceful gestures, modulated voice, elegant expression, appropriate emotion and grace-ful action; wherever you find man as natural and impressive, as audible and interesting as the actor, you will find a full church. Let the preachers work at the people with the same power, intelli-gence and will as the actor is obliged to work at the public; depend upon it their achievements will be in proportion. The actor does not grumble be-cause the people wont come to the theatre. He says: 'I am to blame.' People don't come to church because they are not interested. Let us learn from the actor how to read and how to infuse life into our service.'"

    *   *   *   *   *   *   *

"'Other things beside religion are good. Dickens' works are eternal arguments against in-justice, and in writing novels he was as well em-ployed as in preaching the gospel. Mendelsshon, by his sublime compositions, did better serve the

world than going out as a missionary to China; and
Shakespeare served the world and his Maker better
as a dramatist than as a bishop, preaching sermons
that nobody wanted to hear. The arts and sciences
must go hand in hand with religion and morality."

" 'The charge that religion is scoffed at on the
stage is false. Hypocrites and charlatans occasionally furnish subjects for its characterization.
The cause of religion does not suffer when its
spurious representatives are held up to ridicule and
contempt.' "

" 'The theatre is here to stay. Reform is the note
of the future. Eliminate the bad. Encourage the
good. The shameful postures, the female attire,
or rather the lack of it, the compromising attitudes,
the silly things accepted, the commonplace persons
admired and commended — thunder as much at
these as you will. Let ridicule, sarcasm and
denunciation exhaust their armories upon these
abuses, these positive evils.' "

" 'Can I go to the theatre?' asks the Christian.
I answer: 'If you *can*. Let every man be persuaded in his own mind.' Refuse to do or go
where your conscience forbids, but refrain also
from condemning your neighbor, whose conscience
may not require him to walk in the same path you
have marked out for yourself.' "

" 'All actors are not moral. All preachers are
not moral. There are bad men in all professions.

There are men and women on the stage whose characters are as spotless and their lives as beneficent as any in our churches. Crimes are committed on the stage; so they are in the Bible. Goodness and badness are put in opposition in both books and plays.'"

" ' Charles Lamb once wrote a play for the stage, and he went to see it enacted. The play was condemned, and loudest hissing came from the gallery where Charles Lamb sat, and the audience looked and saw that it was the author of the play who was hissing his own production.'"

" ' If at last we are compelled to look back upon a wasted life, we ourselves will be the severest critics. And remember this, when you go out of this world and your life has been wasted, no encore can ever bring you back to re-enact it. 'As the tree falleth, so it lieth!' Your character in the last moment will be your character through all eternity. Mr. Palmer, the London actor, dropped dead on the stage while quoting the words of the play: ' O, God, is there another and better world?' I do not know what will be your exit, but in that hour there will come before you all that you have been and all that you might have been. O, men and women of the theatrical profession, to whom these words may come, prepare for the closing scenes of this life, when the footlights will be the burning world, the orchestra the resurrection trumpets, the tragedy the upheaval of a world of graves, and the closing scene the dispersing of the audience to their everlasting homes of gladness or sorrow.'"

CHAPTER VII.

"Well, what do you think of that?" asked Fred. "Doesn't that advocate theatre-going?"

He addressed the whole party, but looked particularly at Vera. She answered him.

"It does, and it does not. You see it says: 'Can I go to the theatre?' the Christian asks. I answer: 'If you *can*. Let every man be persuaded in his own mind.'"

"Then I take it that one can go to the theatre and not be in danger of everlasting punishment, so long as their conscience tells them they are all right," observed Jessie, blunt, but to the point. "I don't think my conscience will trouble me much. Isn't that the idea, Vera?"

"I suppose so," answered Vera, thoughtfully. "But what I don't understand is *why* it should seem wrong to some and not to all. I know some good people — Episcopalians and Universalists — who go to the theatre every week of their lives, as regular as clock-work; and they not only go to the theatre, but they go to balls and dance until 2 o'clock in the morning. Sundays they go to church all day and *enjoy* going too, and their lives are all that seem good and just, as they should be."

"Well, those two denominations believe in having a good time," interrupted Jessie. "It's easy enough to belong to *their* church."

"No," argued Vera, "but they are *really* good people; much better than some Baptists that I know. *They* stay at home from all such places from one year's end to the other. If a member of *their* church went to such places their names would be crossed off the church book. How is that? Aren't one class just as good as another? If it is right for people of one denomination to go, why isn't it right for those of another?"

Vera seemed to appeal to Mr. Richards. He answered her.

"I can only use the same quotation you used a moment ago: 'Let every man be persuaded in his own mind.' Speaking of different denominations, I look at it in just this way. Now take the Baptists for instance — and just here let me say, their's is the belief I have the most confidence in, although I have no word to say against any other — their church laws are different from most other denominations. Anyone who enters that church should enter it with their eyes open. They should be ready and willing to accede to the requirements they make. Now, the Baptists do not think that he who has professed himself ready to try to live a Christian life, ought to find pleasure in the enjoyments that the world offers him. You know the

Bible tells us that we cannot serve both God and mammon. Either we must hate the one and love the other, or vica versa. I do not think that it really means that we are to hate in the ordinary sense of the word; but I think it means that we ought to find so much pleasure in serving God and keeping our hearts so full of love for Him, that there will be no room in them for anything else. It is simply impossible for us to live in this beautiful world and not love the things that are in it, and God does not expect or wish us to do so, or he would not have made it so beautiful. It is not that the ordinary pleasures of the world are so *wicked*, but there is danger of our thinking so much of them, that we have no time to think of the giver of every good and perfect gift. That is where the sin comes in — in thinking too much of the world and not enough of God. Now, just for a test. Please do not think me impertinent, for I do not mean to be so, but I want to ask you all a question. How often during the day do you stop to think how good God is to you?"

Not an answer, but over each fair face a burning blush commenced to spread. Fred felt half ashamed and half angry. How long since had Er turned preacher?

"I, myself," continued Erfort, after waiting a moment, "freely acknowledge that I have seldom, in former days, given it a thought. Our days are filled up with something — pleasure, business, almost every moment excitement or work of some kind. What time is left for serious thought? I haven't a doubt but that every one of us say our stated prayers at stated times, but apart from that, what thanks do we give for all our mercies? Forgive me if I have taken upon myself the role of preacher. I would not speak so freely if I did not feel so deeply."

Another pause. Erfort spoke again. "I know I have wandered from the subject somewhat — I beg your pardon for doing so. You asked me, Miss Earle, why it seemed wrong to some and not to others, to enjoy the pleasures of the world. I can only answer for myself. I have always enjoyed society and have always moved in it to a great extent. I have enjoyed both theatres and balls — such things have always seemed perfectly right to me. One must follow according to the dictates of his own conscience."

"Why not follow according to the Word of God?" asked Allie, gently.

Erfort started, then bent his eyes thoughtfully to the floor.

"Look here!" cried impulsive Jessie, "you needn't try to convince me that there is any sin in dancing and going to the theatre and having a good time in general, for you can't do it. There isn't half as much sin in going to see a good play, sitting there and enjoying yourself, and coming away feeling light-hearted and happy and friendly towards everybody — your enemies as well as your friends — just because you have been having a pleasant time, as there is in going to church and hearing, or trying to hear, a sermon that is so dry that it makes you thirsty to listen to it, and so you look about the church and fasten upon any one, or anything, to take your mind up while you're obliged to be there. Just as like enough your eyes will chance to fall upon some one whom you detest and that some one has a hat on that you do *not* detest — quite the contrary — and you sit and hate and admire all in the same moment. Then, while the minister is praying his everlastingly long prayer, you get tired and take another eye-tour around the room, and you see some one else, whom you know to be the most deceitful person in the community, bent almost double in her seat, with her hand on the pew in front of her and her handkerchief up to her eyes, looking as meek a Moses. You come out of that church feeling cross and hateful towards everybody. Now, which is the worst — to go to a place that makes you feel happy, or to one that makes you feel as ugly as sin ? "

" Well, Jess," said Garnet, " it seems to me that the fault, as you represent things to us, lies in the minister. This article here says : 'If vacant seats are so plenty in the church, whose fault is it?

The human mind is the same in the pew as in the theatre.' If the ministers made their sermons as interesting as the actors their plays, there would be no danger of the people becoming disinterested and staying away from church. The fault is in the minister."

Erfort raised his eyes from their thoughtful study of the carpet. "No," he said, gravely, "the fault is not in the minister; it is in our own sinful hearts."

"Oh, get out!" cried Fred, springing from his hassock and commencing a rapid walk around the room. His fair face was flushed, his blue eyes full of doubt and trouble. "You'll get me as nervous as — as a woman, with your funereal talk. Let's drop it and go at something a little more lively. Jess, will you let me try to mesmerize you?"

"Oh, dear! Anything, Fred, to put a stop to this talk. I am as bad as you — it makes me nervous."

Erfort leaned back in his chair, and his face resumed its usual "society" expression. Vera looked troubled; she wished they would talk longer on a subject that was becoming interesting to her. Garnet rose from the sofa; it was difficult to tell what *her* feelings were. She crossed the room with a busy, bustling air that she assumed at times, and that sat very prettily upon her, and when she reached the door she turned and said: "I'll be down in a minute," and disappeared.

"I bet she has gone after the cocoa pot," whispered Jessie to Vera.

Sure enough, in a few minutes Garnet's voice was heard: "Open the door, please." Both gentlemen sprang to open it, and in walked Garnet, both arms laden — the alcohol lamp, the cocoa pot, matches and bottle. Fred raised both hands in mock surprise.

"What's coming!" he exclaimed. "A tea-party?"

"The next thing to it," answered Vera, taking the books, etc., from the table. "Garnet will give you some cocoa that will make you long for more."

And she did. A pleasant hour was spent in talking, laughing, and drinking the delicious beverage, and then the gentlemen left for their hotel, promising to call around in the morning and take the girls to the home of the poor laundress.

CHAPTER VIII.

"Girls," said Garnet, about 7 o'clock the next morning, as they all four lay in bed, trying hard to feel like getting up, "I've made a discovery."

"Found a bedbug?" asked Jessie, yawning; "or a cockroach?" she added, pleasantly.

Allie, who was mortally afraid of both pests, gave a little gasp and turned quickly over on her side.

"Allie has," went on Jessie, taking a wicked delight in her friend's terror. "Is it crawling up from the foot, Al?" she asked, concernedly.

Poor Allie squealed outright, and commenced to squirm, at which Jessie, immensely tickled, laughed immoderately.

"For shame, Jessie," said Garnet, indignantly. "Come and get into bed with us, Allie."

"No you don't," said Jessie, catching hold of Allie's night-dress, as she was about to gladly accept Garnet's invitation. "You just stay here with your mother, young lady, and—" here Jessie took a firm grip of Allie's arm—"she'll keep the nasty little bedbugs and cockroaches away—yes, she will."

"Oh, J-e-s-s-i-e, p-l-e-a-s-e," almost sobbed Allie.

"Oh, no, I won't plague you," said Jessie, quickly contrite. "But what a little goose you are, Al. You should control yourself; pray, control yourself. Doesn't that sound dignified enough to come from the lips of my senior over there? Hey?"

"Stop your nonsense, Jessie, and let me talk," said Garnet.

"Oh, certainly. We will listen to the lips of wisdom now. Attend! Please proceed to article I., Miss Dare, as they say at the Normal," and Jessie cuddled herself down beside Allie and assumed a very attentive expression.

"Now for your discovery, Net," said Vera.

"Well, I have just discovered that this cottage is the same described in 'Megda,' where she and 'Del' and 'Laurie' came that summer, and this must be the very room they occupied."

"Eureka!" cried Jessie. "Garnet, my dear sister, what a great head you have."

"I've read that book," said Vera.

"Which character did you like best?" asked Allie.

"'Laurie.'"

"So did I."

"I liked 'Megda' best," said Garnet, "though 'Ethel' was lovely."

"And *I* liked 'May' best," said Jessie, emphatically. "She was the bravest one of all, for she was brave enough to live and die an old maid for the sake of someone else, and that is what I call a brave deed, *in*-deed."

The girls laughed. "Oh, wait until you read the sequel to the book," said Vera, "perhaps 'May' will be married in that."

"Is there a sequel to 'Megda,'" asked Allie.

"Not yet, but there is going to be."

"An' phwere did yez get the news, Vera?" asked Jessie.

"I advise you to stop practicing that dialect, Jess," said Garnet. "You'll use it some time when you don't mean to."

"Well, I've just gotten so I can talk it pretty well," said Jessie. "I want to surprise Prof. Bancroft when I begin lessons again in the fall."

"What time were our young men going to call?" asked Vera.

"Dear me, if I hadn't forgotten every word about them," exclaimed Garnet, springing up in bed. "Get up, Vera, quick, before I step on you."

"Oh, crawl over the foot-board, Net," yawned Vera.

"You lazy ghost, take that," and Jessie threw a pillow at Vera, and, for a wonder, hit her.

"Re*w*enge," muttered Vera, and arming herself with all three pillows, commenced a vigorous attack on the enemy.

"Are we going to have any breakfast this morning?" asked Garnet, calmly.

"You might know Net had struck upon her feet," cried Jessie, in smothered tones, for Vera was burying her in pillows. "She thinks of her little 'stummick' the first thing. Oh, horrors, Vera, let me up. I never thought before," she said, sitting on the edge of the bed and pushing the hair out of her eyes, "what poor 'Desdemona' must have suffered, and what an old brute 'Othello' was."

"Oh, do hurry, girls," pleaded Garnet. "We certainly won't have time to get breakfast and get cleaned up."

"Well, you and Vera go out and buy the stuff, and Al and I—*won't* cook it," said Jessie, with a hideous grimace.

"That's true enough," said Vera. "We don't want you to. You and Al clear up the room and Net and I will get the breakfast."

"What are you going to give us?" asked Jessie, anxiously.

"What have you down on the bill of fare for to-day's breakfast, Net?" asked Vera.

Garnet referred to her paper with the gravest face imaginable. "Egg omelet," she replied, briefly.

"Egg omelet it is then," said Vera. "And I'm the girl that can make it."

"Conceit," said Jessie, giving Vera's golden braids that were hanging down her back, a loving pull.

"Ready, Vera?" asked Garnet.

"Almost; just as soon as I twist my hair up. You *are* the quickest little thing, Net."

Garnet smiled. She stood ready with her round sailor hat and soft red shawl on. Vera twisted up her beautiful hair, put her hat on, threw her peasant cape over her pale blue wrapper, and announced herself ready.

"Let us go to the market around the corner," said Garnet, as they went out of the house.

"Anywhere," replied Vera.

"How many eggs will we need?"

"Well, to tell the truth, three will be plenty, but I hate to ask for so few, don't you?"

"Yes, but I guess they are used to all kinds of orders. Will you ask?"

"Yes," Vera answered, rather reluctantly. "You have the pocket-book, haven't you?"

"Yes."

The order was given, and the clerk didn't even smile, as the girls were very much afraid he would do. As Garnet took out her pocket-book to pay him, the clerk asked with a smile: "Are you cashier?"

"Yes," answered Garnet.

"And you," he added, turning to Vera, "are the teller?"

Quick as a flash came the answer. "Yes, I tell(h)er what to do."

"Poor Vera! The next instant her face flushed crimson at what she had done. Made a pun before an entire stranger! She felt as though she would like for the floor to open and swallow her. The clerk laughed heartily, and so did Garnet — she couldn't help it. Without another word Vera took Garnet's arm and walked haughtily out of the market. Hiding her embarrassment under a haughty demeanor, you see.

"Don't tell the girls, Net," she said, imploringly, and Garnet promised she wouldn't.

Vera's omelet was delicious. Jessie said, teasingly: "It was a bit thin," to which Vera retorted: "Lave it alone, *thin*."

At 9 o'clock the gentlemen called. "We had better go right down," said Mr. Richards. "She may be too busy to see us if we wait."

The girls put on their hats, took their parasols, and then they started. After fifteen minutes walk Mr. Richards said:

"Do you see that smoke curling up among those trees?"

Yes, they all saw it.

"Well, that comes from her cottage, and there it is."

It was a very small, very poor, but very neat looking cottage, painted brown. A neat wash house stood a few feet from it, and it was from this that the smoke was rising. Thinking that

they would probably find Mrs. Hood in this building, our party walked up to the door and looked in.
The fire was burning, the boiler of water was heat-
ing over it, and the tubs and a large basket of
clothes stood in the middle of the floor, but there
was no one there.

"She must be in the cottage," said Erfort, speaking in a low tone, though he did not know what
made him, unless it was because it seemed so quiet
around there.   There were some tall pine trees on
one side and at the back of the cottage, and they
gave the place rather a lonely look.

The rest followed Erfort as he went towards the
half-opened door, but just as he raised his hand to
knock, a low, moaning sound, fell on their ears.
Erfort dropped his hand, and they all bent their
heads to listen.   Another low, moaning sound, and
a suffering child's voice: "Oh, mamma!" the
very tones of which drew the quick tears to every
pair of bright eyes outside.

"Mamma knows it, darling, and she is so sorry
for her baby-boy. There, lay your head on mamma's
shoulder, precious, and she will sing to you."

The voice was low, sweet and clear. "What
shall mamma sing, dear?"

"The pretty one, please."

> "'Nearer, my God to Thee,
> Nearer to Thee.
> E'en tho' it be a cross
> That raiseth me.

Still all my song shall be,
Nearer my God to Thee,
Nearer my God to Thee,
Nearer to Thee.' "

" Oh, that is pretty, mamma; please sing the next verse. It— O–h ! "

It was a sharp cry of pain, wrung from the suffering child. It cut into the listeners' hearts like a knife, and before Erfort realized what he was doing, he had started forward and pushed the door wide open and they all looked into the room. It was a small, poor room, devoid of almost every comfort, except one or two rockers, a small case of books, and a clean, white bed. On this bed lay a little form; they could just see the outline of it, that was all, for the mother was bending over it in speechless agony and her arms were clasped tightly around it.

" M-a-m-m-a ! M-a-m-m-a ! "

" Yes, yes, darling, mamma knows. Oh, my Father in Heaven, if you would only let me suffer for him ! Robbie, prescious, look at mamma. Don't you feel her arms around you? Oh, my baby, speak to me."

Erfort could bear it no longer—he rushed into the room and the others followed. What they saw they will never forget to their dying day; and Fred, careless, light-hearted Fred—put his hands up to his face and sobbed like a baby, for his thoughtless words of the night before came back to him with cruel force. There lay the "lazy little beggar," "the kid," "the boy who let his mammy do all the work;" oh, how the remembrance of his words wrung Fred's really tender heart.

He lay there, his little slender form writhing in his mother's arms, his little arms clasped tightly around his mother's neck, with the small hands griping each other convulsively. His golden head was on her shoulder, but his face was towards them, and it was terrible to look at — deathly white and distorted, with the blue eyes rolled up until nothing but the whites were seen. But, thank God! the fearful struggle was as short as it was severe; if it had not been, the child could never have lived through it, and the stiffened form nestled back into the mother's arms. Without turning her head, but keeping her cheek pressed against the golden curls, the mother laid him gently down upon the pillow, where he lay with closed eyes and panting a little. The mother's hand brushed softly the pretty hair, all wet with the cold sweat of agony, back from the white forehead. "My baby, my baby!" was all she said, but the tones of her voice spoke volumes.

It was a strange position for our young people to be in, and their voluntarily putting themselves into it was still stranger, but they never thought of that.

They thought of nothing but what was before them, and the mother seemed unconscious of their very presence for some moments, and then she raised her head from the pillow and looked at them, but none of the agony that had been so plainly expressed in her voice was visible in her face. It was pale — very pale — but as pure and shining as at the tabernacle. She smiled at Mr. Richards, and held out a thin, work-worn hand to him. He advanced to the bedside and took her hand with all the manly grace he was capable of, and that was by no means little.

"I hope you will pardon our intrusion, Mrs. Hood," he said, with deep respect. "We did not mean it as an intrusion. The ladies were anxious to see you, and as I knew where you lived I came with them — my friend and I. We — we heard the sounds outside and it made us all feel so badly that we could not refrain from coming in. Will you let me make you acquainted with my friends?"

"Certainly," answered Mrs. Hood. "I shall be most pleased to meet with them, and no apology is needed."

"Thank you," replied Erfort, and then he introduced the girls and Fred.

Robbie opened his eyes just as Jessie stepped forward to shake hands with his mother, and they fell immediately upon her face. He smiled and put up his poor little hand.

"What a pretty lady," he said.

They all smiled, except Jessie, and she leaned over him and kissed him with a tender light in her beautiful eyes, and a softened look upon her brilliant face, which made her, for the moment, perfectly lovely.

"If I could only have her picture as she looks now," thought Erfort.

It may seem strange, but from the moment that Jessie left that humble little cottage her heart was changed, although she scarcely realized it at the time, and, indeed, not for long days afterwards. God has wonderful ways of changing the human heart, and there are scarcely two hearts that experience this change alike. I once heard a minister —an earnest-hearted, zealous young man—give the following experience: "I had a friend, and this friend was one of the happiest christians I ever knew. He was conversing with me one day, and he said: 'Oh, I shall never forget the day that my heart was changed—really changed. I had been feeling tired and discouraged, and I went into my room and I knelt down and prayed. I prayed with all my heart for light, and even while I prayed the light came. It filled my heart and it seemed as if it filled the whole room. It was fairly poured upon me. Oh, I felt so happy! It went through my whole being. I cannot begin to tell how glad and happy I felt.' When I heard him tell me that, my heart sunk within me, and as I went from him, I said to myself: '*I* never had such an experience as that, yet I have thought myself consecrated to the Master's service for a long while. Is it possible that I have been all along mistaken? Has my heart never been changed? Why did not the change come to me as it did to him? I was unhappy. I tortured myself with vain thinking and vain questioning, and then I made it a subject for prayer and the truth was revealed to me. Seldom do two persons experience religion alike. To one the light may come suddenly, as it did to my friend, though I do not think many are blessed with such a manifestation of the Spirit, and to another it may come gradually, yet, thank God! none the less surely."

I have so often thought of this. It answered a question that my own heart had often asked, and never before found an answer to. The light did not burst suddenly upon Jessie. Indeed, the only feeling she was sensible of, was an indefinable one. Her heart felt softened, but she thought it had been touched with pity for the suffering she had seen. So it had, but God was the one who had filled her heart with this pity. He, who is all wise, took this way of manifesting Himself unto her. He had commenced to work the change in her heart and He never makes any mistakes.

Mrs. Hood followed our young people to the

door.   She told them that her boy was nine years
old and had been a cripple and a great sufferer for
four years.   Robin was on a vessel one day and
had fallen down the cabin stairs.   He had never
walked since, and his suffering had been terrible.

Vera could not keep her eyes off the pale face.
There was something about it that completely fascinated her.   It may seem amusing, but all she
could think of when looking at it, was a waxen
taper.   There seemed such a soft luminance upon
it.   Was it to be the taper that would light the path
that Vera's young feet were to tread on their way
to the " better country?"   Was this the light that
would guide her out of the night of doubt and uncertainty into the blessed day of light and glory ?

As they were about to leave the cottage, Mrs.
Hood caught the longing look in Vera's gray eyes.
What made her guess at the desire that was in the
girl's heart, and that she longed to express but did
not dare?   She could not tell ; Vera could not tell ;
no one can tell — only God knew why.

"You will come and see me again," Mrs. Hunt
said.

No one heard but Vera, to whom the question
was addressed, and she answered, quickly : " I
will."

No one talked much going home.   Nothing had
been said about any work being done—it had completely slipped their minds.   As they approached

their cottage, Fred, looking up, caught a glimpse of "Grandpa" and "Mother" standing a little back from the half open door and peering out at them. He turned to the girls with a laugh.

"Our aged friends act as if they had a mortgage on you, young ladies. They seem to keep their eyes upon you."

Jessie stopped short with a little cry, looked rapidly and anxiously into each face, opened her lips as if to speak, and then walked on. They had all stopped when she stopped and looked at her, but Allie seemed to be the only one who had understood. She had answered Jessie's look with one full of self-reproach. Fred commenced to sing in a low voice:

"It stopped — short — never to go again,
And the old man died."

"What was the matter, Jess?" asked Vera. "Have you forgotten something?"

"We've all forgotten something," replied Jessie, with a gravity that was something entirely new for her, and as she spoke she looked at Vera and then towards "Grandpa" and "Mother," still standing in the middle of the kitchen. Vera turned to the gentlemen.

"Thank you very much for your kindness in taking us to Mrs. Hood's," she said, in her stateliest manner.

The gentlemen took the "hint" at once, although Fred, as he said to Erfort afterwards, felt as though he had had cold water poured down his back.

"Wouldn't you like to go down to the beach and watch the bathers?" asked Erfort, as they turned to leave. "The band gives a concert every day at 11, you know."

Vera's red lips curled. "No, thank you," she answered, somewhat curtly. "We do not care for that pastime."

(Fred felt the cold water again.) "You object to the bathing?" asked Erfort, quietly.

"No, I object to the bathers," answered Vera, quickly, and then her fair face flushed scarlet.

"Good-morning," she said, haughtily, and without another word she turned and entered the cottage.

Garnet came to the rescue with her sweet, womanly tact. "Vera is greatly opposed to the manner of bathing here, and I must confess there are some things about it that we all find to object to. "Will you come in?"

The gentlemen declined the invitation, for they knew it had been given only out of politeness, but they asked and obtained permission to call in the evening and accompany the girls to the "band concert."

When the girls entered the cottage they found Vera standing before "Grandpa" and "Mother" with her hat in her hand, talking very earnestly. She turned as they entered.

" I was telling ' Grandpa ' and ' Grandma ' how sorry we were for forgetting what we had promised them last night," she said. "We will sing to them now if they would like to have us, won't we ? "

" Certainly," they answered.

Vera sat down in a chair by the window and drew Jessie down into her lap ; Garnet took the chair at the other window ; Allie seated herself near her ; "Grandpa" and " Mother," each took a large, old fashioned rocker, and then the girls sang to them : " Nearer My God to Thee," " Jesus Lover of My Soul," " Just As I Am," " I Hear Thy Welcome Voice," " There Is Rest For The Weary," "There Is No Name," and " There'll Be No Parting There," and " Grandpa" and " Mother" sat and listened to the beautiful voices, and as they listened their aged hearts were filled with tender memories of the dear old " long ago " when they had sung those same sweet hymns, with voices just as fresh and clear and strong, and before their dim eyes there seemed to rise a picture of the Home they were travelling towards and fast approaching, the beautiful " Home of the Soul" where there is indeed " rest for the weary."

CHAPTER IX.

"Come, Jessie," said Vera, about 7 o'clock that evening, "you won't be ready when the gentlemen call for us, if you don't 'roughe' yourself, as 'Sairey' says."

Jessie was lying on the bed with her hands up over her head and her large black eyes fixed upon the ceiling.

"It doesn't make any difference whether I'm ready or not when they call," she replied, coolly.

Vera turned and looked at her; so did Garnet, who was kneeling before her trunk looking for some lace to sew on the neck of her dress. Allie was standing before the glass, rather listlessly combing out her brown 'bangs.'

"It won't make any difference whether you are ready or not," repeated Vera. "Why — why not?"

"Because I'm not going."

Vera sat down on the edge of the bed, with her handkerchief in one hand and her cologne bottle in the other, and stared at the composed face on the pillow; but Garnet, after that one backward glance, bent over her trunk again, without a word, but her small lips were drawn into their straightest line.

"Jessica Dare!" exclaimed Vera, using the name she always used when particularly astonished at Jessie's vagaries. "*Why* aren't you going?"

"Because," was the "woman's reason" given.

"But why?"

"Because I'm *not*."

"But *why?* Don't you want to hear the concert? You love band music. What is the mattter?"

"Nothing."

"Don't fib, 'Jasmine,'" said Vera, gravely.

"Well, then, I'll tell you," cried Jessie, springing up and turning a very pale little face, lit by two gleaming black eyes, upon Vera. "I'm not going because I'm tired to death of having those two fellows tied to our apron strings everywhere we go. We can't move but what 'the *gen-tle-men* will *call* for us at such and *such* a time.' I'm tired to death of it. When we came down here I thought we four girls were going around together and have a good time. There's no fun when there's a parcel of men around. I wont go out with them again — see if I do. I'll stay cooped up in this room all the time I'm here, first."

It would be impossible to describe the scorn expressed in the fair young face and in the ringing, girlish voice. Vera looked very much astonished at first, and then burst into a rippling laugh.

"Oh, Jessica, Jessica," she cried, swaying her body backward and forward on the bed. "Oh, Jessica, Jessica!"

That was all she could say, and she laughed and laughed. No one could hear Vera Earle laugh very many moments and not be actually obliged to laugh too. Allie leaned against the wash-stand and laughed until she held her sides. Garnet, after a stern, but unfailing effort to keep her face straight, soon lay full length on the floor and spread both arms out in utter abandonment to her mirth, and Jessie, after looking very indignantly at all three, threw her arms around Vera's waist and over they went on the bed together. No one tried to restrain her merriment, and peal after peal of laughter rang through the cottage. "Grandpa" and "Mother" in the back kitchen, taking their quiet cup of tea together, heard it, bent their heads to listen, and looked at each other and smiled. The sound did their old hearts good.

Vera was the first to sit up and dry her eyes. She leaned against the foot-board, utterly exhausted.

"You make me laugh like that again, Jessie Dare," she gasped, "and — and — you'll wish you hadn't."

"For pity's sake, what did I do?" asked Jessie, with big eyes. "I didn't do anything."

"No, I should think not," retorted Vera. "I

hope when you are twenty-seven you will be as indignant at having a ' parcel of men ' around as you are at seventeen. Oh, Jessie, such scorn ! "

" When she's twenty-seven," remarked Garnet, rising from her undignified position on the floor, " she'll be just as indignant over *not* having even *one* man around."

" Oh, she will, hey ? " muttered Jessie, taking the pillow into her arms and hugging it up to her. " Don't you be so sure of that, Miss Dare."

" Jess and I are going to keep ' old maids' ' hall, aren't we, Jess ? " said Allie.

" Well, you better believe we are," answered that young lady. " Let's try it to-night, will you, Al ? "

" With pleasure," replied Allie.

" Oh, don't you want to go out either, Allie ? " asked Vera, rather anxiously.

" No, I would prefer to stay at home with Jessie."

Vera turned and looked doubtfully at Garnet. Garnet's face was flushed and her large, black eyes sparkled angrily, but she tried to speak calmly.

" Well, I must say, Jessie, you are behaving very childishly."

" Well, why ? " flashed out Jessie. " I'm not going anywhere I don't want to go, am I ? "

" It seems not," replied Garnet, still holding her temper under control. " But I think you are doing a very foolish thing."

"Oh, well, we can't all be wise," replied Jessie, changing her high, petulant tone all at once to a low, careless one. "I don't want to go, and I'm not going; so that is all there is about it."

"Very well."

Garnet's voice was low, deliberate, haughty. Jessie sat and looked over her pillow at nothing in particular, with gloomy eyes.

"Never mind," said Vera, cheerfully, getting up and going to the clothes-press for her hat. "We won't stay long."

"Hark! Isn't that your cousin's whistle?" said Allie.

"Yes," answered Jessie, quickly. "I heard him. He whistled 'Little Fisher Maiden.' There he is again. Well, that's one way to call you out," and she slipped off the bed and went to the glass doors. "Shall I tell them you will be down in a minute?" she asked, turning her laughing face towards Vera and Garnet.

She was entirely changed. All traces of petulance and vexation were gone — passed from her face, yes, and from her whole being in that one instant of time. She was her other self now — her sweeter self — bright, loving, happy, warm-hearted. To use her own words, "she felt all right," and took it for granted that Garnet must, and everyone else, for that matter; but Garnet was very grave; her deeper nature — a nature intensely deep in all things — had no sympathy with her sister's light changeable one. She knew this, and didn't think to ask herself if Jessie knew it. Jessie irritated Garnet, and Garnet irritated Jessie. How often are two members of the same family blessed with entirely different natures, and when they come in contact — as they must necessarily do many times a day — they cannot help clashing.

"Yes, tell them we'll be down in a jiff," said Vera, hurriedly and thoughtlessly.

Jessie leaned over the railing. "Hm!"

It was the most delicate little cough imaginable, but Erfort and Fred, walking slowly up and down in front of the cottage, heard and looked up quickly.

They saw a little white face, lighted by two brilliant black eyes and crowned with a mass of dark hair, peering eerily down at them through the branches of the big tree. They raised their hats, but neither spoke.

"Vera says she and Net will be down in a jiff."

O, wicked little sprite! The tone was low, but, alas! distinctly audible to the three girls. Vera held her fleecy fascinator over her golden hair and gazed with horror-stricken eyes out on the balcony; Garnet sank, speechless on a chair. Jessie looked at them over her shoulder from where she stood, but she did not venture in.

"Hurry, girls; they're waiting," she called, softly.

Vera gave her one reproachful look and disappeared. Garnet rose, and if a glance could have sent Jessie over the railing, she would immediately have gone headlong.

"Oh, Jessie, that was too bad," said Allie, as the door closed.

"Oh, phooh! no it wasn't either," replied Jessie, stepping through the door and seating herself on the bed in her favorite attitude. "They ought to be taken down a peg once in a while — especially Net."

"I will make you an apology, Vera, if that will do any good," Garnet was saying in smothered tones, as the two girls hastened down the stairs.

She was extremely angry, but as ever, her voice was under her perfect control.

"Oh, never mind," said Vera, with a little laugh, "the child didn't mean any harm."

"Child!" repeated the low, thrilling voice. "Do you call a girl seventeen years old, a *child*?"

"Jessie is a child in every sense of the word," replied Vera, and then they stepped out into the lighted street.

Fred and Vera walked together, and Erfort and Garnet. The two former chatted gaily and seemed to be becoming friends fast, but with Erfort and Garnet, conversation lagged. Here were two natures very much alike. Neither possessed particularly brilliant conversational powers, but both

were deep thinkers and earnest students of both
" Mother" and human nature, and yet Erfort did
not understand Garnet any more than she understood Jessie, while Garnet, with the natural keen
perception that all women are blessed—or cursed
with — I know not which to call it — understood
Erfort thoroughly.

Her mind was with the late scene in the chamber
and she *could not* tear it away, although she knew
as well as though he had told her, that her companion was putting her down as one very odd and
reserved, if not actually stupid.

Poor Garnet!   Her proud heart beat in hot
rebellion against such judgment, but try as hard as
she would, not one thing could she think of to say,
and her only reply to his remarks — few and far
between — were monosyllables, cut off short and
" spinster-like," from her small, tightly closed lips.

" What a difference between the two sisters,"
thought Erfort, as he spread her gossamer for her
over the seat; and declining with a smile the one
quarter inch of board that she offered him beside
her, leaned carelessly against a tree and waited
for the concert to begin.

" Jessie is as bright and sparkling as the lovliest waterfall, and as brilliant.   She is all life and
fire; but this one —" and he looked down on the
small, dark head that was almost touching his knee,
with a smile, half amused, half disdainful.

The face he could not see, for it was turned completely away from him, but if he had seen it, it would have told him nothing. It wore its usual look of calm, undisturbed repose. Not one trace upon it of the fierce rebellion going on in the poor, passionately beating heart. Even he, who prided himself on his self-control, could not have conceived of such wonderful power as Garnet possessed.

After an hour — during which Garnet had not spoken, except when directly appealed to by one of the others — Vera proposed going home.

"Oh, by the way, Miss Vera," said Erfort, as they turned to go. "I saw Mrs. Hood this afternoon."

"Did you ?" asked Vera, eagerly.

"Yes, and *I* saw something too," put in Fred, eagerly, for he feared a "serious turn" to the conversation. "Guess what."

"Oh, don't ask us to do that," said Vera. "We are not mind-readers." "No ; but that was just what it was," was the rather vague reply.

Both girls turned an inquiring face towards him, and Erfort, stepping forward, gravely put his hand on his friend's forehead.

"Not particularly hot," he remarked, gravely, as he fell back again. "No peculiar sensation there, is there, Freddie ?"

Fred had turned in surprise, but at Erfort's question he broke into a merry laugh. "No," he answered, " but really there is a mind-reader, or clairvoyant, or fortune-teller, or whatever she calls herself — here."

For the first time that evening the ice of reserve in Garnet's face, broke, and she looked up at Fred with flushed cheeks and shining eyes.

" Where are her rooms ? " she asked, almost breathlessly, and then she flushed scarlet and drew timidly back at the teasing smile on Fred's handsome face.

" *Would* you be guilty, my sedate cousin ? " he asked, with mock solemnity.

Garnet did not answer, but Vera said, with sudden dignity : " How can you ask such an absurd question," and her red lips curled scornfully.

" Another cold bath," thought Fred, shrugging his shoulders as though it were a literal one.

" There is something quite wonderful about these mind-readers," said Erfort, thoughtfully.   " The power they possess is really remarkable."

" Did you ever go to one ? " Vera asked.

Erfort smiled at the scorn expressed in her voice. " I must plead guilty," he replied.

" What !   Do you really believe that anyone on this earth can see into the future ? "

" I do not say that.   One who calls himself simply a ' mind-reader,' does not pretend to see into the future ; he sees only what is written on one's mind, and I most certainly do give them credit for much power in that line.   I can't say that I have the least faith in these fortune-tellers though."

"Well, by Guy!" exclaimed Fred, with more force than elegance; "some of these fortune-tellers get things pretty near right, anyway."

Vera laughed softly.   Fred's boyish remarks seemed to please her greatly; the "slang" he frequently indulged in did not offend her, somehow or other—it was always given with such boyish bluntness.

"Giving yourself away, Freddie, my son?" said Erfort, gravely.

"Oh, well, I don't care.   I'm not ashamed to have you all know that all of the simpletons are not dead yet.   I had my fortune told last summer."

"Who told it?" asked Vera.

"Some old hag of a gypsy."

"Oh, tell us about it," pleaded Vera.

They had by this time, reached the cottage. "Shall I go in for chairs?" asked Garnet.

"Oh, no, don't," said Erfort, quickly. "That is, not for Fred and I.   We will sit on the steps."

"The post is good enough for me," said Fred, perching himself on top of it.

Vera sat down on the upper step and leaned her head against the railing of the piazza.   Garnet sat on the second step and leaned her elbow on Vera's lap and her head on her hand.   Erfort took the lowest step.

"Proceed, my brother. You have the floor — or post," he said.

"Well," began Fred, "I'll tell you just how it was."

"Beg pardon, one moment, Fred," interrupted Erfort. "Don't forget to tell us about the future Mrs. Travers, for, of course, the sibyl described her to you."

Fred laughed, blushed and stroked his mustache. "Don't put me out at the start, Er," he said; then proceeded:

"There were a party of us staying in the country and one day we all went for a drive. There were about ten of us. Well, the first thing we knew we came right out onto a gypsey encampment. Just as the fellow who was driving turned around to speak to us about it, an old woman with gray hair, brown, wrinkled face, and the sharpest pair of black eyes I ever saw, came hobbling toward us from her seat by the fire. She was the typical gypsey fortune-teller, toothless, weird and wild. She even had the usual red blanket pinned across her shrunken shoulders. 'Ah, let me tell your fortune, pretty maid,' she mumbled, to Lena Rivers, the prettiest girl of the party. 'It's a lovely fortune you have, my dear, and it's a brave, handsome, dark-eyed sweetheart you have across the seas who is coming home soon to marry you.' Well, it did beat the Dutch that she should hit that right,

for you know Lena Rivers, Er? Well, you know
she was engaged to Le Hazelton, and he was over
to Germany on business for his house at the time.
Well, of course, Lena blushed and smiled and the
other girls looked at each other with their eyes
wide open, and their mouths, too, for that matter,
and the old hag, seeing, of course, that she had
made one, said : 'Just cross my hand with silver,
pretty Agnes, and I'll tell you when the wedding
day will be.' Well, you know, Er, Lena is awfully
pretty and sweet, and all that, but, between you and
me, she hasn't any too much sense — er — not
exactly that — but — er — well, she is just like a
lovely little wax doll, you know, and when the old
woman said that, she drew her hand away and
tossed her head and pouted those red lips of hers
and said petulantly : 'Now you are wrong. My
name isn't Agnes, and I don't want you to tell me
when the wedding day is to be, for I know it
myself.' Well, of course the girls giggled and the
boys — I mean young men — laughed outright. I
verily believe that made the old witch mad, for she
said, quite fiercely : 'Beware, proud lady, your
wedding day is set, but — will it ever dawn?' I
must confess the tone in which she asked this
dreadful question almost gave me the creeps, and
as for poor little Lena, she turned as white as a
sheet and squealed outright. The old witch
promptly followed up her lead. 'I see a proud,

dark-eyed beauty· on the other side of the ocean, by whose side he often lingers, and whose white hand often rests in his. They — ' But just here Lena almost threw herself into the old woman's embrace. 'Oh, don't, don't,' she cried. 'Don't tell me such things; please don't.' 'Ah, but just cross my hand with silver and I'll tell you something that will drive the tears from that pretty face, and bring smiles instead,' said the old woman. 'But I can't,' almost sobbed Lena, 'I haven't my purse with me.' Strange as it may seem to you, not one of us felt like laughing — we were all as solemn as parsons. Somehow or other the place, the time — for it was growing dusky fast — and the weird looking old woman sent a chill over us all. To add to the scene another bent, tottering form came from behind the folds of the tent, hobbled to the fire, and, after stirring something that was cooking in the big kettle, sat herself down and went puffing away at a hideous looking little black pipe, rocking herself forward and backward as she did so. I tell you, it gave us all the shivers. No wonder poor little Lena was frightened half out of her senses. When Lena said she didn't have her purse, we fellows all dived our hands into our pockets, and Roger Comant — you know him, Er — he's a regular old stiff-necked Methodist — was studying for the ministry at the time — took out a half dollar and handed it over to the old witch with

---

a face as solemn as the grave. You would have thought he was paying a forfeit for his own life. Well, as you may guess, Lena's fortune turned out to be a brilliant one. Fruitless efforts on the part of the dark-eyed beauty across the waters to gain the affection of Lena's lover, and his deep, unending love and unswerving faith toward Lena, etc., etc., winding up with a brilliant, happy wedding six months from that date. Oh, after we reached home we had a great laugh over it, of course."

"Well, and *was* the wedding-day six months from that time?" asked Vera, with a long-drawn sigh, raising her head from its resting place."

"It was in little less than three months — in October some time."

"And *was* there a dark-eyed lady across the water?" was the next question.

"No, he didn't get acquainted with but two ladies while he was gone — strange as it may seem — and they were middle-aged and with light hair — regular Germans."

"Oh, phooh!" was the contemptuous reply.

"But where's *your* fortune, Fred?" asked Erfort, as the girls rose to go in. "Didn't you have it told?"

"Yes," replied Fred, with his hand on the knob to open the door.

"Well, describe her to us," said Erfort, with teasing persistency.

Fred bent his head over Vera's little white hand, as he raised his hat in " Good night," and she was the only one who caught his answer.

" Divinely tall, and most divinely fair."

CHAPTER X.

Perhaps it was her running so quickly up the stairs that made Vera's cheeks such a pretty pink when she entered the room, and perhaps it was the lamplight that dazzled her eyes so that she had to cover them for a moment with one hand, and therefore, did not see the slender form coiled up on one of the beds, with its face buried in the pillows, but Garnet, coming in behind her, saw it, and brushed swiftly by her.

"Why Jessie, what is the matter?" she asked, folding her arms about the little form and nestling her cheek between Jessie's hands that covered her face.   Tell Garnet all about it.   Don't cry, dear, but tell Net all about it."

Jessie turned over and put her arms around Garnet's neck and her head on her shoulder.

" Oh, Net," she sobbed, " I've lost my watch — my — dar–ling — lit–tle — watch," and the sobs came thick and fast.

Vera sat down on the foot of the bed and Allie came and stood beside her.   They both looked with pitying eyes at Garnet and Jessie.

" Lost your watch, Jess? " repeated Garnet.
" Well, well, don't cry ; we'll try to find it.   Have

you any idea where you lost it? Do you remember where you had it last?"

"Oh, Allie, you tell them," said Jessie, with a sob between every word. "Oh, my dar–ling — lit – tle — watch."

"She didn't miss it until after we came in," said Allie. "We went for a little walk and came through the park on our way home."

"The park opposite?" asked Vera.

"Yes."

"Let us go over and see if we can find it, Net," said Vera, rising as she spoke. "And, Jessie, while we are gone, you write out a notice and we'll tack it up in the post office."

Jessie looked up and actually smiled through her tears. She was pleased with the idea. In a moment she was sitting up on the edge of the bed brushing her heavy hair away from her flushed, tear-stained face with both hands, and calling to Allie to bring paper and pencil.

"All right, Vera," she said. "I will write a notice and have it all ready for you by the time you get back. But" — and here came one of those wonderful transformations of the little face — "would you offer a reward?"

All three girls burst into a laugh.

"Not a very heavy one, at all events, Jasmine," said Vera. "But I suppose it would be as well to write: 'The finder will be suitably rewarded, etc.,

etc.' Let us hope he or she will be of a big heart, if not of a big purse."

"No such good luck," said Jessie. Now you two girls hurry up and I'll have it ready for you by the time you get back."

Vera and Garnet went down stairs and out into the park. The electric light made everything around as bright as daylight. The two girls walked very slowly, one on either side of the path; they bent themselves almost double in their anxiety to search the grounds thoroughly, but after half an hour they were obliged to give up all hope of finding the watch, that night, at least, and went sadly back to the cottage.

"Poor little Jasmine," said Vera. "I hate to tell her we have not found it, she will feel so badly."

Jessie sprang up from the bed as they entered the room and read their faces with her big, shining eyes. "Oh, you haven't found it?" she cried, sharply, throwing herself back on the pillows. "I knew you wouldn't; it is just my luck."

Garnet went up to the bed and laid her hand on Jessie's. "Don't cry any more to-night, Jessie," she said, in her low, firm tones. "We will try again to-morrow. Now show us the wonderful notice. Is this it?"

She picked up a sheet of paper from the table as she spoke, but had scarcely read the heading before Jessie snatched it from her hands.

"Let me read it for you," she said, and before she finished the tears were once more gone and her face expressed nothing but pleasurable excitement.

"There! How is that?" she asked, with a conceited little toss of her head.

"Splendid!" cried Vera and Garnet together. "Now give it to us and we will go right over to the office and tack it up."

At the door they turned and looked back. Jessie sat with her head leaning on Allie's shoulder. Her eyes were filled with tears again.

"What shall we bring you back that is good, Jasmine?" asked Vera.

"My watch," answered Jessie, quickly.

"I wish we could dear. But won't some nougats be almost as good to-night?"

They were surprised to see the red blood rush to Jessie's face. She laughed a little, and said hastily.

"Oh, something to drink will be better; I feel burning up."

"Some phosa?" suggested Vera.

"Oh, yes; do."

"What made Jessie blush so," asked Vera, as the two girls hurried along to the drug store.

Garnet smiled; she thought she knew, but she only said: "She is nervous, I think."

On their way back they stopped and tacked the notice up beside the post office window.

"There!" said Vera, as she gave the last soft tap to the nail. "If the person who finds the watch sees this and does not give the watch up, I hope the ticking of it will drive him crazy."

"What a heartless wish," laughed Garnet.

As they entered the room once more Jessie came towards them with both hands held out. Vera stopped with her phosa bottle held high in the air.

"Here, take them. They are all I have left," said Jessie, and she dropped two nougats into each girl's hand. "Al and I bought them while you were at the concert. Al wanted to save some for you, but I was a little pig and wanted to keep them all for ourselves."

The girls laughed heartily.

"Well, and why didn't you keep them?" asked Vera.

"Oh, because I was ashamed of myself for being so selfish when you are so good to me."

Little, tender-hearted Jessie! So full of your faults, yet so childish and innocent withal! It would seem impossible to chide you.

"Vera," whispered Garnet, about half an hour after they had gone to bed, and the regular breathing heard from the other side of the room proved that both Jessie and Allie were asleep. She laid her hand lightly on Vera's arm as she spoke.

"Yes," replied Vera, in the same soft tone, and she turned over and put her face close to Garnet's.

"You remember what Fred said to-night about that clairvoyant who has rooms on the avenue?" Garnet's whisper was tremulous with excitement.

"Yes," answered Vera.

"Well, I'm going to her to-morrow."

If Garnet had said: "I'm going to jump off the wharf to-morrow," Vera would have been but little more startled. She gave a little jump and sat up in bed, but Garnet drew her hurriedly down again.

"'Sh; don't waken the girls. I would never hear the last of it if Jess were to get hold of it. I have fully made up my mind to go, and I'll go if I have to go alone; but I wish you would go with me; will you?"

Vera's heart commenced to beat quickly. The idea filled her with a strange excitement.

"But do you really believe she will tell you anything worth listening to, Net?" she whispered.

"I don't know; but I am going."

Garnet's tones, though necessarily low and soft, were full of quiet determination. Vera knew she meant what she said. She could not think of allowing her to go to such a place as that alone.

"I will go with you," she said. "But I shan't let her tell me anything."

"No, you needn't; only go with me."

Five minutes later Garnet was sleeping peacefully, but Vera's eyes remained wide open for an hour or more. Spiritualism, mesmerism, and clairvoyance always seemed to her so unreal and full of secret horrors, that the thought of meddling with them — testing their powers — was as far away from her thoughts and inclination as — well, as the power that the people who deal in such arts profess to have, is away from them. She knew but little about them, and had never allowed herself to become interested in them. Gypsey fortune telling was bad enough, though it seemed more silly than really bad; there was fun to be gotten from it anyway. If Vera had been going to have faith in anything of that nature, she would have chosen palmistry. But the idea of a person going into a trance and pretending to read one's future to one — why, it was preposterous. Vera was not sure but that it was downright wicked. How did they dare pretend to see into the future! No one but God could do that. She wondered if Garnet really had faith in it, and raised herself up on her pillow to better look into the face lying so near her own. It was very quiet, very serene. The breath came softly and regularly from between the small lips.

But it seemed to Vera's excited imagination as though she saw under the richly colored skin something that passed and repassed swiftly, until it changed the quiet of the face into broken, troubled unrest. Vera heaved a little sigh of impatience as

she lay down and settled herself determinedly to
sleep. "That woman won't go into a trance for
me — that is sure," was her last thought before she
drifted off into dreamland.

How the two girls ever escaped the watchful
vigilance of Jessie's bright eyes the next morning
was a wonder to themselves, but at 10 o'clock they
were walking slowly and sedately up Circuit avenue. Had their feet kept pace with their quickly
beating hearts, they would have run all the way.

"Madam Hazel, Medium," read Vera, suddenly; and then the two girls found themselves passing up a long flight of steps. At a door, which
bore the same words as the sign outside, they
paused and looked silently at each other. Vera's
face was very pale, even to the lips, but Garnet's
remained unchanged, only the small lips were
drawn into their straightest line. She put out her
hand and pressed Vera's very closely for a second,
then she pressed the button and the next moment
they were ushered into a small, but handsomely
furnished parlor.

"Madam Hazel will be at liberty in a moment,
ladies," said the attendant — a colored woman.
"Please to take chairs;" then she disappeared.

Vera looked at Garnet and Garnet looked at
Vera, then both looked around the room. There
were two long windows facing the avenue, draped
with lace curtains. Between these windows was a

small parlor organ.   On one side of the room was a handsomely draped mantel with fireplace ; on the other, what seemed to be a cabinet, draped with garnet plush.   Both girls wondered to themselves if that was where the " spirits " were kept, and Vera even found courage to say to herself : " Perhaps one could smell them if one could put one's nose through the draperies."   In the center of the room was a small table.   But that which the girls looked at the longest, was a curtained alcove at the back of the room.   The heavy draperies were drawn closely together, but they were sure that that was the " mysterious chamber " — Madam's " sanctum sanctorum."

After they had been seated about ten minutes, a door leading into an apartment beyond opened, and a tall, large woman came slowly into the room. She had a fair, pleasant face, dark hair and small blue eyes.   She was dressed in a loose wrapper.

" Good morning, young ladies," she said, and her voice sounded fresh and cheerful; indeed, quite like other human beings.   " Please excuse my wrapper, but my husband has been quite ill for the past two or three days, and I was up with him the greater part of last night."

Her husband !   Then she was human enough to get married.   Vera wondered if she had mesmer- ized her husband and he had married her while under the " spell."   And he was sick and she had been nursing him; had even stayed up most of the night with him. Human, more human. She spoke with a certain amount of tenderness in her tones — doubtless she loved her husband well. Human, more human, most human. Her next remark set the girls' hearts a-fluttering.

"Did you wish to consult with me?"

"Yes, ma'am."

Both girls replied, but their voices together would not have made one good one.

"On anything in particular? Matters of business; or relating to health?"

No, the girls were not particular about either of these. Madam looked at them a little coldly. Vera caught the look and her pride came to the rescue. She drew herself up haughtily.

"My friend would like for you to give her a sitting, Madam Hazel," she said, in her clearest tones. "But she is not particular about its relating to either business or health. Simply tell her what — what — " Vera paused, not knowing how to express herself, then added, desperately, "what is shown to you."

Madam Hazel rose from her seat, and walked over to the curtained alcove. She drew the draperies aside and turned to Garnet.

"In here, please," she said.

Garnet walked very meekly past Madam, and Madam followed her, drawing the draperies closely together, but the next moment her head appeared through a small opening.

"Excuse me, Miss, but do you play on the organ?"

"Yes, ma'am," answered Vera, with a promptness born of surprise.

"Well, will you please play softly while I am talking to this young lady? My 'spirit' does not like for a third party to hear what she tells me."

Then the head disappeared, and Vera surprised and displeased, but with no choice left, rose slowly from the chair and seated herself on the stool. Her hands dropped aimlessly on the keyboard, and she gazed vacantly at a picture over the organ.

"Begin at once, please," came from behind the draperies.

Vera gave a little jump and struck out desperately on "The Old Folks at Home."

"Not quite so loud, please," again came from behind the draperies. "You disturb my spirit — she cannot talk with me."

Thus corrected, Vera closed the swell and played on softly and sweetly. She felt very indignant at first, and as Madam's tones came indistinctly to her, mumbling off some jargon or another, she felt angry and ashamed of herself for coming, but by and by the comicality of it all — Garnet in close communication with Madam and the "spirit," and herself posted upon the organ stool, playing anything and

everything that came into her mind — dawned gradually upon her and changed her angry feelings to
those of amusement.

"What *would* anyone think if they were to
come in here and see me stuck up on this stool,
playing away for dear life, while that nonsense is
going on in there — behind the scenes. They
would probably think — and I don't know as I
would blame them if they did — that I am hired by
Madam for so much an hour to play while she goes
into her trances and reveals the future to anyone
who is foolish enough to pay her for doing it.
If such a thing were possible as one of my friends
coming in here and catching me, I would die of
mortification. I wonder what Mr. Travers and
Mr. Richards would think, especially the latter."

The very idea of anything so dreadful, caused
her to stop playing. Madam's voice stopped at the
same time, but Vera did not notice it. After a moment Madam called out:

"Keep right on, squaw; I'm not quite through
yet."

"Gracious!" exclaimed Vera to herself. "A
queer trance *she* must be in to know when I stop
playing, and scream out to me in that way. And
what does she mean by calling me 'squaw.'"
Aloud she said: "But I have played all I know."

"Then begin over again and go through with the
same pieces, please," replied Madam, pleasantly.

Vera obeyed, smiling a little grimly as she thought: "Serves me right for coming."

She was in the middle of "Home, Sweet Home," and heartily wishing herself there, when the door bell rang. Vera's heart gave a jump. The woman who waited on the door came into the room. Vera turned to her.

"Will they come in here?" she asked, in an agitated whisper.

The woman smiled. "They will only pass through."

Then she opened the door, and Vera almost twisted her head off in her anxiety to turn her face completely away from the door. In doing this she looked squarely into a looking-glass, and not only that, but she looked squarely into the face of the gentleman who was entering the room — Mr. Erfort Richards.

But Mr. Richards' eyes were cast downward. Vera drew a long breath as she saw this. He hadn't seen her! Oh, joy! But what was he there for? What was *she* there for? *She* came with Garnet; but what was Garnet there for? Mr. Richards came alone, so there was no question as to his errand. Well, of all things! Such a grave, dignified, sensible young man as he seemed to be! If it had been Fred — Vera's fingers wandered lightly into "Beautiful Blue Danube." She played on, one waltz after another, a smile on her

red lips.   She did not know that Madam's voice
had ceased; she hardly realized where she was,
until she felt a light touch on her arm, and then
she started and turned around, and there was
Garnet standing close beside her, drawing on her
gloves.   She looked very grave and quite pale.

"Well?" questioned Vera.

Garnet gave her a most expressive look, at which
Vera laughed nervously.   This is how Garnet
looked:

She opened her eyes wide, and rolled them
slowly upward, drew her lips closely together, and
wagged her head solemnly.   The look said, as
plainly as words could speak:

"Oh — h, Vera!   She is w — o — nderful.   Try
her!"

And Vera, under the spell of that look, turned
and walked quickly into Madam's presence.

CHAPTER XI.

Madam Hazel rose from her chair to draw the draperies together.

"It is *your* turn to play now," she said to Garnet, in the pleasantest voice imaginable.

"But I don't know how," said Garnet.

Madam's face fell. "Can't you play at *all*?" she asked.

"Well — well — er, no; not much. Nothing, to speak of. Only chords," burst out Garnet, nervously, and then she grew more nervous still at hearing Vera's soft giggle.

Madam's face cleared; she smiled brightly. "Oh, well, that will do. Play chords," and then she drew the curtains together, and poor Garnet, feeling more foolish than Vera had dreamed of feeling, sat herself down on the stool and went to playing "chords." Tum, tum, tum; tum, tum, tum. One thing right over and over again. If she only knew enough about playing to change the chords, but, alas! she only knew the accompaniment to one piece,—"Last Night,"—and Jessie had taught her that because she — Garnet — had liked it so well. Oh, dear! What would anyone in the house think to hear that monotonous drumming. If she only dared to change it! After fifteen minutes of absolute torture to herself, Garnet, rendered desperate, closed her eyes, spread out her hands as if desirous of taking the whole keyboard in, and brought them down again slowly, but not the less surely. Horrors! What a wail! It turned her own blood cold to hear it. With nervous haste she proceeded once more to "Last Night."

Meanwhile, Vera was passing rapidly from one excited state of mind into another. Now feeling ready to burst into laughter, and now unpleasantly alive to a creepy feeling up and down her spinal column. The room in which they were, was a very small one. The only articles of furniture were the sofa — on which Vera sat — and a small table with a chair drawn up before it. Upon this chair Madam had seated herself.

" Let me have the glove from your right hand, please," she said.

Vera drew it off mechanically, and Madam, taking it, commenced to turn the fingers inside out and roll and twist the glove in her hand, talking softly and rapidly as she did so, and slightly swaying her body backward and forward.

" Now you must know that the spirit with which I talk is that of an old Indian squaw. Sometimes she will tell me everything clearly and easily, and again, she is very stubborn and will scarcely tell me a word. At these times I have to be very care-

ful how I speak to her. After I tell you everything
my spirit tells to me, you may ask me any questions
you choose and I will answer them for you. The
old squaw sits at the door of her wigwam, and
when I ask her a question she writes the answer to
it on a slate, and I read it from it. Sometimes it is
very misty around the slate and I cannot see the
writing, but if — dis a quee bushee din a pree
fumoo — "

Vera gave a little jump as Madam very suddenly
went from English to a jargon which Vera, after a
moment, supposed to be Indian dialect, but which
sounded to her just as I have written it. She
stifled a nervous desire to laugh, and paid close
attention to what Madam, with ever moving hands,
proceeded to tell her ; first in broken English, then
in perfectly plain.

" Now, my fair-haired squaw, I see you velly
plainly. No, not so velly plainly, for ze light that
am shining around you am not bright like ze sunlight, but paler, like ze moonlight. You am standing all alone in ze tall grasses, and all around you
am — am — oh, (here Madam passed her hands
rapidly over each other several times and made up
a most comical face, as though she could not find
words to express her meaning,) oh, zey look like
cobwebs ; zee? Zey mean that you am surrounded
with difficulties and troubles, and you do not know
which way to turn or what to do. The clouds are

heavy over you, but by and by they begin to break and roll slowly away, and a little star appears and shines brightly down upon you. In a little while the moon begins to peep through the clouds, a little at a time, a little at a time, until by and by it shines down upon you, and makes the way clear before you. Then you begin to break with your own hands, one by one, these cobwebs that are about you. No one helps you, you do it all yourself, and in a little while you break them all, and walk away. You come to a gate, and as you pass through, a dark-eyed brave come towards you. He is about thirty years of age. He will try to influence your life, but, squaw, have nothing to do with him, for his influence will not be for your good. Then I see two more figures coming towards you; a tall, fair brave, leading a dark-eyed squaw by the hand. You know the brave, but you do not know the squaw. This brave, squaw, will be the one you will marry, but his squaw will not die for a year and a half yet. I see that you are a person who is possessed of a large amount of will-power. But be careful, for in a little while you will lose a good amount of it. Now, squaw, one thing is certain. You will marry a brave whose squaw has gone to the happy hunting grounds. You will have a beautiful home and will be very happy, although you will never have children. But before this change comes to you, you will pass through considerable trouble and perplexity, but it will all come out right at last. Now, squaw, am dere any questions you would like to ask me?"

Vera, half ashamed, half angry, and wholly disgusted, had a great mind to reply with a curt "No," but then thought she would ask a few questions just for fun.

"How old am I?"

Madam leaned forward, as if listening, with her head on one side and her mouth pursed up. Then she said slowly:

"Squaw, the slate says, 'twenty two.'"

Vera's heart beat a little quicker; the answer was right. Madam still sat with her eyes closed. "She is reading my mind," thought Vera, suddenly. Aloud she asked:

"What is my occupation?" and she said to herself, over and over: "Writing," "writing:"

Madam leaned nearer to her. Her face twitched, and she screwed it up so tight that Vera could see nothing but nose. Presently she said:

"Squaw, the slate says, "Writing," "writing," oh, so many times."

Vera smiled in a superior manner.

"With whom do I live?" was her next question, and immediately after asking it she fixed her eyes on space and her mind ditto. She did not think of anything. Her mind, for the time being, was a perfect blank. The twitching in Madam's face became something quite alarming. She moved nearer yet to Vera; she breathed quickly, and her breath touched Vera's cheek. Her hands worked nervously; she twisted and wrung Vera's glove into a perfect rag. The expression of her face became perfectly beseeching, but Vera used all the will-power that Madam had truly given her credit of possessing, in keeping her mind in its blank state. She *would not* yield one inch. At last Madam dropped the glove in her lap and spread out her hands towards Vera with a pathetic gesture.

"Ah, squaw, the slate is misty. I cannot see the writing upon it. My "spirit" is growing tired, and she will not tell me anything."

Vera said nothing. In her own mind she was satisfied. The mystery of clairvoyance was, for her, clearly explained.

"Have you any more questions to ask, squaw?"

Madam was meekness personified, and her tones were timid. Vera rose from her chair.

"No, thank you; no more."

She stood, with one hand resting on the table, looking at Madam. Madam raised both hands up over her head, clasped them tightly together, yawned once or twice, as if waking from a deep sleep, stretched herself, rubbed her eyes like a sleepy child, allowed one or two slight quivers to pass through her body, and finally sat upon her chair and looked up into Vera's face with blinking eyes. Vera did not allow her natural politeness to be entirely swallowed up in her disgust.

"How much is it?" she asked, but her tones were what Garnet always said made her think of "sweetened ice."

"One dollar."

Vera took the money out of her purse and handed it to Madam, picked up her glove from the table, bowed haughtily and swept in her most dignified manner out into the parlor. Garnet turned on the organ stool and looked at Vera with wide open, questioning eyes. Vera replied with an expression that drew Garnet from the stool and out of the room, as the magnet draws the needle.

Never a word said Vera as they went down the stairs, but once on the street, and at a safe distance from the crowd, and she turned to Garnet with scornful eyes.

"Garnet Dare, we are two big simpletons."

"Amen!" said Garnet, but her tones were not cordial, and Vera, looking at her, knew that whatever inclination Garnet had had to believe in the power of the medium, that inclination had been strengthened by the things that had been said to her by Madam.

Vera was reserve itself, even with her most intimate friends, but as she looked down into the strong little face beside her, the question sprang abruptly to her lips:

"What did she tell you, Net?"

Garnet looked before her with dreamy eyes. She paused a moment before answering, for Vera was her dearest friend and they loved each other well. Then a quick flush spread itself from brow to neck.

"Oh, lots of foolishness, Vera; nothing worth mentioning."

Vera appeared satisfied. "There is one thing about it; we'll have to go without something else, now. The idea of throwing away a dollar on such foolishness. But, Net, I have something to tell you. Do you remember of hearing the bell ring, while Madam was talking to you?"

Garnet looked surprised. "Did it ring?" she asked.

Vera laughed. Were you really so carried away that you didn't hear it? Well, it rung, and a gentleman passed through the parlor."

Vera stopped and looked at Garnet. Garnet lifted calm eyes. "Yes?"

"Well," repeated Vera. "Guess who it was?"

Garnet stood perfectly still. They had turned off the avenue and were walking along the beach.

"Not Fred?"

"No; not he."

Garnet looked earnestly into Vera's smiling face, then she commenced to walk slowly on with her eyes fixed on the sand.

"It wasn't, was it, Vera?"

Although Garnet mentioned no name, Vera understood. "Yes, it was, Net," she answered.

They walked along the beach for half an hour or more, both very silent. Vera was wishing she had her dollar safe back in her purse again, but Garnet's thoughts, to judge from the expression of her face, were of a more romantic nature.

At last Vera exclaimed: "Oh, mercy! how hot this sun is. Let us go home." As they entered the cottage by the kitchen door, Jessie came rushing from the parlor to meet them, her face sparkling with smiles. In her hand she swung lightly to and fro, the silver fob to her watch. Allie followed close behind, and she, too, was smiling.

"My watch, girls; my watch!" cried Jessie, and threw an arm around the neck of each.

"Where did you find it?" both asked at once.

"Oh, the strangest thing!" said Jessie, breathlessly. "Come into the parlor and I'll tell you all about it. There! you three sit there on the lounge and I'll stand up before you and tell it all off. I'm so excited I can't sit still. You know, just a little while after you two *sneaked* off this morning, (she stopped long enough to roll her eyes reproachfully around at Garnet and Vera,) somebody knocked on the front door. "Grandpa" went to the door, and there stood a lady. She wanted to see the person who had lost the watch, so of course "Grandpa" called me. Well, when I came down, of all the sights *I* ever saw! I suppose she was a woman, because she had on a woman's dress and hat, but there all the likeness to other women ended. She had short hair and big brown hands, and she took long steps like a man, and her voice was 'ugh, ugh, ugh,' (Jessie made her voice as gruff as possible,) and upon my word, girls, she had a mustache that any man might be proud of. Twice as heavy as Fred Travers'; and the color was what you might call a fast black. Well, she eyed me over as cool as you please. The mean old thing didn't bring the watch with her, but she said it was at her cottage on Ocean avenue, and if it belonged to me I could have it by coming for it. She found it last night in the post office. Well, Allie and I trotted up to her cottage with her, like two little puppy dogs, and she left us in the reception room while she went for the watch. My! but wasn't that house furnished though! B-e-a-u-ti-ful! She was gone quite a while, but when she came back she had the watch. I almost forgot all about the reward, but I pulled out my purse as grand as life, and took out the big sum of one dollar and passed it to her, and I declare if she didn't take it.

Jessie's eyes fairly snapped. So did Vera's and Garnet's. "No, you don't mean it, Jess!" they both exclaimed.

"Yes, sir, she did — the stingy beggar. Worth her millions, probably — she's just cranky enough to be — and take a dollar from a poor little pauper like me. I can't have any more nougats now all the rest of the time I'm here. But I don't care. I've got my darling little watch back again." And Jessie laid her little scarlet cheek against the pretty toy and kissed it.

Vera was indignation itself. "Well, if she isn't what I call meanness personified. The idea!"

A knock sounded on the closed blind door. Jessie ran to open it. They saw her start, then draw herself up haughtily and press her lips together. Then they heard a gruff voice say : "Excuse me, but I have come to bring back the dollar you gave this morning. I don't care for it."

They saw a big, brown hand put a silver dollar into the little palm that Jessie mechanically held out, then the gruff voice said : " Good Morning," and Jessie closed the door and came back to them with big, black eyes.

" Of all things ! " was all she could say, and then all four burst into a merry peal of laughter.

After many conjectures as to what induced the strange woman to bring back the dollar, Jessie declared that the other ladies in the house *made* her do it; that she was a loon, or half a one anyway; and then she went dancing out of the parlor, crying : " I'll treat the crowd on nougats now, to celebrate my double good luck. Come on mit me, Al."

Garnet looked at Vera. " It has made her forget to ask us where we have been. Fortunate, eh ? "

And Vera replied with a little squeeze of the hand.

CHAPTER XII.

The next morning, as the girls were putting the finishing touches to their toilet, a low, soft, trembling knock sounded on their door. They looked at each other with smiling faces and their lips simultaneously formed the word, " Mother."

Vera opened the door. Yes, there she stood on the threshold, a smile on her fair old face, one hand resting on the door, the other holding back " Grandpa."

" Good morning," said the girls. " Come right in and take some chairs."

" Thank you, dears," replied " Mother," her face flushing with pleasure at the pleasant manner with which she was received. She and " Grandpa " had even so soon learned to love " their four girls," as they called them. " We won't come in, thank you ; but Mr. Atherton and me wanted to ask you if you would as soon come down to the kitchen before we have breakfast, and sing something to us."

" Yes, girls, if you would come, ' Mother ' and I would be so happy," quavered " Grandpa," from the background.

"Why, certainly we will come," said the girls.
The look on the old faces was thanks enough.
"Mother" pushed "Grandpa" towards the stairs.

"Now we'll go right down, Mr. Atherton," she
said, primly. "Perhaps the young ladies are not
quite ready."

But the girls declared they were, and in a few
minutes they were all seated in the kitchen singing
the same hymns they had sung every morning —
old, but ever new to "Grandpa" and "Mother."

"Girls," said "Mother," suddenly, "you have
all given your hearts to the Saviour, haven't you?"

The question was a great surprise to the girls.
Vera, Garnet and Jessie could only look down into
their laps and smile nervously. Allie surprised
them as much as "Mother's" question had done.

"I have never confessed my love for Him before
the world," she said, softly, "but I do love Him
with all my heart."

"Amen. Thank God!" quavered "Grandpa."
"'Mother,' let us pray."

Side by side knelt the two bent forms. Allie
slipped quietly from her chair to her knees, and the
other three, after a quick look at one another, did
the same.

"Our dear Father and our God, who has heard
what this, Thy precious daughter, has testified to
us and to Thee, take her forever close to Thy heart,
so close that she can never wander away from it,

and fill her young life with the strength that can only come from constant intercourse with Thine own holy self.   Dear Father, Mighty Redeemer, hold her close, close.   Many and great are the temptations that will come to her in this life.   Thou knowest this, for Thou hast lived upon the earth and passed through it all before us, and we cannot tell Thee anything Thou dost not know.   But we know that it is very precious to Thy loving heart, to have Thy children ask Thy help; Thy help which Thou art always so glad to give.   Oh, Father, dear Father, bless her, keep her, shield her from all harm.   And, dear Father, touch these other young hearts that are beating before Thee; they are such true, pure, lovable hearts, dear Father, capable of containing such strong feeling; turn them in these, their early days, towards Thee and towards the only true life.   We love them so dearly, Father, that we cannot find words with which to pray for them, but Thy love for them, which is so much stronger and greater than ours can ever be, is able to do all and much more than any words of ours could ask for.   Help us through this day and the days — many or few as Thou wilt — that are to come, forgive us our many sins, and save us at last for Jesus sake, Amen.

*   *   *   *   *   *   *   *

"Where are you going Vera?" asked Jessie about 4 o'clock that afternoon, as Vera came into the room and took her hat down from its nail.

Jessie looked tired. She was sitting in the rocking chair, with her head leaning against the back of it, rocking. Garnet and Allie were out on the piazza.

Vera stood still in the middle of the room, and ran her hat-pin through the lace on her hat.

"Oh — not far — just for a little walk."

"Well, I'm awfully lonesome, somehow or another," said Jessie, with a sigh. "Don't you want me to go with you?"

Strange to say, Vera hesitated. Jessie opened her eyes in surprise.

"Don't you want me, Vera?" she asked, childishly.

"Of course I do, Jasmine," replied Vera, lovingly. "Only — perhaps, when you know where I am going, you won't care to go."

"Well, tell me; then you will know."

"Well, I'm going to see Charlotte Hood."

Vera fully expected a burst of scornful laughter. What was her surprise to see Jessie spring to her feet, clap her hands softly and run for her hat.

"Oh, Vera, that is perfectly lovely. Of course I want to go. I have been thinking of her all this afternoon, and wishing I might see her and hear her talk. Whatever made you think of going there?"

" Well, to tell the truth, I had the same desire that you have confessed to having — I felt just like it."

"Net and Al are out on the piazza, talking to those two boys," said Jessie, a little contemptuously. "They rode up a few minutes ago on their bicycles. Let's go out the side door and they won't see us."

Vera stopped irresolutely at the foot of the stairs. "Perhaps they would like to go with us. I feel as though I ought to tell them where we are going."

Jessie gave her lace mitten an impatient jerk. "Oh, come along, Vera ; don't, for pity's sake, ask those two boys. I'd like to go somewhere once, without them tagging at our heels."

Vera smiled and followed Jessie out of the house. The day was beautiful. It was a little cool, so the girls wore their plush shoulder capes over their light dresses. It seemed as though all Cottage City were out promenading, or riding the wheel. The cool sea-breeze made everyone feel bright and joyful. Gay laughter and merry voices sounded everywhere. A little fellow in a smart sailor suit and cap rode his miniature bicycle close to Jessie's dainty muslin dress, and then raised his cap in laughing apology. He was not more than ten years old. Ordinarily Jessie would have corrected him sharply for his carelessness, but now she smiled and nodded pleasantly back to him and watched him with wistful eyes as he spun gaily down the avenue.

"How poor little Robie Hood would enjoy doing what that boy is doing," she said; and Vera, looking at her in surprise, saw tears in the sweet eyes.

"Oh, Vera, it doesn't seem right, does it?"

Vera looked very grave. "What doesn't seem right, Jess?" she asked.

She knew what Jessie meant, but wanted to draw her out. She never remembered to have seen her in such a mood before, and it pleased, while it perplexed and saddened her. Bright, laughing, careless little Jessie, to be so touched and grieved.

"Why, that such a woman as Mrs. Hood should have so much care and trouble, and that darling little boy should suffer so. He never did a bit of harm in all his life, I know, and just see the life he is living. I wonder if it is all right. It can't be, for where is the justice in it?"

Vera could not tell her; she didn't know herself. Had Jessie asked for her opinion on the justice of "King Arthur" leaving "Guinevere" to her fate in the nunnery, she would scarcely have been able to talk fast enough, her thoughts would have come so rapidly. But on this subject she was dumb. She was dumb because she was ignorant. She had never thought about the justice of God, and so she could not pass an opinion on it.

"I have never once thought about such things before," went on Jessie. "And I don't suppose I would now if I hadn't happened to go there the other day: but since then I haven't been able to get that child out of my mind. I can see his little face just as it looked on his mother's shoulder. Oh, Vera, wasn't it dreadful!" and Jessie grasped Vera's hand. Vera returned the clasp and they walked along in this manner.

"I've always been such a selfish little thing," went on Jessie. "Getting mad over the least little thing. If I want the sun to shine and it rains, I rave and tear around as if some terrible thing had happened; and there that poor little boy has to lie in bed in all kinds of weather — fair as well as foul — and besides that, suffer such terrible pain all the time. Now look at that handsome carriage ahead there; see that lady lying back in it with that nasty little poodle on her lap. And see the gentleman opposite to her, half asleep on his soft cushions. He looks as though he had been up half the night. I don't suppose they have anything in this world to do but laze around, eat, sleep, drive out and enjoy themselves. And there is this poor mother working herself to death in order to get food enough to keep her and her child from starving; lived a good, christian life all her days, I suppose, and the child — little lower than an angel — suffering untold agony every hour of his life. Not even able to crawl to the door and get a breath of fresh air. Nothing to amuse himself with, the few moments he is not suffering, but a few miserable little toys. Why, Vera, he even has to stay in the house alone while his mother is gone for the clothes. O, it is dreadful, dreadful! Don't you suppose he is as precious in God's sight as that poodle lying in that lady's lap?"

Jessie turned her glowing face to Vera as she sharply asked this question. Vera recoiled in shocked surprise.

"Why, Jessie, what a question! Of course he is."

"Then why does He provide better for the dog than for the child?"

Vera was mute. She was shocked, grieved and troubled. Jessie was all hot resentment, but she was seeking for light, poor child!

"What do you *think*, Vera? You are educated and have always been considered more than commonly intelligent. You are a great reader and a great thinker. Tell me what you think about it."

Alas, proud Vera! Well informed on all the important topics of the day, she was totally unable to answer Jessie's simple little question. She could tell the author of almost any book that anyone might mention, and be able to give a fair synopsis of the book itself. Her opinions on this and that subject — slavery, dress reform, woman's rights, pro-

hibition, etc., etc., her criticisms on art, ancient as
well as modern literature, public speakers, and
even her really enviable knowledge of the manner
and customs of foreign countries and the government of her own — in all these she had gained for
herself recognition from the cultivated society in
which she moved.   But this thing of which Jessie
spoke was beyond her comprehension ; she could
find no words with which to answer.   And Jessie,
who disliked all deep reading and who did not read
a poem once a year, except in her elocution, had
commenced to think out the deep mystery of life,
and Vera — learned Vera — had no help to give
her.   She looked into the little quivering face and
her own grew sad at the thought.

" It isn't right, Vera ; it isn't right," Jessie repeated wildly, and then she stopped suddenly
before a toy-shop and her face grew laughing once
more.

"Come in here a minute, Vera ; I'm going to
get a ' Noah's Ark ' for Robin."

" You go in here, Jess," said Vera, " and I'll run
across the street and get some of those nice looking
bananas."

The two girls, as they neared Charlotte Hood's
little brown cottage, both realized plainly that
there was a new feeling in their heart ; a quiet,
softly happy, contented feeling that they did not stop
to analyze, but which was very pleasant, indeed,

to them. They did not mention it one to the other, but it was there in each heart.

Mrs. Hood answered their knock on the door. Her face lighted up at the sight of her visitors and she invited them into the room where Robin lay, in her most cordial tones.

"This is one of my boy's good days," she said, smoothing the white pillow that his golden head rested upon. "Robbie, darling, these young ladies have come to see you."

But at the first sight of Jessie, Robin's face had broken out into a bright, merry smile, and Jessie, so pleased to see this — for it made him look more like other boys — stepped quickly to the bed-side, and taking both his little, thin hands in one of her's, smoothed the clustering curls back with her other, and kissed him twice, once on each cheek. And when she lifted her head, the pleased mother saw tears standing thick in the glorious eyes. Vera's kiss on the white cheek was very sweet and gentle, and the boy smiled up into the fair face bent over him with a childish, trusting smile, that deeply touched her.

In a few moments more they were all three watching Robin with happy faces, as he sat propped up in bed, his 'Noah's Ark' spread out before him, a large banana in his hands, which he kept offering to his mother now and then, and from which she took little bites to satisfy him, and his beautiful, pale face glowing with an almost healthful glow.

The mother sat in a chair close to the pillow, Jessie sat on the bed, and Vera in the low rocker beside it. For an hour Robin played with the pretty toys and prattled gaily as he did so ; then, by and by, he laid them down with a little happy sigh, and slipping his hand into that of his mother's, turned his face toward her on the pillow and said, a little wearily :

" I'm tired, mamma, but I'm happy, too. Sing the pretty piece, mamma."

She was oblivious of everything but her child, and she sang to him the "pretty piece": "Nearer, My God To Thee," just as though they were there alone. And as she sang, his hand, wandering lovingly among the toys, touched Jessie's hand as she timidly put it in his way, and nestled there ; and so with one hand clasping his mother's and the other clasping Jessie's he sank into a sweet, untroubled sleep.

For a few moments after they knew he slept, they were very quiet, for fear of waking him ; then all at once Jessie said in a very low, but passionate tone :

" Oh, it seems cruel. It can't be right. There is no justice in it."

The mother's eyes, that had been feasting themselves hungrily on the little face so close to her own, turned towards Jessie, and Jessie's sank before the light in them.

" Oh, don't dare to say it," breathed the low,

thrilling tones. "It is God's will, and He is an all-wise and an all-merciful God."

Jessie stared at her in utter amazement, so did Vera, and Mrs. Hood looking first into one face and then into the other, read the secret of each heart as plainly as if it had been written upon each face, and drawing her hand gently away from her boy's clasp, motioned the two girls to go with her to the other end of the room, away from the bed, and sit beside her at the window.

CHAPTER XIII.

"I feel that God means for me to speak to you now, in this place and at this moment," she said, in low, vibrating tones. "He is moving my heart very strangely, and I feel that it is so I may, through His guidance, move yours. You do not know what it is to have the Saviour for your friend? You have never given your hearts to him?"

Both girls shook their heads.

"I knew it, for if you had, you would never have said what you did."

She stopped a moment and looked at them. She was very pale indeed, and her lips were trembling, but the look that Vera had seen on her face in the tabernacle was on her face now.

"Let me tell you the story of my life," she said, suddenly. "It is something I have never told to anyone before, but it seems as tho' the Lord were commanding me to tell it to you. Would you like to hear it?"

"Oh, if you would, Mrs. Hood," said Jessie; and Vera said: "Yes, please, if you are willing."

Mrs. Hood looked over to the bed where her boy lay sleeping, and commenced her story.

"I was one of a family of eight children — six girls and two boys. Our home was on the Cape — Cape Cod. My father was a sea captain, and up to the time I was fifteen years old I did not know what it was to want for anything. I had three sisters older than myself — Hannah, Emeline and Deborah. Hannah and Emeline were very handsome girls, but I loved Deborah the best. After me came the brother whom I almost worshipped — Johial. Then Thankful, then Mercy, then little Warren, named for father. We were a very happy family. Father was away from home a great deal, of course, but when he came back from his trips — oh, what happy times those were! Such syrup as he used to bring home. I have never tasted anything like it since; and whole barrels of almonds. I cannot begin to tell you how happy we were. My three older sisters went to dancing school, evening parties and entertainments, and I was always looking forward to the time when I could go. No serious thought ever entered my head, until when I was about eleven years old, there came a revivalist to West Dennis, (my home was in South Dennis).

"Hannah, Emeline and Deborah used to go over to the meetings every night, but they only went for the walk home with the young men after meeting. Child though I was, I saw that easily enough. I begged and teased mother to let me go with them just for one night, but the girls said they would not

be bothered with me, and mother let them have
their way about it. But I had made up my mind
to go, and go I would. I had heard the girls tell
of things the revivalist had said, and Deborah, who
was a very good mimic, had once or twice acted
him out to us younger ones. I had made up my
mind as to how he looked. I imagined him to be
a tall, large man, with long, floating, black hair,
fiery, dark eyes, and a stern mouth, out of which
proceeded terrible words about sinners dying and
being thrown into a lake of fire, where they burned
forever and ever. I was wild to see and hear, and
on the last night of his stay I crawled out of the bed
where mother had tucked Thankful and I an hour
before, and, dressing myself rapidly, glided down
stairs and out of the side door, just as my sisters,
with cousins Abbie, Modina and Patience, went out
of the front gate. Fortunately for me there was no
moon, but the stars shone beautifully bright and
clear, and the May night was delightful. The
girls kept up a continual chatter, and they neither
saw or heard me as I glided along, a little dark
figure, in the shadow of the whispering pines. It
was a good two miles and a half walk, and when
we reached the church we found it nearly filled.
The girls managed to get seats together, and I
squeezed myself between two fat old ladies in one
of the seats opposite. We had not been there long
before half a dozen young men, who haunted our

house like so many spirits, came in and took seats back of the girls. I can safely say that it was very little of the preacher's words that those girls and boys heard that night, for as far as I could see, they did nothing but eat wintergreen tablets, lozenges and peppermints. The boys wrote on pieces of paper, put them into the singing books, and passed them slyly over the shoulders of the girls. The girls took them, held them in their lap very innocently for a moment or two, then took them up and carelessly turned the leaves. Of course the slip of paper fell out, but the girls did not seem to notice this for a while, but my childish eyes, watching them sharply (for reasons of my own which I will tell by and by), saw them read the notes surreptitiously, with blushing cheeks and pouting lips, but looking vastly pleased all the time, and then, under cover of the leaves of the book, wrote a word or two on the back of the paper, put it into the book, and returned it to the boys over their shoulders with the sang froid worthy of society women of twice their years. I know now that the boys had asked to 'see them home,' and the girls had written back: 'Certainly.'"

" But now I was looking eagerly around for the ' preacher,' but I didn't see anyone whom I thought could be he. The congregation sang two or three pieces and then the pastor of the church stepped down from the platform, and a tall, slender man

took his place.   He was the 'preacher.'   Did he
look as I had pictured him?   Not at all.   His face
was mild and fair; his white hair was brushed
simply back from a broad, beautiful forehead.   His
eyes were blue, and although he must have been
seventy years old, they were as bright and clear as
any man's of forty.   When he opened his lips to
speak no terrible words of 'death and fire and eternal
banishment' came from them, but just this, softly
and tenderly spoken: 'Come unto me, all ye that
are weary and heavy laden, and I will give you
rest.'   That is all that I can clearly remember, but
the effect these words had on my childish heart, I
will never forget.   There were no loud groans
from excited hearers, such as I had expected to
hear; everyone was very quiet, but upon many a
tired face, there gradually settled a look of rest and
peace, and the softly spoken words fell upon and
soothed many an aching, sorrowing heart.   I can
only remember how *my* heart was filled with a happy
longing — I felt like crying and singing at the
same time.   When the meeting closed with the
hymn, 'Blest be the Tie that Binds,' I could hardly
realize where I was or how I had gotten there, but
the truth came to me only just in time, for as I
turned to leave the seat, Emeline's dark eyes, glancing carelessly around, almost lighted upon me.
I dodged behind the tall pew door not a moment
too soon.   When I peeped out she was passing my

hiding-place and her eyes were cast down beneath the admiring blue ones of Elnathan Rogers. I slipped out and was soon fluttering along in the shadow of the old pine trees once more. But now my heart was beating strangely. I could not think clearly of what the 'preacher' had said; I only knew that he had told us of a Father in Heaven — a loving, tender Father — who cared for all His children alike. He had taken just such little ones as me up in His arms and said: 'Suffer little children to come unto Me, for of such is the kingdom of Heaven.' He had told of a beautiful home up above the skies, where all who had been His faithful children here, could come and live, by and by, when He called them. There, all things that seemed wrong here, would be made right. There was no crying there, no pain, no parting; all was happiness, peace and rest. The 'preacher' had spoken so simply, albeit with great eloquence, that I had understood plainly what he had said, and I was thinking of it very earnestly, as I walked along with my eyes cast down, so earnestly in fact, that I had entirely forgotten everything else, until I was suddenly ' brought back to earth ' and my surroundings by walking right into the midst of the young couples, who had stopped and were regarding me with rather suspicious glances, until I lifted my face to theirs, and then — such a torrent of exclamations as burst forth, such as : 'Of all things !' 'Well, if I don't give it up!' 'Charlotte Mehitable Phillips, where did you come from?' I was mute until Hannah grasped my arm, not any too gently, and said sternly: 'Charlotte Mehitable, tell me the truth this instant. Where did you come from?' All the softened feelings that had been filling my heart, left it as I twisted myself out of her grasp and cried, breathlessly: 'I cum from the meetin', and you just let me alone Hannah Abbie Phillips, *or I'll tell mother how you girls never listened to the preacher one single bit, but et candy and wrote notes to the fellers every blessed minute.*' Great is the power of the infant terrible! A hush fell upon the group as they eyed me, small conquerer! facing them all with a little flushed face and shining eyes. Then Deborah, slyly thrusting a checkerberry wafer in my hand, said: 'Well, well, never mind Charley; tell us all about it, that's a good girl.' Thus 'approached,' I graciously complied. When I finished, Hannah took me between her and Theophalus Baker, and said, as we walked along: 'Well, we'll let you run in at the front door and get up stairs to bed, and *this* time we won't tell mother about it, but don't you ever dare to do such a thing as this again. Mercy! It's a wonder something awful didn't happen to you.' I don't think mother ever knew about my going to hear the 'preacher.' I never told her and I do not think the girls did. Although Hannah made a great show of 'letting me off,' as she called it, yet I secretly believed, and do now, that I was the lenient one."

Mrs. Hood stopped talking and sat looking at Robin with a smile on her face. The room was full of shadows, for the twilight was deepening. Vera and Jessie had been much interested, and could not bear to think of going without hearing more, but the supper hour was very near. Mrs. Hood seemed to realize all at once how late it was growing, for she suddenly rose from her chair and said:

"Why, you must excuse me for keeping you here in the dark. I will light the lamp."

The girls had risen at the same time, and Vera said:

"Oh, please do not light the lamp for us; we must go now. We have enjoyed it all so much. Can't we come again and hear the rest of it?"

"Yes, indeed," answered Mrs. Hood. "I want to tell you it all."

"When will it be most convenient for you to have us come? *Our* time is all our own, you know."

"Yes. Well, I am generally at liberty about this time every day. I call this hour 'Robin's hour,'" and the mother glanced lovingly towards the bed.

"Then we will be so glad if we can share 'Robin's hour' with him," said Vera, and Jessie asked slyly: "Would you be willing for the other girls to come and hear it too, Mrs. Hood?"

Vera looked at Jessie in surprise, but Mrs. Hood replied :

"Certainly, I would be very happy to have them come, if they would like to ; and your two gentlemen friends, too."

"Thank you," said Jessie, simply.

The girls kissed Robin softly.   He still lay asleep, holding an animal tightly in his little, thin hand.

"How was it you asked if Net and Allie might come, Jess?" asked Vera, as they walked swiftly towards home.

"Oh, I knew they would enjoy it so much," replied Jessie.

"And the young men?" said Vera, slyly.

Jessie tossed her head.   "Oh, let them come if they want to.   It may do them good."

CHAPTER XIV

"Well, my dears, if you have no particular objections to telling, we would like to know where you have kept yourselves all the afternoon," was Garnet's greeting to Vera and Jessie as they entered the kitchen where she was spreading the cloth for the evening meal. Allie stood near by with the cups and saucers in her hands.

"*Guess* where we have been," said Vera, taking her hat and cape off and laying them on the other table.

"Haven't the least idea," said Garnet, smoothing out an extraordinary large wrinkle in the tablecloth. "You might as well tell us first as last."

"Well, we've been to Mrs. Hood's."

Garnet turned on her way to the closet. "*To Mrs. Hood's?*" she asked, in amazement. "What ever induced you to go there this afternoon? It was rather sudden, wasn't it, not to say — sly?"

"Now, Net Dare," said Jessie, "we hadn't the least idea of being sly, so don't make that charge against us. You and Al were having it all to yourselves out on the piazza, and while I was up in our room trying to imagine what pleasure you could find in boys' society, Vera came in and commenced putting her things on. I asked her where she was going and if I couldn't go with her. To make a long story short, we have been to Mrs. Hood's, and, oh, girls"— here Jessie's cheeks grew red — "she is going to tell us the story of her life up to the present time; that is, a good part of it; she told us a little of it this afternoon and we are going again to-morrow at the same hour, and she is going to tell us some more, *and* she has given you and Allie an invitation to come too, and — oh dear! I suppose I must be truthful and tell you that your two young gents are invited too; though mercy knows their room would be better than their company, to *me*, at least," and Jessie sat down in "Mother's" old fashioned rocker and leaned her head against its high back.

"Well," said Garnet, turning once more to her work. "I'm sure that I shall be more than delighted to accept her invitation. Won't you, Allie? How did you find little Robin?"

"You tell them about him, Ve," said Jessie, closing her eyes wearily, and beginning to rock with all her might.

Vera told them everything, and when she spoke of Jessie's wishing to carry Robin something, she saw Garnet's thoughtful face light up with a glad, surprised smile, and the next moment she crossed the room with her light, quick step, and put a soft, cool little hand on Jessie's forehead.

"Head-ache, dear?" she asked.

Jessie rubbed her forehead against the hand, like a kitten.

"A little bit," she murmured, lazily. "But its because I'm so fearfully hungry."

Garnet smiled; she seldom laughed aloud. "That is a good kind of head-ache to have," she said. "You shall be satisfied in a very short time."

"I don't know about being *satisfied*," said Jessie. "What have we got for supper? If you love me, Net, *don't* tell me it is the usual bowl of crackers and milk. I want something more solid than that to-night."

"Well, to tell the truth, Jess, that was what we were going to have, but if you feel like having something else, you shall have it. What would you like?"

"Oh, something; I don't much care what. There's lots of canned stuff over to the store. Why not try some, just for a change? And I'd like to know — " here Jessie sat upright in her chair — "when we are going to have another good, square meal. It seems a year since we've had one."

The girls laughed. "I'm with you, Jess," said Vera. "It *is* about time we patronized some restaurant. 'Grandma' says they give very good dinners at the Brockton House, right back here, at very reasonable prices, too. Suppose we go there to dinner to-morrow. 'Grandma' says they have five or six courses."

"I second the motion," said Jessie, emphatically.

"Well," said Garnet.   "Do you know what they ask?"

"I'm not quite sure, but I think only thirty-five cents.   Not more than fifty, anyway."

"Phooh! money's no object," said Jessie, throwing her empty purse into Vera's lap.

"You'll have to draw on the bank soon, won't you Jess?" asked Vera, pinching the purse.

"I'll draw on something or somebody by and by if I don't have something to eat.   Thought you were going out purchasing, Net."

"Well, so I am," said Garnet, taking her hat and shawl down from the nail behind the door. "Who wants to go with me?"

"Not I, thank you," said Jessie.   "I'm weary."

"I'll go," said Vera.

When the two girls stepped out on the street, they were surprised to find a fine mist falling, and looking in the direction of the ocean, they saw the heavy fog come rolling up.

"Why, what a sudden change," said Garnet. "This dampness strikes deep."

"It was commencing to cloud over when Jess and I came in," said Vera.   "I guess we won't go to the concert to-night.   Do you think we had better?"

"No; we wouldn't enjoy it very much.   The boys wanted to know if we were going, and we told them we expected to, so they were going to call for us. But they can stay and spend the evening instead, and we'll give them some cocoa."

"Suppose we get some canned salmon, if they have any," said Vera, as they went up the steps to the store. "Do you like it?"

"Very much; and so do Allie and Jess."

The salmon was purchased, and while Garnet was paying for it, Vera looked around the store. The next moment she nudged Garnet softly. Garnet looked in the direction indicated by Vera's eyes.

There stood "Mother," dressed in her best black dress, shawl and bonnet. She was standing directly under one of the oil lamps and peering anxiously into an old leather pocket-book she held in her hands. While the girls looked, she shook the pocket-book gently and moved her long, thin fore-finger back and forth in one of the pockets, as if feeling for change. Her glasses rested on the extreme end of her nose, and either for this reason or because the light was so poor, she could not see. Finally she succeeded in bringing to light a piece of money, which she turned over and over, held it up to the light, felt of it, and then stood looking at it.

"Change, madam," said the clerk, and Garnet turned with a start. Vera stepped quickly over to "Mother."

"Can I help you, 'Grandma?'"

Poor "Mother" turned at the sound of the sweet, young voice, and her dim eyes brightened.

"Oh, is it you, dear? I'm trying to find a ten cent piece, and I don't know whether I've got it or not."

Vera looked at the piece of money. "Yes, that is ten cents," she said.

"I want to get a loaf of bread for supper," went on "Mother." "I've been doing some shopping — buying some cloth to make into pillow cases. I've got a few pair, but I'm afraid I shall need some more before summer is over."

"Mother" was evidently considerably excited over something. Her soft wrinkled cheeks were faintly pink, her blue eyes had quite a sparkle in them, and her manner was more than usually nervous and flurried. Vera couldn't help smiling as she looked at her, and thought that she must have been a great beauty in her younger days.

"Let me get your bread for you, 'Grandma,'" she said.

"Well, if you will, I'll be much obliged to you," said "Mother."

"Is there anything else you'd like?" asked Vera.

"Mother" turned and took up a large bundle from a barrel that stood near.

"Let me carry that for you," said Vera.

"Thank you, thank you; it *is* rather heavy. No, there isn't anything else I want to-night. Is that cheese over there?" she asked, suddenly.

"Yes; would you like some?"

"Well, now I would. Me and Mr. Atherton are both very fond of cheese."

"Shall I get half a pound?"

"Well, now, I would like it so much, but I haven't got another cent of change with me."

Vera smiled at the dear old lady's innocent, but broad hint. "Never mind, the change," she said. "I'll get it for you. Net," she whispered, "'Grandma' wants half a pound of cheese. Can we draw on the 'bank' for eight cents?"

"I guess so," whispered back Garnet, with a smile.

After the cheese was purchased and paid for, "Mother" insisting on carrying that package herself, they passed out of the store and down the steps. "Mother" walked in the middle, with her left hand drawn through Vera's arm. The girls were obliged to walk very slowly to accommodate their steps to her's. When fairly on the street, "Mother," first looking cautiously over each shoulder to see that no one heard the great news she was about to impart, said eagerly:

"Well, girls, we have got a new lodger."

Vera and Garnet smiled encouragingly, as "Mother" turned her pleased face, first to one, then to the other. "Oh, that is nice. Who is it?"

" Well, now, I can't think of his name — he told it to me. Let me see — what was it? Well, I can find out when we get home, for it is printed on the lining of his coat, and he left that hanging on a nail in his room. It is a very nice coat, too — the braid is all sewed on by hand, and the coat is lined with good strong satin. He's a young man, and I don't think he is married — he doesn't look so."

The girls, secretly wondering what mark distinguished the married from the unmarried man, asked what room had been given to him. They asked questions, partly because they were really interested, but principally to please " Mother." She took such a childish delight in being " important."

" I've given him the room right opposite to your's. I told him I had four girls staying with me, and that your room was across the hall from his, but he said he didn't mind that."

The girls opened their eyes at this. The new lodger was evidently a cool young man. Vera felt very much like saying : " Well, if he won't mind it, perhaps we will," but she did not like to hurt " Mother's " feelings, so instead she asked :

" Are you expecting many lodgers this summer?"

" Oh, yes, by and by. You see the season has scarcely set in yet; they don't really get here until the first of August. We always have our rooms all taken."

" Then we might as well make hay while the

sun shines," thought the girls. "By and by we won't have the privilege of occupying every room as we do now."

"You seem to understand the business, 'Grandma,'" said Garnet, pleasantly. "You like it, don't you?"

"Oh, yes, dear; very much. Yes, me and Mr. Atherton understand letting rooms pretty well. You see, our home is in Cambridge, and we used to let rooms to the students at Harvard. Then my grandsons — three of them — used to live with us while they were attending college there. Its lots of care, though — lots of care."

Vera opened the gate to let "Mother" pass through. "Yes, it must be quite a responsibility," she said. "But you understand making it very pleasant for your lodgers, 'Grandma.'"

"Mother" smiled proudly as she took her loaf of bread from Garnet, and went up the steps that led to the summer kitchen, where she and "Grandpa" took their meals.

"Where would you like for me to put this cloth, 'Grandma,'" asked Vera.

"Oh, would you just as soon take it up to my room?"

"Certainly."

"Then me and Mr. Atherton can go right up after we have some tea and tear off the pillow cases, and I can lay the hem before I go to bed."

When Vera and Garnet entered the kitchen, Jessie looked up at them with reproachful eyes.

"Well, now I call you two girls perfectly heart-less, to be gone so long when you knew I was on the very verge of starvation. Have you been making it?"

"Never mind, Jess," said Garnet, while Vera ran lightly up the stairs to "Mother's" room with the cloth, "one taste of this delicious salmon will more than repay you for your waiting."

Jessie peeped over Garnet's shoulder and watched her as she undid the wrappings.

"Oh, have you got some canned salmon?" she exclaimed. "I do love that."

"So do I," said Allie, as she leaned her folded arms upon the table and watched proceedings.

"Have you told them about the addition to our family, Net?" asked Vera, coming down stairs.

"Haven't had a chance," said Garnet, giving the salmon the place of honor on the table, viz: the center.

"Who's coming now?" asked Jessie. "Dear me! I was in hopes we would have the cottage all to ourselves while we stayed here."

"Oh, what a selfish Jessie," said Vera. "You ought to think of 'Grandma's' pocket-book."

"Phooh! They've got money enough to keep them the rest of their days — don't you fret," said Jessie, with superior wisdom. "These people who pretend to be so poor are just the ones that have the full pocket-book."

"*Do* you think 'Grandpa' and 'Grandma' have any money?" asked Allie. "They don't dress nicely at all, and just see how pleased they are when we give them any little thing we have left over from our meals."

Jessie laughed merrily. "Hear Al," she said. "Anybody'd think we were some of the tonies. How much do we generally have left over, young lady? I believe we had a few lobster claws last night, and — *were* there any herring tails left over from breakfast this morning?"

All the girls laughed as they seated themselves around the table.

"I think 'Grandpa' and 'Grandma' have quite a sum of money put by, from the few things that 'Grandma' has let drop when she has been talking with me," said Garnet. "Don't you know, as some people grow old, they get into the habit of thinking that unless they count every penny, and make it go as far as they can, they will end their days in the poor-house. One would imagine to see 'Grandpa' and 'Grandma,' that they were very poor, indeed, but I am quite sure they have a plenty to keep them comfortably the rest of their lives."

"Just what *I* say," said Jessie, holding up a piece of salmon on the end of her fork and eyeing it admiringly before putting it into her mouth.

"How strange it seems to be eating by lamp-light," said Vera. "But it grew dark early to-night."

"By the way," said Allie, taking her cup of cocoa from Garnet's hand.   "You didn't tell us who the new lodger is."

"Prepare yourself, Jess," said Vera. "I don't mean to be cruel and spoil your supper, but — its a *man*."

"*What's* a man?" asked Jessie, with charming directness.

"It; the new lodger."

Jessie dropped both knife and fork, and sank back in her chair with an expression of complete discouragement on her face, but suddenly, bethinking herself of the delicious salmon on her plate, she immediately straightened herself in her chair, only saying:

"Well, I might as well stop trying now."

"Stop trying what?" asked the girls.

"Oh, keeping you girls away from the men, or the men away from you — I don't know which."

"Don't, Jess," said Vera, in mock dismay. "Perhaps we'll never have another chance of asso-ciating with the fascinating creatures.   You know they are rather scarce articles up our way."

"And just as well for you that they are," retorted Jessie. "What is that now?" she asked, suddenly. "If that doesn't sound like Fred Travers whistling 'Little Fisher Maiden.'"

Garnet laughed.

" *Is* it, Garnet Dare?" asked Jessie, sternly.

" Well, I suppose it is. We were intending to go to the band concert, but it is so misty and damp we'll let them come in and spend the evening instead. So run and let them in, while we clear this table — that's a good little girl."

" If I let them in I won't have to help clear the table, will I?" asked Jessie, standing irresolutely.

" No. Run; quick!"

" Nor wash dishes, either?"

" No."

" Nor wipe?"

" No, no, no! Hurry!"

Jessie disappeared.

"You go in there, too, Allie," said Garnet, suddenly. " Jess will commit herself in some way or another if she is left alone. She is as bad as 'Miss Edith, who helped things along.'"

The girls did not stop to wash the dishes, and when they entered the parlor they found Fred and Erfort apparently enjoying themselves greatly, and very much at home, indeed. Jessie's tongue was going rapidly; her cheeks glowed, and her eyes flashed. Allie was listening smilingly.

" I'm telling them all about our visit this afternoon, Vera," said Jessie. " And they say they will be glad to go with us to-morrow."

" That will be pleasant," said Vera, taking the low, willow rocker that Fred handed to her.

CHAPTER XV.

"Miss Jessie has interested us deeply by her pleasing account of your visit to Mrs. Hood and Robin, Miss Earle," said Erfort. "We shall be most happy to continue our acquaintance with them."

"Oh, I am sure you will enjoy listening to her," said Vera, earnestly. "I think she is a most lovely woman."

"But the poor little boy," said Fred, with a seriousness that was entirely new with him. "I don't know when I have felt so sorry for anyone."

"I know it," returned Vera. "He is a perfect little hero."

"Well, he is," replied Fred, heartily. "He makes me ashamed of myself. I have thought about him a great deal since the day we were there."

"Little Robin is a hero, and his mother is one of earth's noblest heroines," said Erfort. "How she can bear her heavy cross as she does, I can't imagine."

"I know," said Jessie, softly, and with a bright blush.

All turned and looked at her inquiringly.

"She has some one to help her," said Jessie, with the blush growing deeper. "I said to her to-night, that 'there was no justice in it,' and she said: 'Oh, don't dare to say that. It is God's will, and He is an all-wise and an all-merciful God.'"

Jessie's voice was very low. Fred looked at her in astonishment, for a moment, then he drew his chair a little nearer to her and rested his hand on the back of her rocker.

"How can anyone doubt the satisfaction the christian derives from his or her religion?" said Erfort, earnestly "Even the most skeptical cannot but see and acknowledge the great comfort it brings to them."

"I wonder," said Fred, "how anyone feels when they experience religion."

"Haven't you ever heard one say?" asked Garnet?"

"Yes, I have heard different experiences, but, really and truly, it has seemed to me that every one I have ever heard were not sincere."

"Why, Fred Travers!" exclaimed Jessie.

Fred's face flushed. "I know I've no right to judge," he said quickly, "and I don't mean to. But that is really the impression they gave me. Not one of them ever made me in the least feel that I would like to meet with the change."

"Then your heart was not right," said Erfort.

"Do you mean to tell us, Fred, that you have lived to be twenty-four years old, and have never felt like being a christian?"

Fred's blue eyes looked steadily back into the dark ones so earnestly fixed upon his face.

"I never have," he said.

All were quiet for a moment, then Erfort said: "I have."

The dark, expressive face wore a very sad look. Vera said, impulsively:

"Won't you tell us about it, Mr. Richards?"

"There isn't very much to tell. I attended a prayer-meeting at one of the smaller churches at home one Sunday evening. Now, please do not imagine that this was a rare thing for me to do, for it was not. I have always attended Sunday services very regularly ever since I can remember. Of late years I have gone more to please mother than anything else, but I have gone nevertheless. It was not a revival meeting; if it had been I am positive I would not have had the desire that I am about to speak of. If I am ever converted it will not be at a revival — I don't like them, and I have no faith in conversions that take place under such influences. The speaker was an old gentleman, rather slow and prosy, too. The singing was something dreadful, but there was a poor old lady there — I can see just how she looked now. She had on an old, rusty, black dress, shawl and bonnet, and when she stood up she trembled so that she was obliged to hold to the back of the seat in front of her. I don't, and I didn't that night, know of but one thing she said, and that was : 'Oh, the Lord is such a *true* friend.' I wish you could have heard her say that—I shall never forget her voice and the expression of her face. I cannot tell you the effect it had on me. I longed to rise to my feet and ask them to pray for me, that I might have Him for *my* friend, but I didn't dare to. I was president of one or two societies, and secretary of our club at college. I had made more than one after-dinner speech — had been judge in the famous 'Mock Trial' we fellows gave, and had even made quite a lengthy speech on the common one Fourth of July on 'The Independence of the American Citizen,' but the simple act of standing up before those few uneducated people, was something that I did not dare to do. My heart beat quickly, and my face burned. I was afraid that if I did rise, some one else would rise at the same time, and that seemed to be a terrible thing to me. I put it off and put it off until at last it was too late. The meeting was closed, and I had to go ; but I *did* shake hands with the old lady at the door, and—" Erfort stopped suddenly, and they saw the rich color showing under the dark skin.

"*Please* tell us," said Vera, softly.

"Well, I walked home with her, and at her

door she turned and put her hand on my shoulder
and said : 'God bless you, whoever you may be.
There must be a happy mother somewhere.' I
have never forgotten that," said Erfort, looking
around on the earnest faces.   " It has had its influence on my life.   I have heard," he continued,
after a pause, " as doubtless you have. many times,
that each one has his or her chance of redemption
— only *one*.   I don't believe that.   I think so long
as one lives, it is never too late to receive the blessing.   I think that the longer one neglects to see to
his soul's salvation, the harder it is for him to do it,
but the loss is all his.   He loses many years of
deep happiness.   If one feels the desire to become
better — if their hearts are really touched — if they
realize fully, as I did, that an opportunity has presented itself, and they give themselves up, then and
there, I think they receive a deeper, richer blessing, than they do if they wait years, months, or,
perhaps, only weeks, for the second opportunity,
and then, besides, they have all that time in which
to grow in grace.   It is dangerous to wait for the
' second opportunity,' for sometimes one is called
away before it comes.   I have always deeply
regretted my lack of moral courage."

   " Don't you think," said Jessie, " that you
thought of *self* too much, that night? "

   The others were surprised to hear such a grave
question from " little Jess," but Erfort answered,
quickly :

"I know I did, Miss Jessie. If I had only looked away from self and thought only of Him and asked Him to give me strength, I would have been all right. And what I did, thousands of others are doing every day. It is a fearful mistake."

"Haven't you ever felt the desire since?" asked Fred.

"No; but I am sure that I will, and before it is too late. I feel it."

"When *is* it too late?" asked Jessie.

"Never," answered Erfort, firmly. "Not until the breath has left your body."

"And after that?"

"I do not know."

There was a pause, and then Jessie said: "I am going to ask Mrs. Hood. *She* will know."

"I want to tell you all," said Allie, "that I am sure that I have found the Saviour."

"Oh, Allie," cried Jessie, throwing both arms around her neck, "I believe you have always had Him, for if you hadn't, you never could have borne with my horrid, hateful temper, as you have always done. You never snapped me back in your life."

Smiles gave place to the tears that Allie's words had brought, at impulsive Jessie's speech, and her manner of delivering it. Erfort and Fred gave Allie's hand a warm, friendly clasp, and Vera said:

"You have found Him the first, Allie; but, perhaps, you can help us find Him, before long."

"If I only could!" murmured Allie, fervently.

Garnet just touched Allie's hair lightly with her little hand, and then she commenced to clear the table of its books and small articles.

"Cocoa?" asked Fred, gaily, springing to his feet and assisting her. "Oh, Er, *aren't* you glad you are living?"

"We are to have a new lodger, to-morrow, boys," said Vera, putting the cups on the table. "And 'Grandma' expects more in a few days; so drink your cocoa and be happy while you may."

The boys' faces fell. They would miss the evenings in the bright little parlor.

"Oh, what a shame!" said Fred. "That will spoil all our fun. Who is coming to-morrow?"

"A m-a-n," said Vera, impressively.

Fred made a movement of disgust. "He'll be cutting us out, Er," he said, half meaning what he said.

"Now, you *won't* give him cocoa, too; will you?" said Erfort, watching Garnet's busy little hands as she prepared the delicious beverage.

"Perhaps he will not care to have us," said Vera, remembering what "Mother" had said about the gentleman's "not minding them."

"Well, we'll hope for the best," said Fred. "But I guess 'Barkis will be willin' enough.'"

Vera clasped her hands. " Oh, Mr. Travers, *do* you read Dickens?"

Fred made a wry face. " No, thanks."

Vera looked disappointed.

" I do, Miss Earle," said Erfort, noticing her look of disappointment.

" Oh, *do* you? Isn't he perfectly splendid?"

Vera's eyes shone and she involuntarily drew her chair nearer to Erfort's. Fred immediately determined to commence to martyr himself the first thing the next morning. A few of Dickens' works were in the " Library " — he would get one and read it if it sent him to the insane asylum.

" If you want Vera to love *you*, *you* must love Dickens," said Jessie, innocently. " It is 'love me, love my Dickens,' with her."

" I will worship him immediately," said Fred.

" Nonsense! " said Vera, scornfully, and then she turned eagerly to Erfort.

" Which of his books do you like the best, Mr. Richards?"

" Martin Chuzzlewit."

" Oh, do you? Well, that *is* a splendid story. One meets with a great many ' Pecksniffs ' in this life. (Vera spoke with the air of an octogenarian at least.) But my favorite is ' David Copperfield.' I have read that so many times that it really seems as though the characters were real living beings. They seem much more real to me than people with whom I meet in real life. Poor little 'Dora!' I love her—well, much better than some real people that I know."

Erfort smiled. "You are an enthusiast. But do you think it is well for you to feel so intensely, what is, after all, only imagination?"

Vera looked serious. "I have asked myself that question more than once, and have never answered it satisfactorily. I can tell no one what a peculiar effect the reading of Dickens' books has on me. They do not make me dissatisfied with real life; but while I am reading them, it seems just as though I am living in a world peopled only with Dickens' characters. I can see and talk with them all. I love, like, respect, dislike, despise each one, according to the impression he or she makes on me. 'Dora,' 'Agnes,' 'Uriah Heep,' 'Miss Betsey,' 'Rose Dartle,' 'Steerforth,' 'Little Em'ly,' 'Pecksniff,' 'Mercy,' 'Charity,' 'Martin,' 'Mark Tapley,' 'Little Dorrit,' 'Dolly Varden,' 'Emma Haredale,' 'The Maypole Cronies,' 'Barnaby Rudge,' 'Nicholas Nickleby'— oh, dear! all of them," and Vera leaned back in her chair with a deep sigh.

"I saw the questions: 'Who is Dickens' noblest character?' and 'Who is his worst character?' in an educational paper once," went on Vera. "And I answered 'Little Dorrit' to the former, and 'Jonas Chuzzlewit' to the latter. What do you think?"

"Your answers were good," replied Erfort. "I think Dickens goes to extremes. He either makes his characters — his principal characters — either very noble, or most despicable."

"Oh, but there are mediums. 'Pet Meagles' was quite a natural character; there was nothing very angelic, or very bad about her. Her worst fault was in loving a handsome face."

Vera looked very scornful.

"*Did* she love him for that alone?" asked Erfort, quietly.

"Undoubtedly. But she wasn't to blame for that; it was all there was about him to love. But what a peculiar character 'Miss Wade' was! I don't know whether I greatly pity, or greatly blame her."

"Her life was what she made it. She would accept neither pity or love from anyone. She called herself indifferent, but she was simply ugly."

Vera opened her eyes a little at Erfort's earnestness.

"Well, I don't know but you are right."

Just here Jessie came to them with a cup of cocoa in each hand.

"Can you tear yourselves away from Dickens long enough to drink this?" she asked.

"We would prove ourselves sadly deficient in *taste* if we couldn't," said Erfort, quickly, at which

Jessie made a little face and went back to Allie and Fred.

"May I come and talk, too?" asked Garnet. I also, am an ardent admirer of Dickens. As an acquaintance of mine says: ' I love Dickens *very* dearly.'"

"What a deuced happy chap that old fellow ought to be," said Fred, who, from the table, overheard Garnet's remark, "to have all the ladies in love with him."

"He is dead, Fred," said Garnet, with rather more solemnity than the occasion warranted. Indeed, her voice was full of awe.

"Oh, I beg his pardon," said Fred, meekly, and took a cup of cocoa.

"Who do *you* think is his noblest character, Miss Dare?" asked Erfort.

"' Little Dorrit.'"

' And his worst? "

"' Jonas Chuzzlewit.'"

Erfort looked from one to the other. Vera smiled.

"We have discussed those questions before," she said.

"Why do you think ' Jonas ' his worst character? There is ' Daniel Quilp.' Surely nothing could be more repulsive. And ' Bill Sykes ' and ' Fagin ' — how despicable ! "

"Yes, we know," said Vera. "But ' Jonas ' did not have one redeeming quality. He was ugly, mean, cowardly, deceitful, lying, bullying, fawning — all that was bad. He fairly hated himself, abused his wife, tried to murder his own father, *did* murder his friend, and finally murdered himself. But one could easily forgive him that last crime. ' Quilp' was repulsive, but he possessed a certain kind of spirit, even if it wasn't of the right quality. He didn't take particular pains to hide his true colors. And 'Fagin' — well, he *was* a terrible man, but he paid the penalty ; and ' Bill Sykes,' he suffered a lifetime in the few last hours he lived."

" I said that ' Little Dorrit' was his noblest character," said Garnet, " but do you think she is any more noble than ' Little Nell?'"

" The character of 'Little Nell' is not natural," said Erfort. " It is greatly overdrawn."

" I think so, too," said Vera. " Very pretty and pathetic to read, but nothing natural about it; although I've read that the original was Dickens' wife's sister, of whom he was very fond. What do you think of ' Rose Dartle?'"

" I always called her ' Dickens' wild woman,'" replied Erfort, with a smile.

" And very appropriate, too," said Vera. " I never read about that visit she made to ' Little Em'ly' without getting so angry that I can scarcely resist the temptation to throw the book at something, and wishing it were ' Rose Dartle' herself.

Horrible woman! But do you know, nothing that Dickens has written amuses me more than the 'Maypole Cronies,' in 'Barnaby Rudge.' Weren't they too comical for anything? especially John Willet."

"The wise John," said Erfort. "We see a good many such as he. How they did like to gossip. But you have not told me what you think of 'Edith Granger,' in 'Dombey and Son.'"

"I always feel like shaking her," said Vera. "She acted very foolishly. To use an expression that is more adaptable than elegant, it always seemed to me that she 'bit off her nose to spite her face.'"

"That is true," said Garnet. "But I pitied her."

"That is just like you, Net," said Vera. "Pity the foolish ones."

"I pity the *bitter* ones," said Garnet. "Those who have lost faith in everything and everybody, even in themselves. When *that* time comes, life cannot be worth the living. Nothing seems so sad to me, as not being able to trust anyone. I say, hold on to your faith in people as long as you possibly can. There can be no happiness where there is no faith."

"You agree with 'Frances Anne Butler,'" said Vera:

> " ' Better trust all and be deceived
> And weep that trust and that deceiving,
> Than doubt one heart, which, if believed,
> Had blessed one's life with true believing.
> Oh! in this mocking world, too fast
> The doubting fiend o'ertakes our youth;
> Better be cheated to the last
> Than lose the blessed hope of truth ! ' "

" She expresses my sentiments, exactly," said Garnet.

" It is a blessed thing to be able to trust those whom we call our friends," said Erfort. " I think nothing changes a man's whole life — not to say his character — so throughly, as having his trust betrayed. Unless one's will-power and strength of character is very great, indeed, finding one's self deceived in one's friend — that is, a friend one has loved very dearly and trusted implicitly — makes one very bitter and skeptical, and spoils one's whole life. It is wrong, for the whole world ought not to be judged by one; but it is hard to trust when you have once been deceived."

" But it is sinful to allow the infidelity of even a dear friend to spoil one's whole life," said Garnet. " One's pride ought to keep them from that, if nothing else would."

" Pride will do a great deal for one," said Vera. " If I were ever deceived in anyone, no one would ever know how badly I might feel. Of course it is a terrible thing to happen to anyone, but there is no need of letting the whole world know of it, or of its making your life miserable. By the way, Mr. Richards, that makes me think of a little ditty of Tennyson's, in which he proves traitor to his sex."

"What is it? Please repeat it."

"Oh, you must have read it."

> " ' Sigh no more ladies, sigh no more,
> 　Men were deceivers ever ;
> One foot in sea, and one on shore,
> 　To one thing constant, never.' "

"There is a case where the man was most deplorably lost in the poet," said Erfort. "I am ashamed of my Lord Tennyson."

Just here Jessie came over to them, with a grieved expression on her face.

"*Aren't* we going to have any fun to-night, girls? I think you are real hateful to get off by yourselves in this way and talk on your horrid, dry subjects."

" Well, bless her little heart," said Vera, smoothing the wrinkles away in Jessie's forehead, " we'll do anything you say for half an hour, now. What is it? "

" Play ' Consequences,' " said Jessie.

When at 9.30 the young men went to their hotel, it would have been hard to tell which of the young people was in the greatest hurry for 4 o'clock of the next day to come, that they might go to the home of Charlotte Hood, and hear more of the interesting story of her life.

CHAPTER XVI.

On the following afternoon, at about 3:30, the girls were sitting on the front piazza, waiting for Erfort and Fred. A tall, broad-shouldered man came through the gate, and just glancing at the girls, crossed the lawn and knocked at the door of the parlor where the girls "served their cocoa." Vera, knowing that "Mother" was up in her room, looking over a big chest of bed linen, and that "Grandpa" was out in the summer kitchen, whispered to the girls:

"Shall I tell him?"

They nodded their heads and Vera rose from her chair and went towards him. He turned his head, and seeing her near him, raised his hat. "Uriah Heep," went like a flash through Vera's mind. She bowed in a dignified manner, and said:

"You would like to see the lady of the house?'

"If you please."

The gentleman's manner was pleasant enough, but Vera did not like the expression of his eyes. They were not mates in color, one being blue and the other gray, and they were set too close together. But then, the poor man could not help that.

"If you will take a chair," said Vera, motioning to the one she had been occupying, "I will call Mrs. Atherton."

"Thank you," replied the gentleman. "You are very kind."

Vera went out to the kitchen and notified "Grandpa," and then up stairs to "Mother."

"Mother" was flustrated at once, and the thin, nervous, white hands went up to the pretty hair immediately.

"Oh, it must be Mr. Wild, my new lodger," she said, and her voice trembled with excitement. "Will you pass me my cap, dear, and is my hair smooth in the back? I'll put on this black silk apron. Dear, dear! it's a blessed thing I made up his bed and put his room to rights this morning. Now I'm ready, I guess. Did you say he was out on the piazza?"

Vera replied that he was, and helped "Mother" down the stairs. "Grandpa" was hovering in an uncertain manner between the stairs and the door, but "Mother" very soon made his place known to him.

"I'll speak with him, Mr. Atherton," she said, primly, and the thin hand held him back.

The gentleman, who had been making himself agreeable to the girls, rose as "Mother" and Vera appeared in the doorway, and bowed low with his hat in his hand. "Mother" invited him into the

house with the air of a duchess. Seeing Erfort
and Fred appearing in the " near distance," the
girls went to meet them.

" I don't like that man's face," said Jessie, as
soon as they had left the piazza. " He looks like
a sneak to me."

" 'Sh, Jessie," said Garnet. " We ought not to
judge. He may be a very nice man."

" Don't believe it," said Jessie, stoutly. " He
looked like a wolf when he grinned."

" *I* didn't like the looks of his hands," said
Garnet, meditatively. They made me think of
' Uriah Heep.' "

Vera turned quickly. " Just what I said to myself when I spoke to him," she said. " I believe
there was really a ' Uriah ' and this man is a de-
scendent of his."

" How do you do, ladies," said Fred. " What
is the subject of discussion this afternoon? "

" We have just had a glimpse of our new
lodger," said Vera.

" What is the impression received? "

" Not particularly favorable."

" Good! I guess we are all right for the
cocoa."

" Is he a large, smooth-faced man, with a 'Uriah
Heep-like' face? " asked Erfort.

The girls broke into a merry laugh, and in reply
to Erfort's look of surprise, Garnet explained to

him the reason of the laugh, and they all commenced a lively discussion as to the advisability of
allowing an acquaintance to spring up between
them and the new lodger. It was done more for
the sake of something to talk about than for anything else, and although no good came from it, yet
no harm came from it either.

But right here let me warn my readers against
practicing this habit — discussing the qualities,
good, bad and indifferent, of your friends and acquaintances, or even people whom you know only
by sight, merely for the sake of something to talk
about. Better let your tongue keep silent forever,
than run the risk of hurting anyone in the eyes of
others. How often have we read the valuable
advice — although I cannot now recall the one who
gave it: "Never speak of a person unless you
can say something good of him. If you know of
nothing good, then say nothing." It is very
seldom, if ever, that we meet with anyone who has
not *one* good quality. Make the most of that
one good quality, then, and it will surprise you
how much pleasure you derive from doing this.
We have all heard, of course, that "Money is
the root of all evil." I would like to change the
word "Money" to that of "Gossip." "Gossip is
the root of all evil." Methinks I hear a loud
"Amen!" from the many persecuted ones.

When our party reached the cottage of Charlotte Hood, they found the door wide open. As they stood hesitatingly on the steps, Mrs. Hood called to them from the sitting-room to come right in. She was propping Robin up in bed. The little childish face was unusually pale and drawn to-day, and there were deep shadows under the beautiful eyes. The temples, too, looked sunken. It was a sad, sad sight for our young people to see, and their hearts were softened and filled with pity. Poor little baby sufferer! It could not seem right to them for this thing to be. But Mrs. Hood greeted them with a bright smile, as she placed the " Noah's Ark " within reach of the little thin hands.

" Come right in and be seated, please. My boy has not had a very good day so far, but he is better now, and so glad to see you all."

Robin smiled as each one stopped at his bedside and spoke to him, and he put up his mouth as Jessie bent over him. The glowing girlish face was pressed tenderly against the thin, pale one, and the red lips touched lovingly the white, parched ones.

Erfort and Fred seated themselves on the lounge, Vera took the rocking-chair, Allie sat on the foot of the bed and leaned against the foot-board, Garnet took a low chair and rested her elbow in Vera's lap, Jessie sat in a high chair close to Robin's pillow, and Mrs. Hood, with her mending basket by her side, sat near the open window. Jessie proceeded at once to the " business of the afternoon," with her usual charming directness.

" Please begin right away, Mrs. Hood, we want to hear you so badly, and it seemed as if the hour yesterday afternoon fairly flew. We have told the others what you have told us, and they are as eager to hear more as Vera and I."

Garnet looked almost scandalized at Jessie's abruptness, but Mrs. Hood seemed pleased.

" One hour *isn't* very long sometimes," she replied. " I am very happy to have interested you all and will continue my little story with pleasure : After the revival meeting which I told you about, I felt very strangely. I was exceedingly happy, yet quietly so. I was submissive to my older sisters and cousins, which was something so very wonderful that they were more than surprised, and spoke of it many times. At last, one day, about a week after the meeting, it seemed to me as though my heart would burst with its weight of love and happiness. Mother sent me up stairs to the porch chamber after some pieces for a rag carpet, which she was making. I entered the room and closed the door. I sank down on my knees in the middle of the dim, dusky garret, and called on God to help me, out of the very depths of my untutored, childish heart. Oh, I will never forget the glory of that moment. As I prayed, the room was filled with a bright light, which almost dazzled my eyes. It was not imagination, and I was not foolishly excited. It was something that was *real*. I have never had just that same experience since, though I have had many glorious moments. I do not know how long I had been in the garret, but all at once mother's voice sounded sharply at the foot of the stairs: ' Charlotte, where be you? I'm waitin' for them rags.' Ah, the glory faded in a second; the light was all gone from the room, but it still lingered in my heart. I sprang hastily to my feet, snatched up the rags from the floor, and hastened down stairs; eager hope in my heart, eager words trembling on my lips. But as I entered the kitchen, the sight of Betsey Ann Doane — the gossip of the town — sitting in the big cushioned chair, needles and tongue running a race together, met my eyes. The words died on my lips, and as I placed the basket of rags at mother's feet, the bitterness of the disappointment brought the tears to my eyes. I ran from the room for fear the small, snapping black eyes of Betsey Ann would see them, and in a few moments I was lying full length on a soft bed of pine-needles, looking up through the green branches to the blue sky and wondering why God, if He knew how I felt and how I had longed to tell mother all about it, should have put it into Betsey Ann's heart to make us a call on this particular afternoon. I was young — nothing but a child — but I had so soon commenced to question God's wisdom, and I have done it, oh, so many times since — God forgive me! I did not have a chance to speak to mother that night. Mother's tasks were many, and she had few moments to spare for 'talks' with her children. Several days passed, and still no opportunity presented itself. My feelings were undergoing a change. I felt afraid to speak to mother now — afraid that she would laugh at me, and tell me I was too young to think about such things, that I had been excited; and as the days went by I commenced to feel that I *had* been excited. The tender, *good* feeling was passing slowly, but surely away, and in a short time had disappeared altogether. I cannot tell how I have mourned over those wasted years. I might have lived such a different life if I had only had the help of my Heavenly Father. But some one has told us that there is no such thing as ' a thing that *might have been.*' All things that are best for us *will be*; there is nothing that '*might have been.*' But I think that a great many of the things we have to grieve over, are brought on by our own thoughtless, foolish actions, and by our lack of moral courage. God many times puts noble ideas into our minds; it is our own fault if we do not convert them into noble actions. The summer that followed was an unusually happy one for us. Father made a prosperous trip and brought us home many pretty, as well as useful things. We wanted for nothing, and a happier

family than our's could not be found on all the
Cape.   In the fall our cellar was filled, as usual,
with everything that was good, for the following
winter's use.   In November, father made a trip to
New Orleans, and it was while he was gone that a
very sad thing happened.   Hannah, Emeline and
Deborah had commenced to go to dancing school,
and they were all carried away with the pleasures
of it.   They cleared the floor of the porch chamber,
and they, with cousins Abbie, Modina and Patience,
would get up there in the evening and practice the
round dances.   Sometimes Johial and I would
creep up the stairs, and with our heads just showing over the top one, would sit and watch them.
They never saw us, until one night they were trying a new step.   Hannah, our most dignified sister,
slipped on the smooth floor, and in her efforts to
save herself, went through with such a comical
gymnastic exercise, that I giggled and Jo burst into
a loud laugh.   Hannah wouldn't let us watch any
more, although I teased hard, for the young men
came after that and practiced with them and I
wanted to watch the fun.   The girls were always
fixing over their dresses, to wear dancing-school
night, and one evening we were all sitting around
the table.   Mother and the girls were sewing.   Deb
was at work on a very pretty brown poplin dress,
with pink ribbon, on which I looked with admiring,
covetous eyes.   I had teased hard to sit up until 8

o'clock and watch the work go on, and mother had let me — for a wonder.   Of course if *I* was going to sit up, *Jo* was, but as he wasn't longing for a brown dress with pink bows, the making of it didn't particularly interest him, and long before 8 o'clock he was lying on the floor, under the table, fast asleep.   Oh, I can see him now !   He wore a colored apron with long sleeves.   He had taken off his shoes and stockings, and he lay with one arm thrown up over his head, and his little brown legs drawn up.   My precious little brother !   How the terrible thing that happened was done, we hardly knew, but one of the girls pushed her chair up against the table, as she bent to pick up a spool of thread that had fallen on the floor, and the next moment the lamp rolled off the table, and went crashing down right on poor little sleeping Johial. Another moment and he was one cruel blaze.   We all screamed, and that is about all we did do for a moment.   Emeline went towards the door with an idea of running over to get Aunt Thankful. As she passed the sink she saw the pail of water that was always left in it at night, and, seizing this, she threw the water on Joe.   It extinguished the flames at once, but, oh, the poor, little, darling boy !   It seems as if I can hear mother's cry now, as she bent over him and took him up in her arms.   She carried him into her room and laid him on the bed, and then Aunt Thankful and one of the neighbors,

whom the girls had called, came in, and in their
excitement they hardly knew what they did. They
did not think to unbutton the band around his
wrists, but pulled the sleeves right over his hands,
and I screamed as I saw the tender flesh come with
it. They sent me out of the room then, but I hid
in the corner near the door, and when the doctor
came I slipped in with him, and they were so busy
they didn't notice me. The doctor must have been
a very ignorant man, for he swathed Jo in cotton
from head to foot. He had to lie in this way for a
long while, and for weeks he could not open his
eyes. How I longed to bear the pain for him, and
how patient he was! When they took the bandages
away, his fair, soft skin was disfigured for life with
cruel white scars, but he was Jo just the same;
scars would never change my brother to me, and
when he opened his blue eyes and looked at me
with the old, sweet, loving smile, I just lay down
on the bed beside him, and put my arms around his
neck and cried for joy. When he got so he could
sit up, I used to go out into the snow and make a
regular little clown of myself, just for the sake of
seeing him laugh. I would make believe slip up
and would go rolling over and over in the deep
snow. I would dance the 'Fisher's Hornpipe.' I
even went so far as to turn a somersault, and then
how Jo did laugh! When I got ready to go out,
mother would lift him from the lounge to the big

green chest in front of the window, and with the
sugar tub at his back to prop him up, Jo would sit
and watch me by the hour. It was the latter part
of March before he was able to go out, and for a
long while he was obliged to limp along with a
stick. One of his legs had been so badly burned
that it would never be the same as before. The
doctor said that it would gradually grow stronger,
so that in a few months he would be able to go without the stick, but he was afraid that there would
always be a slight limp. I think I suffered almost
as much as Jo. It seemed as though I could not
bear the thoughts of my darling brother being
almost a cripple all his life, besides having his beautiful face marred by the scars."

Mrs. Hood stopped for a moment and looked at
Robin. "Ah!" she said, almost passionately,
"do not think it strange that I should worship
him as I do, for I am loving two in one. My
brother lives again in my boy." Then she went
on more quietly:

"Jo was a proud child for one so young, and for
this reason his affliction seemed all the harder. I
used to sit and watch him when he slept, and many
times I have fallen on my knees beside his lounge
and almost cried my heart out. I didn't pray to
God to help us both, but I blamed Him for sending
this great trouble to Jo. 'Why had He done it?'
I used to ask, with passionate pain and anger.

'What had my innocent little brother ever done to be punished in this way?' He had always been a much better child than I — sweeter-dispositioned, more obedient, more lovable. I reproached God bitterly out of the anger and pain of my childish heart, but instead of punishing me for it, I think He pitied me, for He knew how well I loved my brother, and how unselfishly. During the month of January there was the heaviest snow storm there had been for many years. Father had gone with Uncle Daniel, his youngest brother, and the favorite child of both grandfather and grandmother, up the Kennebec for lumber. We knew they were out on the night of the storm, and none of us slept for the night. He was to have been home that same week, but the days passed and he did not come. Child though I was, and usually a thoughtless one, I saw how mother was suffering from suspense, although she never murmured once. She was then, as always, a 'silent sufferer.' She never once neglected her children to sit down and mourn, but many a time I had seen her steal away to the clothes-press, in the spare room where father's clothes hung, and, taking the garments, one by one, hold them close to her face for a moment and then put them back lingeringly and lovingly, and when she came out there would always be a happy smile on her face. I could not imagine why she did this. I wanted to know, but did not dare to ask her. One day Deborah saw me watching. Deborah was always kind to me, and I was never afraid to have her catch me doing what I ought not to, though I think she was going to correct me this day, but I said eagerly : ' Oh, Deb, what does mother do that for?' Deborah knew what I meant, but she said : ' Do what?' ' Why, rub father's clothes against her cheek.' Deborah's eyes filled with tears, but she smiled at my question and said : ' She was not rubbing them against her cheek.' ' What was she doing?' ' Smelling of them.' My eyes must have been perfectly round with astonishment, for Deborah smiled even more, as she asked :· ' Don't you know what she does it for?' I shook my head emphatically. ' Why, to see if father is — is — drowned — or — not.' Deborah's eyes overflowed, now, and she sobbed bitterly. I cried, too, but my curiosity had been much excited and demanded gratification. ' And — how — can — she — tell?' I asked, between my sobs. Deborah waited a moment, until she could speak without crying : ' Why, if his clothes smell like dead folks, he is dead, and if they don't, he is living.' I was much awed by this information, and then I happened to think that mother's face had always worn a smile every time I had seen her come from the room, and I cried, gladly : ' Well, he isn't drownded, Deb, for mother always looks glad, after she has

smelt of his clothes.' Of course I had to tell Jo
all about it, and for the next two or three days I
spent the most of my time in the spare-room clothes-
press, smelling of father's clothes. No one knew
it except Jo. One night, just before lamp light,
about three weeks after the storm, the family were
all sitting around the open fire-place in the kitchen,
except Jo, who, had been put to bed, but he lay
where he could look out at them all. Betsey Ann
Doane had ' dropped in' to console with mother
and hear the latest news, if there were any. Aunt
Thankful, too, was there, and her girls. I was in
the clothes-press for about the twelfth time that day.
All at once I heard the outside door close. There
was nothing in that, of course, but, somehow
or other, it made my heart jump. I ran from
the room, and, as I stood in the long passage-
way that led to the kitchen, the inside door
opened and closed quickly. Then I heard one
cry—not a loud one, but more like a half moan,
and I reached the kitchen door at a bound. All
I saw was a tall, broad-shouldered, snow-cov-
ered form, for the head was bent over mother, and
the arms were wrapped tightly around her. Yes,
it was father come home again. Oh, how we all
cried and hung upon him, kissed, hugged and
almost strangled him. There had been loud
screams from the girls and both younger children.
Emeline even went so far as to faint away ; but

Emeline was always the lady of the family, and we none of us thought it strange that she should be the one to do this lady-like act. Mother, with the worried look all gone from her face, bustled around to get father's supper, while the girls unbuttoned Emeline's dress and held the camphor bottle to her pretty nose. I drew father into the bed-room to see Jo, and when mother called him to supper, he appeared in the kitchen with Jo wrapped in blankets, in his arms. 'Don't scold, mother,' he said (as if there were any danger of it on that night of all nights!). 'It won't hurt him, and I must hold my little man to-night, anyway.' After supper father drew his chair to the fire and said, gravely: 'I have something to tell you all.' I knew there was something that had happened, for father's usually merry blue eyes had looked so sad, even when he had been smiling. We were all anxious to hear what had happened to keep him away for so long. Of course Aunt Thankful and the girls had stayed to hear, and so had Betsey Ann, though she had feebly suggested going home to tell the folks that 'Cap'n Phillips had cum hum all right,' when father had sat down to supper. I knew that wild horses couldn't have dragged her away until she had heard the whole story; but I was too happy to care how long she stayed, and so we all drew near the fire to listen."

CHAPTER XVII.

'It was a terrible storm. As we sailed up the Kennebec, the sleet and snow flew into our faces, the wind blew icy cold, the waves dashed over the deck, but we managed to keep our way until the darkness came settling down upon us. And such a darkness! The air was just one white, whirling mass, that beat against our faces and stung them. We could do nothing but cling to the railings and let the old ship take her own course. The storm grew wilder. All at once the vessel gave a great lurch. I was thrown flat to the deck, where I clung, the Lord only knows how, for it was one glare of ice. It seemed to me that I was first on my head and then on my feet; the vessel heaved and plunged and tossed from side to side and then, with a great lurch, that almost drove the breath out of my body, she settled herself between two large cakes of ice, and there she stayed. When I got on my feet I stared around me. I couldn't see a thing, and I called out: 'Where are you, boys?' 'Here,' some one shouted back from the other end of the vessel. 'Is that you, Dan'l?' I called. 'Yes. Where are you?' 'At the head of the cabin stairs.' 'All right; I'll try and crawl over to you.' He

got over to me, after a good deal of slipping and
falling, and we sat on the stairs the rest of the night,
almost frozen, but not daring to stir. It seemed to
us as though the vessel was turned almost upside
down. About 5 o'clock the next morning, the wind
commenced to go down, and it didn't snow nearly
so hard, but the cold became unendurable. As it
grew light we saw that the vessel was lying over
on her side, between the two great cakes of ice.
None of the boys were left on her; Dan'l and I
were the only ones there.' Father stopped here
and brushed the tears out of his eyes. Mother put
her apron up to her face, the girls gave little gasps
of horror, and Betsey Ann exclaimed: 'The Lud
have mercy on us! What be you a-tellin' of us,
Warren Phillips?' Then father went on, only
interrupted now and then by Betsey Ann exclaim-
ing: 'What be you a-tellin' of us, Cap'n Phillips?'
'Me and Dan'l sat on the stairs and groaned with
the cold. We longed for the vessel to right herself
— we wouldn't have cared much if she had gone
over the other way and sent us to the bottom with
the other boys, we were suffering so. Along
towards 10 o'clock we felt the water 'heave
under us, the vessel commenced to move gently
from side to side; we knew that the ice was
separating. We waited. As far as I was concerned I wouldn't have given a shuck if we had
both been pitched into the river, I was so cold.

But we were not. She slowly righted herself, and then she commenced to drift along. The masts were gone; we could do nothing but move slowly about to get warm. The deck was like a looking-glass. We slipped along on it for a little while, and at last Dan'l sank down on it all of a heap. 'I'm freezing, Warren,' he said. I didn't know what I was doing, but I commenced to dance on the slippery deck, and I shouted: 'Dance, Dan'l, dance!' 'I can't, Warren,' said he, and he stretched himself out and closed his eyes, and in a little while he was dead.'* Mother threw her apron down from her eyes and seized father's arm with both hands. 'Warren!' she cried, 'Dead! Dan'l dead! Oh, poor mother!' and she commenced to cry. So did the girls and we younger ones, and Betsey Ann rocked back and forth in her chair and wrung her hands and the stocking she was knitting, and groaned: 'Oh, Lud! Oh, Lud! Oh, Lud a mercy!' 'Yes, he died. Poor Dan'l; poor boy!' said father. 'And I watched him die while I danced to keep myself from dying, and when I saw that he was dead, I strapped him to a plank and let him down over the side of the vessel into the water, then I lay down on the same place he had been lying, and didn't know anything more until I opened my eyes to find myself on board a vessel bound for New Orleans. They had come along

---

* A fact.

and found me just in time to save me, and that was all.'* Father stopped again and leaned back in his chair. He closed his eyes, but I saw the big tears slowly roll down his face. We were all too horrified to say a word for some little time, and then mother asked: ' Have you been to mother's, Warren? Does she know?' 'Yes; I stopped there on my way home.' ' And how did she take it?' Father shook his head. ' Poor mother! I might as well have taken a knife and drove it, clean through her heart. She worshipped that boy!' After that we didn't talk very much, only mother said she would go over to see grandma early the next morning. It would do no good to go that night; it was snowing hard, father was almost sick himself and grandma's house was a mile and a half away. Betsey Ann rolled up her knitting work and put it into the big bag she always wore at her side. Mother got down the lantern and lighted it for her. ' Wal, Warren,' said Betsey Ann, tying her hood snugly under her sharp chin, ' you hev my sympathy, and so does Sally Ann. (This was grandmother). She thought an orful sight of that boy — I shouldn't wonder if it killed her; she's gettin' along in years.' Then she turned to mother. ' The land sakes, Emeline, ef I wasn't agoin' off with nothin' but my cloth shoes on. Where be my rubber boots? Oh, here they be in

---

* Fact. The occurrence related here is true. It actually happened.

the corner. The Lud! I'm so upset I'd forget
my head ef it wasn't fastened on.' Johial and I
watched Betsey Ann's light as it twinkled down the
path, through the gate and up the long white road.
It looked like a little glow-worm, shining through
the snow. None of the women ever thought it
necessary to be escorted home from a neighbor's,
after dark, no matter how late it was. Such a thing
as a tramp was never heard of on the Cape, so the
most timid of us never had any cause for fear,
although if there ever was a place that seemed the
very home of hobgoblins and ghosts, the pine
woods that stretched themselves for a mile or more
between our house and the village, was the place.
I don't think I need tell you of the sad time
after father came home. Grandma's grief was
pitiable to see, but I was too young to realize very
deeply. I will skip over the next four years of my
life to the time I was fifteen. They were happy
years, free from care and trouble. Jo grew
stronger, but he never was as well again after his
sickness. I'll never forget the whipping I gave
David Bassett — a big, cowardly boy, who lived in
the village. I was about twelve years old. Jo
and I were out in the yard one day. Jo was
sawing wood and I was packing it into a basket
and carrying it into the wood-shed, for I was a
strong child. David came along and stopped to
talk with us. He didn't like Jo, for he thought

that Jo was proud and felt above him. Jo wasn't proud.   His misfortune made him timid and re-served — that was all.   David commenced to say little hateful things to Jo, but Jo never answered him back, only kept right on with his work.   David edged along toward the road, and when at a safe distance, he called out: ' Limp-leg, limp-leg !' and took to his heels. My heart gave a great leap. I just caught a glimpse of the painful flush that dyed Jo's face, and then *I* took to *my* heels and fairly flew down the road after David. He didn't hear me coming until I was close up to him, and then, coward that he was, he ducked his head and put himself right in my path.   I couldn't stop then, and so of course I went heels over head, and rolled over in the dust.   I heard David's laugh and his ' Neow, gosh take ye,' and then in my anger and desperation, I caught hold of his bare leg, as he started to run, and held on for dear life.   He wrig-gled and twisted ; he slapped me in the face ; he even kicked me with his free foot, but I twined my arms around his leg, and in another moment he was down in the road.   Then I scrambled to my feet and slapped, pinched and pounded him to my heart's content, until he cried like a great baby. I looked up and saw Jo hurrying towards us, as fast as his lame leg would let him.   I let him get near enough to get a good look at his fallen tor-mentor, then, with a parting pull at David's white

hair, and a mocking ' Neow, gosh take ye,' I
strutted off to meet Jo — a dusty, rumpled, but
proud little conqueror. I never would have thought
to fight for myself, but he had cruelly insulted Jo,
and he had to suffer the consequences. Jo's face
was quite white when he met me. ' Oh, Charley,
did he hurt you?' he asked, putting his little arm
about me, and despite a black eye and a rapidly swelling lip, I replied, carelessly : ' Hurt me?
Well, I guess not. It will take somebody a little
bigger than that white-headed lunk to hurt *me*.' My
vocabulary of loving (?) epithets must have been
very limited, for that was the only one I could think
of that was sufficiently bad and strong to express
my feelings. I remember how the girls applauded
and scolded me all in one breath after I reached
home. Mother was out, but Hannah put a piece
of raw beef on the black eye and Deborah rubbed
some mutton tallow on the swollen lip, and Emeline
let me hold her pretty camphor bottle, and insisted
on my smelling of the contents of it every other
minute. I didn't feel a bit faint — try as hard as I
did to do so — but I leaned languidly back in the
big rocker, and closed my eyes and played the fine
lady and the heroine to my heart's content. Jo sat
at my elbow and once in a while I would open my
one eye slowly, and after taking in to the full his
loving, admiring look, would close it again and
languidly lift the bottle to my nose. Oh, homage

is dear, even to a child ! * * * I went to school
until I was fifteen years old. Never was a girl
happier than I ! Blessed with a good, kind father
and mother, loving sisters and brothers, a perfectly
healthly constitution, and a gay, happy disposition,
with every comfort that a girl could ask for ; what
had I to worry about? Nothing at all. I went to
dancing-school the winter I was fifteen. I even
had beaus come to see me on Sunday evenings —
boys who went to dancing-school with me. 'I remember one night I was obliged to stay at home
from dancing-school, on account of a very severe
cold, and loud were my lamentations, for a new
step was to be taught that evening. Deborah
consoled me by saying she would go in my place
and learn the step and teach it to me. I lay
awake until after 10 o'clock, in spite of the strong
mixture of niter that mother had given me, and
when Deborah came into my room with her candle,
I muffled myself up in a big shawl and sat up in
bed to take my lesson. Deborah hummed the tune
to me once or twice, and I attempted to hum it after
her, but after one or two feeble croaks, I gave it up
and whistled it instead. It seems as though I can
see that picture now. The large, unfinished cham
ber, dimly lighted by Deborah's candle, that she
had placed on the big chest, the low trundle bed in
the corner, under the rafters, in which slept Jo, the
little sleeping Thankful by my side, and Deborah

with her skirts tucked up, moving slowly and gracefully up and down the space before my bed, with
her shadow, grotesque and large, for her partner.
I hate to leave this brightest part of my girlhood
days, but I must, and come to the saddest one I
had ever known; the day when mother received
the letter that changed all our lives; that turned
our morning into darkest night. Father lay dead
of yellow fever in New Orleans, and we were left
almost destitute. If we had had what belonged to
us we would have been comparatively comfortable,
but cruel men cheated us out of every cent, and we
poor, helpless women did not know enough, then,
to fight for what belonged to us. Well, we went to
work. Hannah took in dress-making; Emeline
went up to New Bedford and learned tailoring, but
her beautiful face soon won for her a husband, and
she never came back to us. Deborah and I went
out as nurse or governess or whatever you might
call it; mother went out nursing; Hannah took care
of Thankful, Mercy and little Warren, and did her
dressmaking beside, and Jo, well, this is Jo's sad
story: Deborah, after a short time, married Captain Hersey Nickerson, a good man and kind.
Very soon after, when I was eighteen years old,
I married Isaac Chase, a young man of twenty-one.
Hersey was in command of a good vessel. Isaac
went with him as first mate, and Jo had the chance
of going as cook. But the poor boy begged of

mother not to send him to sea, but mother, with her heart almost breaking, was obliged to do so as there was nothing else for him to do. So he went — my precious Jo!"

Mrs. Hood's voice broke here, and she hid her face in her hands. The girls drew nearer to each other and clasped each other's hands. The room was almost dark. Vera was about to say: "Do not tell us any more, Mrs. Hood, if it hurts you," when Mrs. Hood went on, but she seemed to forget that she had listeners.

"At no time of my life had I felt so rebellious as I did then. At no time had I questioned God's goodness as I did then. I was wild with hopeless misery. I had two little girls at this time, and I loved them with all a young mother's unreasonable love. The 'boys' were to take some government stores to the soldiers, for it was during the last year of the war. They went away one cloudy day in the last of March. That night a terrible storm came up. I lay awake all night and listened to it. I loved my husband, but I worshipped my brother Jo. Was this the reason that God saw fit to take him from me? It was just and right for Him to do so, for I loved Jo better than I did God. Our 'boys' never came back to us. That storm swept them away from the face of the earth, and we saw them no more — only a wreck was left off the coast of Cape Hatteras to tell us of the end they had made.* But I love to think that when the boat went down, and my Jo's·fair, scarred face was hidden beneath the cruel waters, that God sent His life-boat to save them and take them safely across to the golden shore, and that when Jo stepped out of the life-boat and grasped the hand of Him who died to save, the face he lifted to that Other's was white, and pure, and unscarred, as when he was my baby brother and nestled his cheek to mine. Only I know it is a hundred-fold more pure, for the light of everlasting peace is upon it."

The hush of the room was broken by low sobs from the girls, and, could the boys' faces have been seen, the tears in their eyes would have been seen also. The sobs recalled Mrs. Hood to herself. She rose from her chair and tried to make her voice cheerful, as she said : " Now I have made you feel badly and you will not care to come and listen to me again."

" Oh, we will, we will ! " came the reply, in choked, but earnest, voices.

" Please do not trouble to light the lamp for us, Mrs. Hood," said Fred, in a queer voice. " We can find our way out."

Dear Fred ! He need not have been ashamed of the tears, for the girls thought twice as much of him for having them.

---

* Fact.

"May we come again to-morrow?" asked Jessie, as she clung to the hand that Mrs. Hood gave to her.

"Yes, indeed. I shall be so glad to have you. But do not let my story grieve you. There is nothing to grieve about, for my life is a very happy one."

The girls had no reply to make to this. How could her life be happy? was the question each asked herself, but Erfort's grasp of Mrs. Hood's hand conveyed to her an answer that she understood as plainly as though he had spoken. *She* knew that *he* knew.

CHAPTER XVIII.

There was not much said on the way home. Each seemed to feel that at such a time, " silence spoke louder than words." Probably not one of them, unless, indeed, it were Erfort, had ever felt and thought so deeply on the subject of religion, and now their thoughts were but half formed. Their sympathy for Charlotte Hood was deep and heartfelt, and now they were wondering if it were really her religion that was bearing her up so wonderfully.

" How can it ? " was all the question they could think to ask themselves.

At the cottage the boys took leave of the girls, after asking permission to come back and spend the evening with them ; a permission they readily granted. At the supper table Jessie seemed unusually silent ; she didn't even protest against the usual bowl of crackers and milk, although Vera, fearing that she would, said :

" Never mind, Jasmine ; to-morrow we are going to have another good square meal at the restaurant, and to-morrow night we'll vary the monotony of the regular supper fare with huckleberries."

" Crackers and milk are good enough for me," was the unexpected reply, given with a meekness that surprised them all.

Vera looked at her, and the thought flashed through her mind : " Little Robin is teaching her patience," and she was right.

A strange teacher for bright, sparkling, wayward Jasmine ! Truly " God moves in a mysterious way His wonders to perform."

After supper the girls felt a little livelier. Not that they were forgetting what they had listened to that afternoon, or that its influence was leaving them, but the youthful spirit in them was strong and would assert itself, and it was well and right that it should do so.

" I suppose if those boys are coming," said Jessie, leaning on the back of the chair from which she had just risen, and watching the others clear the table, " that there will be no band concert for this party to-night."

" Now, Jess," said Vera, pointing a spoon impressively at her, " You know you enjoy their company."

" Oh, well," replied Jessie, carelessly, " they are a little better than the common run. Nothing *very* foolish about them." Then she seated herself in the big rocker, saying : " Hurry up with those dishes, so we can go out on the piazza — it's too lovely to stay inside."

" ' Many hands make light work.' Suppose you help ? " said Net.

" Too many cooks spoil the broth," retorted Jessie, with a reckless disregard of adaptiveness.

" You had better go out on the piazza now," advised Net, gravely. " It must be too warm in here for you."

" All right," replied Jessie, only too glad. " Come on, Al ; you are looking a trifle flushed.'

When Vera and Garnet joined them a few moments later, they found Erfort and Fred already there. They were surprised to see them so soon, and Jessie, leaning lazily back in her chair and rocking in her usual rather violent manner, looked over her shoulder at the girls and said easily :

" I've just been asking them when they ate their supper — they must have swallowed it whole."

Garnet, shocked, slyly tweeked Jessie's hair as she leaned on the back of her chair.

" Ow," squealed Jessie, putting her hand up to her head. " Gracious ! Net Dare, let my hair alone ; you've given me the head-ache ! "

Fred couldn't help it — he laughed outright, and over Erfort's face flitted that shadow of a smile, only it was dark and no one saw it. Net sank down in her chair, angry at first, and then she joined in the laugh, her only revenge being :

" You are worse than any child, Jessie," for which reproof Jess cared not at all.

Strange as it may seem to some, the subject of Charlotte Hood and her story was not alluded to, yet every one was thinking of it. So it is. The thoughts that lie nearest to our heart are those it is the hardest to speak of. To have heard their light talk and laughter, one would have said that they had not one serious thought.

"By the way," said Fred, rather loudly, "what has become of Uriah Heep? Haven't seen the the gentleman this evening. Where does he keep himself?"

"'Sh!"

A warning from Net, delivered with such energy, that the gentleman, walking leisurely up the path, could not fail to hear it, even if he had not heard Fred's inquiry; which, by the way, he had.

"Good-evening, young ladies."

Fred, in his consternation, tried to draw into himself, and become as air, but he loomed up against his post "as large as life and twice as natural," and the gentleman had his eyes fixed upon him curiously.

Vera rose to do the honors.

"Our friends, Mr. Richards, Mr. Travers," and at the word *friends* Fred straightened himself and bade defiance to a hundred "Uriah Heeps."

The gentleman seated himself. Vera had not given his name, for she was not sure of it, and the gentleman after taking the chair she offered him, said:

" My name is Wild — Prof. Wild, of Boston. It doesn't seem to me necessary to stand on ceremony at such a place as this, particularly when we are fellow lodgers."

" Unfortunately we can not lay claim to that pleasure," said Erfort, " though we come as near to it as we possibly can."

" Told the truth for once in your life," said the incorrigible Jessie, sotto voce.

In the course of conversation that followed, our young people learned that their new acquaintance was a professor of phrenology, and he became a wonderful man in their eyes at once, especially in Garnet's.

" But *do* the bumps on anyone's head tell what kind of a person one is, or what profession, or — or what work one is best fitted to do?" asked Jessie, rather incoherently.

Prof. Wild held up both hands with a supplicating gesture. " Bumps! Miss Jessie! Oh, please do not call them that!"

" What *shall* I call them?" asked Jessie, not a bit abashed.

" Organs."

" Well, organs then. ' But a rose by any other name would smell as sweet.'"

Jessie seemed possessed to drag in quotations of questionable appropriateness, into her conversation that evening.

"The study of phrenology is a most interesting one to me," said the professor. "I have devoted myself almost exclusively to it for the past twenty years."

"He must be quite ancient," thought the girls.

"What is the distinction between phrenology and physiognomy?" asked Garnet, who knew, but wanted the professor's definition.

"Phrenology is the science of the functions of the parts of the brain. The theory of Gall is, that the mental faculties are shown on the surface of the head — in the different organs. Physiognomy is the science of discerning the character of the mind from the features of the face. Not many of the people of to-day have much faith in this latter theory, but it attracted considerable attention among the ancients, tho' it was, with them, rather a fanciful art than a natural science. Pythagoras and his disciples believed and practiced it, and Plato mentions it with approbation in 'Timæo.' Aristotle is said to be the author of a treatise on it. When the physiognomist, Zopyrus declared Socrates to be stupid, brutal, sensual and a drunkard, the philosopher defended himself saying: 'By nature I am addicted to all these vices, and they were restrained and vanquished only by the continual practice of virtue.'"

"Brave Socrates!" murmured Erfort, who was an ardent admirer of the ancient philosopher.

Prof. Wild smiled in a rather superior manner, and continued.

"You know the remark of Julius Cæsar on the physiognomy of Cassius and Antony is : "

" ' Would he were *fatter* : but I fear him not ;
Yet if my name were liable to fear,
I do not know the man I should avoid
So soon as that spare Cassius.   He reads much
He is a great observor, and he looks
Quite thro' the deeds of men.
He loves no plays, as thou dost, Antony ;
He hears no music :
Seldom he smiles, and smiles in such a way
As if he mocked himself and scorned his spirit
That could be moved to smile at anything ;
Such men are never at heart's-ease
While they behold a greater than themselves
And therefore are very dangerous.' "

"Poor Julius Cæsar !"   said Erfort.   "To be murdered by his friend !"

"Yes it was sad," replied the professor, who evidently did not have the interest in "things ancient" as did Erfort.   "A wonderful man was Caius Julius Cæsar."

"As Longfellow has it," said Erfort :

" ' Truly a wonderful man was Caius Julius Cæsar.
Better be first in a little Iberian village
Then be second in Rome, and I think he was right
when he said it.

Twice was he married before he was twenty and
many times after;
Battles five hundred he fought, and a thousand cities
he conquered
He, too, fought in Flanders, as he himself has re-
corded;
Finally he was stabbed by his friend, the orator
Brutus!'"

"What a pretty way Longfellow has of telling
things," said Vera. "I think that 'The Courtship
of Miles Standish' is one of the most beautiful
poems that was ever written."

"It contains good advice for us all," said Erfort.
"And it is given in very few words."

"If you wish a thing to be well done, you must
do it yourself, you must not leave it to others,"
quoted Garnet. "Very good advice, but Miles
Standish did not not practice what he preached in
one instance. If he had — "

"It would have made no difference," interrupted
Vera, with her wisest air. "Priscilla never would
have married him. She preferred John Alden.
And no wonder that she did."

"Why?" asked Erfort, with a smile.

Vera opened her gray eyes. "What a question,
Mr. Richards! Is it strange that a young girl like
Priscilla would prefer a handsome young man like
John Alden to a rough old fellow like Miles Stan-
dish? Besides, he ought to have asked her himself.

instead of sending John Alden to do it. I would have said with Priscilla 'If I am not worth the wooing, I surely am not worth the winning!'"

As Vera sat there with the electric light shining on her golden hair and fair face, Fred thought to himself that she was decidedly worth the wooing and he determined to do his best to both " woo and win " some day.

" We have somewhat strayed from our subject." said Garnet, who had been longing all this while to continue it.

" Just one moment, please." said the professor.

" What was it Priscilla said to John when he was pressing the suit of Miles Standish upon her?"

"' Why don't you speak for yourself, John?'" said Vera, archly.

" My name is John," said the professor calmly, and there wasn't the ghost of a smile on his face.

Vera " drew back into her shell," feeling that she had been taken advantage of in some way, and when Jessie giggled and the others couldn't help smiling (except Fred who only glared at this rather strange gentleman). Vera took her revenge by calling him fiercely to herself: " Uriah Heep!"

" Do let us come back to physiognomy," said Garnet. " Please tell us some more about it, Prof. Wild."

" Whether we believe in physiognomy or not," said the professor, " we must admit that we judge the quality of things by their outward form. Appearences are said 'to be often deceitful.' They seem to be so at times, but I think that generally it is our observation that is at fault. Now you take a lady's face that is fair and peaceful looking; the blue eyes are mild and pleasant, the smooth brow has no wrinkles, for no frowns ever appear on it to make the wrinkles. The whole surface of the face speaks plainly of the calm, mild spirit beneath it. Take another face — a dark, frowning face. The lips are set in an ugly pout, the black brows meet in an ugly frown, the whole face expresses a sullen, hateful temper. Are we often mistaken in our judgement of two such faces ? "

" Yes we are."

It was Jessie who spoke — bluntly and emphatically, much to the surprise of everyone.

" You have drawn the picture of two faces we have at home — the faces of two girls that we are well acquainted with, and the one with the ' dark, frowning face,' has the tenderest heart and the sweetest, most lovable nature of any girl in our 'set,' and the one with the ' fair, calm face,' is the biggest spit-fire that ever walked — in her private life — but when you meet with her in society, oh, dear me, she is s-o n-i-c-e and so s-w-e-e-t. (Jessie put a vast amount of expression in these words.) Butter wouldn't melt in her mouth. A deceitful minx, if *I* ever saw one. You can't tell *me* that you can judge by appearances. I know better. A poor body isn't to blame for having homely features. There isn't a soul living but what would have a classic nose and mouth if they could, but one's disposition is not necessarily ugly because one's nose happens to be."

When you touched on noses, you touched on Jessie's sorest point. Not that her nose was ugly — far from it; only it was little — not much of it, but what there was, was very pretty.

Erfort clapped his hands softly at Jessie's generous burst, but the professor looked at her much as he would have looked at a little kitten that had spit at him.

"You believe what you have said, no doubt," he replied. "But you will see differently when you get older."

Now, wasn't that provoking? Garnet saw the dangerous light leap into the beautiful black eyes, and she rose hastily, overturning her chair as she did so. The professor picked it up.

"Thank you," said Garnet. "Don't you think it is a little chilly out here? Perhaps we had better go in."

They all rose. The gentlemen took the ladies' chairs, and Garnet led the way into the parlor. Jessie put her arm around her neck and whispered fiercely in her ear:

"Don't you give that mean old thing a drop of cocoa."

" Jessie ! "

" You hear me.   If you do, *I* shan't pay a cent towards the next can."

Then Jessie slipped back with Vera, and they exchanged sympathetic pressures of hands.

The professor had gone down a good many degrees in *their* estimation.   Poor man !   He was totally unconscious of it, or appeared to be, as he sat in a low rocking chair and sipped the cup of cocoa that Garnet had given him — despite Jessie's threat — with an air of thorough enjoyment.

It did seem to Vera and Jessie as though he would have shown to much better advantage if he had taken a higher chair, for his legs being very long, and the chair very low, there was not room for them between the chair and the floor, so he wrapped them around the rounds to get them out of the way. Vera could hardly help laughing as she looked at them, but she fervently hoped that Fred would not see them.   Alas !   She had scarcely composed her face at Jessie's whispered :   " Isn't he a regular ' daddy-long-legs?' " when she became aware of Fred's painfully apparent efforts to attract her attention.

He was sitting on a high chair on the opposite side of the room, and he commenced by fixing his eyes earnestly upon her face and giving vent to a a loud "Ahem !"   Vera, of course, wouldn't look, although it seemed almost impossible for her to

keep her eyes away.   Then he rattled his cup
against his saucer, at which Garnet asked him
kindly, " if he would like more cocoa."   This
rather disconcerted him for a moment, for no young
man would like even his cousin to think that he
would take this childish way of asking for more
drink.   " I have plenty, Garnet, thank you," he
replied, keeping his eyes on Vera's rapidly crim-
soning face.   Then he went to the rather extreme
measure of stretching his own long legs half way
across the room and literally wagging his feet, (if
such an expression would be allowed) at Vera.

Poor Vera!   Her eyes fastened themselves on
the wagging feet, as though fascinated, and followed them as they were slowly drawn up to their
rightful place under the chair.   Then, quick as a
flash, they twined themselves round and round the
rounds of the chair in such an alarming manner
and in such an absolutely ludicrous imitation of
the unconscious professor's, that Vera, finding herself on the verge of an hysterical burst of laughter,
rashly took a drink of her cocoa, when — we all
know what followed, some of us from experience.
A gurgle, a gasp, a violent effort to send the cocoa
on its right road down, and only succeeding in driving it *out* — over the floor, her dress, and everything
around her, and a precipitate retreat into the back
parlor, where she is followed by Garnet, Allie
and Jessie, who take turns in slapping her on the

back and anxiously asking what is the matter. The gentlemen do not dare to follow, except Fred, who is really frightened, so much so that he throws all prudence to the winds and ventures to the open door. Vera catches sight of him and gasps out: "Send that boy out."

Poor Fred! The punishment is severe. To be called a boy, and before that hateful professor! Oh, Vera, cruel, hard-hearted Vera! Fred goes back to his chair thoroughly subdued.

The girls repair to the kitchen for a few moments of explanation. They all sympathize with Vera, and tell her not to care, but to go back into the parlor and act as though nothing had happened. Garnet makes this possible by saying:

"You know you can do it, Vera. Don't give that foolish boy the satisfaction of thinking he can upset you altogether."

That was appealing to Vera's pride, and she immediately arose, put her handkerchief in to her pocket, and herself led the way back into the parlor. Jessie went dancing after, hugging herself with both arms to think that it was not she who had disgraced herself. "Net would have taken my head off," she thought.

Not another word or glance would Vera bestow on poor Fred the rest of the evening, although the pleading looks he gave her must have haunted her dreams that night.

Prof. Wild was the first to leave the room, and as he rose from his chair, he said :

" If you would like to have me — that is, if you think you would enjoy it, I will examine your heads some evening. Explain the different organs to you. You may derive some pleasure, if not benefit from it."

They thanked him and agreed to have it done the next evening. Garnet was so pleased with the idea that her eyes shone like stars. Vera looked skeptical, and the professor, quick to see it, turned to her.

" Would you like for me to tell you what you ought to be, if you are not ? "

" If you please."

"A school teacher."

Vera started. How did he know? No one in the house knew of it except their own party — not even " Grandpa " and " Mother."

" You love music, too, and are a very good singer. You do not play much in public, but you love to play and sing for your own amusement. You are — but I'll reserve the rest for to-morrow evening . Shall I ? "

"As you wish."

Vera was certainly surprised, but she wasn't going to let him see it.

" What am I ? " asked Jessie.

"You are a school-girl now," was the answer,
but you will take up the study of elocution, and do
wonderfully well with it, too."

"Shall I?"

The little face glowed and the big eyes shone.
That was Jessie's one ambition — to be an elocutionist. She was on the point of pouring out a vol-
ley of questions, but he turned to Garnet. He
looked into the strong little face for a long while.
So calm, so untroubled, so firm in its expression of
self-control, outwardly. Beneath — did the professor see what there was? He passed over to Allie
with the brief words: "To-morrow evening."

"You are a little home-body. You are interested in housework; you love it and you do well
with it. Your father could not get along without
you; you help him in his accounts; you help your
brothers and sisters with their studies. You are
very necessary in your father's home, and — you
will some day be a wife — a minister's wife."

At this rather startling information, Allie blushed
a rosy red, and the others laughed. .

"I will see the gentlemen another time. And
now, good-night," and with a low bow this rather
strange professor went hurriedly out of the room,
and in a moment or two they heard — alas, that it
is necessary in this matter-of-fact world to *be* matter-of-fact — his boots come down pretty heavily on
the floor overhead. Fred wafted a kiss Wild-ward.
"Pleasant dreams to you, Oscar," he said.

As the girls stood on the piazza saying "good-night" to the boys, Fred stepped up to Vera, and said:

"Won't you *please* forgive me, Miss Earle?"

"It was very wrong of you," said Vera.

"I know it," said Fred, eagerly. "But I'm very sorry."

Vera could not help smiling at the boyish face and tone. "Won't you do it again?"

"Never!"

"Then I forgive you *this* time."

So they parted friends.

"Say girls," said Jessie, unlacing her shoes up stairs five minutes later. "I'd like first-rate to hear what the old fellow has to say about my elocution, but I'll be snooked — excuse me, Net — if I want his cold hands on *my* head."

"Ugh!" shivered Vera. "It makes me crawl to think of them. But I *would* like to hear what he has to say about me."

"He seems like a kind-hearted man," said Allie, always seeing the best in anyone.

"Net's all carried away with him," said Jessie. "I see it in her eyes."

"You'll get something in your own eyes if you don't shut them and go to sleep," said Vera, raising her pillow.

All Garnet said was: "Be careful, girls, he will hear you. His room is right opposite, you know."

"Oh, to-morrow afternoon," said Allie, with a happy sigh. "We'll hear more of Charlotte Hood's story."

"A happy thought to go to sleep upon," said Garnet.

CHAPTER XIX.

The next morning the girls were "up betimes,' (as the story-tellers have it,) each one looking eagerly forward to "Robin's Hour," although not speaking of it.

"Who's going to get breakfast this morning?" asked Jessie.

"Who's going to get breakfast this morning?" repeated Garnet.

"That's what I said," said Jessie, calmly, diving under the bed after one of her shoes.

"The ones who get it every morning," and Garnet gave her curls a parting brush, and commenced to take the clothes off the bed.

Jessie made up a face at Allie from behind the shoe she had captured. "That's you and I, Al,' she said, in a stage whisper.

"Yes, I should say as much," said Garnet. "You haven't done a thing towards getting breakfast a single morning since we have been here."

Jessie opened her eyes wide and made an " O " of her lips. "Why, Net Dare, what a big lie! I help every morning, so there now!"

"Why Jessie!" Garnet's tones were full of reproach.

" I do. You ask Vera."

" I can swear to that," said Vera, who had her head down and was braiding her golden hair into one thick, heavy braid, preparatory to coiling it on the top of her head. " Jess puts her chair up to table every morning, and sets the omelet in a particular spot, viz: You all know where."

" Close up to her plate," said Garnet, while Jessie cried:

" You mean thing, Vera Earle. I beat the eggs for you two or three mornings, and it isn't any fun to do that, I can tell you. But that's all the thanks I get. You can beat them yourself this morning and see how you like it," and Jessie gave her shoe-string such a jerk that it broke, and she came very near falling over on her back, a mishap that didn't improve her temper any.

" Jasmine's cross this morning," said Vera, trying not to laugh at the comical figure Jessie cut in her gymnastic performance, while Allie hastened to her trunk to get a shoe-string.

" Never mind, Jess," said Allie. " Remember where you are going at 4 o'clock this afternoon."

How quickly the clouds were banished from the little face, and brightest sunshine filled their place! The angry words were forced back, and as Allie handed over the shoe-string, Jessie smiled one of her rare, sweet smiles, as she looked up into Allie's gentle face and said: " Thank you, Allie."

Perhaps Allie understood that the thanks were for something more than the shoe-string. I think she did, for she looked so pleased.

" I have heard soft, faltering footsteps on the other side of the door several times this morning," said Garnet, " and I have my suspicions as to whose they are."

" The professor's ? " asked Jessie.

" Mercy, no ! Can you imagine *his* footsteps being soft and faltering ? "

" I can imagine them being soft in correspondence with his head," said Jessie, who had not forgotten last night's injury. " But it's my belief he would falter at nothing."

" Not even murder, hey ? " said Vera. " Then he could have our heads to put into alcohol for future use."

" All he'd want would be the pianos," said Jessie.

" The what ? "

" The pianos."

" What are those ? "

" The bumps."

" You mean organs, Jessie," said Garnet, absent-mindedly, at which they all laughed.

" An' did the innocent think I didn't know ? " cried Jessie. " Begorra but I knowed they were some kind of an insthrumint, an' phwy not pianners as well as orgins, now ? "

Just here the soft, faltering footsteps that Garnet had spoken of, were plainly heard outside the door. Jessie paused, comb in hand, and looked at the others.

" Mother," she whispered.

Vera opened the door, and sure enough, there stood " Mother," with " Grandpa " behind her.

" Do please excuse us, dears, for intruding ; but we were so afraid you would forget to sing to us this morning, so I says to Mr. Atherton, ' I'll go up stairs and see if they are up yet.' Now I'm sorry if I have intruded. Mr. Atherton, you go right down, and I a-coming," and " Mother " put her hand upon " Grandpa's " arm and moved slowly towards the stairs.

" You have not intruded at all, " Grandma," cried the girls. " We are going right down."

" Yes, yes ; thank you, thank you," and " Grandpa " quavered an echo.

" Do you call that man hen-pecked ? asked Jessie, gravely, as Vera closed the door.

Vera laughed. " I suppose some would call him so, but I don't know."

" ' Mother ' is evidently the head of the house." said Garnet, " and I should think had always been so, but ' Grandpa ' seems to take it calmly enough."

" I suppose it has gotten to be second nature to him by this time." said Vera.

"Are we all ready?" asked Allie. "If we are, let's go down so as not to keep them waiting."

They found "Grandpa" and "Grandma" sitting in their respective chairs. "Grandma" in the big rocker, "Grandpa" close beside her in the old arm-chair, his Bible on his knee, his spectacles on his nose. The girls seated themselves and the usual morning service proceeded.

I do not think the girls, before this morning, realized how peacefully, quietly happy they felt during that half hour, when they sat with those two aged pilgrims, whose journey through life was almost ended, and listened to the precious words from the "Holy Book" and sung the sweet songs of the Gospel. I am sure the memory of those half-hours will never leave them while they live.

"I do believe it is going to rain," said Jessie, as she stood in the door-way after breakfast. "Won't it be too bad if it rains this afternoon."

"It needn't make any difference to our going to Mrs. Hood's," said Vera. "I've been to dancing-school nights when it has rained pitch forks, and I guess I can go as far as Mrs. Hood's and not hurt myself. Dear me! I'll never forget one night when I went to dancing-school — oh, how it did rain! Mother didn't want me to go, but I didn't want to miss a lesson, and then we always did have such fun. Well, you know Madge Weld, Net? she was with me. We got off the train and started down Main street. Oh, that street was perfectly dreadful — just like a river, and here and there were small places that were icy. Ever so much worse than as though the whole street had been slippery. Well, we were hurrying along as fast as we could go, when all at once an old lady — not so very old either; not more than fifty-five, but very fleshy — slipped upon a piece of ice about the size of a sheet of writing-paper, and down she went, right on the back of her head, with her feet up in the air. You know how quickly the gentlemen offer their assistance, at such times — well, one gentleman who had been looking in one of the shop windows, ran eagerly forward, anxious to do the polite, when, if you will believe me, he slipped up on that same piece of ice, and down he went, giving the old lady the awfullest kick in the back! It must have hurt her twice as much as the fall did. I just leaned against the railing of the window and laughed until I cried, for his hat fell off, showing a miniature skating-rink, and he rolled his eyes around at me with such a look of agony, entreaty, rage, humiliation and laughter, all combined, that I thought I should die. Well, that isn't all. When I managed to start on again, if *I* didn't slip up on that same mean little bit, and the gymnastic exercise I performed in trying to save myself was twice as comical as though I had gone down. My feet sprawled all over the sidewalk, I threw both arms up wildly — umbrella and all — in the air, hitting a man on the head and knocking his hat off, thus causing him to commit sin by mentioning a place where ice is unknown. How in the world I kept from going down I don't know, for my hair came in such close contact with the sidewalk that it was slightly damp with the moisture thereon. Madge declared she was going to tell Prof. Starkland that I had originated a new step, but I told her to beware as she valued my friendship."

"Isn't it fun to dance?" said Jessie, after they had finished laughing at Vera's account.

"Yes, it is," answered Vera, with such a heavy sigh that the girls looked at her, whereat Vera laughed nervously and blushed.

"To tell the truth, girls," she said, "I for one, would hate to give up dancing."

"Who said anything about being obliged to?" asked Jessie, rather sharply.

Vera paused a moment, and then said quickly, as though half ashamed:

"I was thinking of what 'Grandpa' and 'Grandma' said to us, the other morning, about our not caring for things that we care for now, when we get to be as old as they are —"

Jessie interrupted Vera with a ringing laugh, "Well, I should say as much. Whoever would imagine 'Grandpa' and 'Grandma' wanting to waltz! Ha, ha, ha! and 'Polka!' and 'Military Schottische!' and the 'York!' Ha, ha, ha! and the 'Highland Fling,' while you are about it. Oh — h — h!" and Jessie leaned forward in her chair, with her hands on her sides and laughed until the tears rolled down her cheeks, and the others couldn't help laughing in sympathy.

"Oh, Vera Earle, you'll kill me," gasped Jessie, rolling her head from side to side and lifting eyes that were heavy with tears. "Can't you imagine them hopping around here? Swing you partners! First couple in the centre and eight hands around! All waltz! Oh — h — h!" Jessie fairly doubled up in her chair and came near being hysterical, so much so that Garnet said, rather sharply for her:

"Jessie, keep still. How can you make fun of poor 'Grandpa' and 'Grandma!' and Vera said:

"You didn't let me finish, Jessie. I was going to say, rather, that we would not care for such things when we cared more for — for — "

"Our Heavenly Father," said Allie, softly, and Vera breathed a sigh of relief at Allie's coming to the rescue.

Vera could talk upon any other subject, but at the very thought of speaking the Saviour's name aloud her face burnt and her heart beat fast.

Jessie came out of her merry fit in an instant.

"Oh, nonsense," she said, sharply. "Don't be so foolish. Just as though any one couldn't be just as good when they danced as when they didn't. It doesn't hurt anyone to shake their foot a bit — it does them good. It does me, anyway," and Jessie sprang out of her chair and waltzed lightly around the room.

Vera leaned against the table and watched her. How lightly and gracefully the slender, girlish form glided over the floor. Jessie looked over her shoulder at Vera, as she danced. Her cheeks were crimson and her beautiful eyes were flashing.

"I would dance to-night if I knew I was going to die to-morrow. It's no sin, and I would go to Heaven just as quick. Don't look so sober, Vera. I don't mean to be wicked, but I'll dance, dance, dance, though the Heavens fall," and with an extra whirl and trip Jessie danced out of the room.

"That child will never be anything *but* a child," said Garnet. "And a spoilt one at that."

"Jess says a great many light things to hide her real feelings," said Vera. "She thinks more than we gives her credit for doing."

"That is true," said Allie, emphatically. Jessie is a noble girl."

Garnet looked almost scandalized. "Why, Allie Hunt, what an idea!"

"Oh, but she is," said Allie, with soft persistence. "You'll find it out, some day."

"Well, I really hope I shall," replied Garnet, "but I doubt it."

That afternoon, at 3 : 45 o'clock, Fred and Erfort presented themselves at the cottage, punctual to the minute. Strange to say, it was the first time, they had been there that day, and Jessie greeted them with :

"Well, what's going to happen ? Have you been sick, or what, that you are just showing yourselves ? "

"We are sorry if we have disappointed you," said Fred, wickedly. "If we had known you were anxious to see us, we would most surely have exerted ourselves and come before."

Jessie flashed a contemptuous look at him.

"You needn't bother about exerting yourself on *my* account, thank you. I can manage to exist without your delightful company. Of course you had to stay in your room and rest to-day, after your effort of last evening." And with this parting shot Jessie slipped her hand through Allie's arm and hurried on ahead.

"You will learn better than to apply a match to *that* piece of tinder," said Vera, laughing, as Fred, rather disconcerted, walked by her side.

"True. She is rather quick at taking fire, isn't she ? "

Erfort, over whose face had flitted the strange smile, walked with Garnet, and she stole a look at him to see if he was utterly shocked. He didn't seem to be, certainly.

"Jessie is so childish," she began, apologeti-
cally, but he turned to her with one of his quick,
eager looks that always tied her tongue, somehow
or other, and she stopped.

"Your sister is the most charming lady I have
ever met," he said.

And Garnet was so utterly astonished that she
didn't speak another word voluntarily during the
remainder of the walk, but, she did a vast amount
of thinking.

"What a perfectly insane remark," she thought.
"And coming from such a grave, thoughtful, dignified young man. It can't be he is falling in love
with her." At the very idea of this dreadful thing,
Garnet's sisterly heart took fright. Of course not
— it couldn't be — Jessie was nothing but a baby.

"But I'll watch him just the same," she said to
herself, just as they came in sight of the little brown
cottage; "and if I see any signs of it, I'll — but
what can I do? I can't send her home, though I'd
want to, and I can't say anything to her to warn
her — it would put foolish ideas into her head, and
would do more harm than good. Besides all the
thanks I would get would be the advice to mind
my own business. Perhaps mother will write
that she must come home. I almost hope she
will, and still the dear child would be dreadfully
disappointed. Well, I can only keep still and
hope for the best."

Oh, Garnet was a wise little body if ever there was one. Little trouble would there be in this world if *she* had the brewing of it.

Mrs. Hood met them at the door. They could see she was feeling unusually happy, and she soon explained it.

"Robin hasn't had any pain to-day," she said, with almost childish eagerness. "It is the first time for months. Oh, God is very good!"

Surely the patient faith of this woman was something wonderful and her entire goodness was a thing that could never be doubted.

Jessie had already seated herself on the bed beside Robin. Her arm was about him and her head touched his lightly as it rested on her shoulder. He smiled at each one as they came in and held out his little thin hand, but after they were seated he nestled close against Jessie's side, his hand holding tight hold of her's, and hardly moved while his mother proceeded with her story.

CHAPTER XX.

" After the news of the wreck, that had been seen off Cape Hatteras, reached us, we all knew that we would never see our boys again in this world, yet we kept hoping that some other news would come.— that they had been picked up by some other vessel or something. Deborah and I went home to mother. The stage used to pass the corner near our house, and night after night I have seen mother go to the door, and stand with her hand shading her eyes, watching for it to come around the corner, but it never turned the corner to come to the house, but always passed on. Oh, those were terrible days! I have often wondered how we ever lived through them. I have known since where mother went to find strength to endure, and found it; but then my heart was hard and bitter. I think suspense is the hardest thing of all to bear, or if not the hardest, the most trying. It was hard to lose husband and brother together — yes, *two* brothers, for Hersey was very near to me.

Well, time passed on. Mother went out nursing and I kept house for her, for soon Hannah married and went to a home of her own, and Deborah went to New Bedford to Emeline's. Seven months after the storm, another little girl was born to me, and when I heard its first little wailing cry, I turned my face to the wall and the tears rolled down my cheeks. Poor little baby! Never in this world to look upon its father's face! Why was it born? I asked myself this question over and over again. For two or three days I would scarcely look at it, I felt so sick, and tired, and miserable, and then one night I heard Betsey Ann (who was by this time, a little shriveled old woman) talking to mother and Aunt Thankful, and I heard her say: 'Yes, it's a great pity the child was born. Seems to me, Emeline, ye had enuff trouble without this one a-coming. It's one more mouth to feed.' And mother, although she didn't say anything, sighed once very deeply, and that sigh went straight to my heart, for it spoke louder than words could have done. Then Aunt Thankful spoke. 'It beats all how sum folks hez an awful sight of it and it all comes to once. I didn't know how in the world Charlotte was ever goin' to git along with two children, and neow another one's come, I don't know what she *will* dew. Tew bad, tew bad!" Just then baby cried —a little plaintive cry that no one heard but myself —and it's little head moved slowly from side to side on my arm. Then something in my heart seemed to give way. I gathered the tiny form close to me and kissed it and cried over it. And from that hour I loved it more than anything I had ever loved before — except Jo. Yes, even more than I loved my other little ones, for I had to love it for so many, you see. It's welcome in this world had been such a cold one, even from its own mother. I felt as though I never could love her enough. But as she grew older her sweet face won everyone's love. She had the most beautiful eyes I ever saw, large, bright, and a deep brown. But it was their expression that made them so beautiful; such a sad, wistful look; even when she was laughing their sadness never left them. We called her Hope. When she was two years old Emeline sent for me to come to New Bedford. Her husband was a merchant tailor, and he would give me employment. Deborah was to live with me and keep house. So I packed my few household goods and went. My head troubled me very much at this time. I suppose it was because I used my eyes so steadily and thought so much; but all my thoughts were how to make both ends meet. The two oldest children went to school, and never shall I forget the times when they used to come home and ask me to buy for them things which the other little girls were having — some of them really necessaries. Many times I have been obliged to refuse them, and at others I have gone without things I actually needed that they might have what they asked for. Oh, no one but a mother can know how a mother's heart aches when she is obliged to deny her children even the ordinary comforts of life. All this time my heart had been growing more and more bitter towards God. What crime had I ever committed that my life should be one long pain — one long struggle for mere existence? Existence not only for myself but for those who were infinitely dearer to me than life itself. I heard a sermon one Sunday. It was considered to be one of the ablest sermons ever preached in New Bedford, but to me it was nothing more than a mockery, and I went home with my heart full to overflowing with hate and anger. Only one thing that he had said could I remember, and that kept repeating itself over and over again: 'God doeth all things well, and ye who dispute His righteousness and goodness are of a sinful nature and do err wickedly; for which eternal punishment shall be inflicted upon you at some future day.' How did he dare to say such words as those to one who had known nothing but sorrow for many a long day? It was well enough for *him* to say that 'God doeth all things well,' for all things *were* well with him. He had a beautiful home, a loving wife, beautiful children — everything to make a man thankful; why *shouldn't* he declare God to be good. Let *his* home and money be taken from him, let *him* lose his wife as I had lost my husband; let *him* know what it was to hear his children asking him for food to eat, that he

could not give them; let *him* work until his head
felt like a piece of lead and his eyes like balls of
fire; would he be so quick to tell to miserable
creatures that they were in danger of hell's fire if
they doubted the goodness and justice of God? It
was all very well to be thankful when you had
everything to be thankful for, but wait until misfortune comes, and then see how long one's thankfulness will hold out. . . . These were my
thoughts as I walked home from church on that
beautiful autumn Sunday night. When I entered
the house Deborah was sitting in a chair holding
Hope on her lap. Her face was flushed and her
eyes unusually bright.

'Oh, Charlotte, I am so glad you have
come,' she said 'My head aches so that I can
hardly see and my back is almost broken off. I
think I'll go to bed.' I was very much frightened
for Deborah was always so well, and even when
she felt a little sick she never complained. I forgot all about the sermon and everything else in my
anxiety. Deborah was, and had always been, my
dearest, best sister. I commenced scolding myself
for leaving her alone with the children, but she
stopped me immediately. 'It was right that you
should go out. You must have a rest some time and
Sunday is your only day. I can go out every afternoon in the week if I want to. Take Hope — she
doesn't seem very well either — and I'll go to bed.

I'll be all right in the morning. Marjie and Lillis are both asleep, but Hope wanted rocking.' I wouldn't let her go until she had taken some hot drink and put her feet in mustard water, for I thought she must have taken a severe cold; then I sat down and rocked and sang to Hope until I was half asleep, but it was 10 o'clock before she stopped moaning and lay quiet in my arms. I sat and looked at her a few moments before putting her in her crib. She was four years old now. She looked like a little angel as she lay there. She was very pale, and her bright hair clung in little damp rings to her forehead; her long dark lashes rested on her cheek. But her little hands were clenched and she kept grinding her teeth as though she were in pain. I took her up stairs and laid her on the bed beside Lillis, who slept with me, deciding to keep her beside me that night, then I undressed and got into bed. It didn't seem as though I had been asleep but a very short time before Lillis wakened me, crying. 'What is the matter, darling?' I asked, putting my hand over and resting it on her arm. It burnt me like fire. 'My head aches dreadfully, mamma.' I was out of bed in an instant and lighted the lamp. 'Oh please don't, mamma,' cried Lillis. 'The light hurts my eyes.' I placed a book before the lamp to shade the light, then went over to the back side of the bed and took Lillis in my arms. 'Tell

mamma all about it, darling. Where does she feel
sick?' 'In my head, mamma, and my back. Oh,
mamma!' ''Sh, 'sh, don't cry darling; you will
waken Hope. Let mamma smooth her head and it
will make it well.' My brave little darling stifled
her sobs against my neck, but I could feel her little
form quiver with them. I smoothed her head and
sang in a low voice to her and by and by she fell
asleep. A strange feeling came over me. I felt
as though something was coming — I didn't know
what — but I must be ready to meet it. I dressed
myself and sat on the side of the bed and fastened
my eyes on my darlings' faces. First one would
moan in her sleep and then the other and I would
sooth and hush them in turn. About 3 o'clock,
hearing Deborah talking, I went into her room.
Marjie met me at the door, holding her trailing
night-dress up with one little hand, and looking up
into my face with her large dark eyes full of wonder. 'Oh, mamma!' she whispered. 'Auntie is
talking awful fast, and saying such funny things.
I guess she thinks I'm Aunt Hannah because she
calls me by her name.' I hurried to the bed and
there lay Deborah with her arms tossed up over her
head and her eyes rolling all around the room. I
knelt beside her. 'Debbie.' She looked at me
and commenced to laugh. 'Debbie dear, don't
you know me?' She put one hand out and
touched my face. 'Where did they see the wreck,

Hannah ? I've been looking for it since morning, and now it is evening, and I have not found it.' How I remained calm I do not know, but I did. 'Don't you know me, Debbie ? I am Charlotte. Don't you know where you are ? See, here is Marjorie too.' She took her hand from my face and flung her arms up over her head again. 'The wreck ! the wreck !' she moaned, and that is all she would say. I turned to Marjie. She was nothing but a child, only eight years old, and very small and slender, but she was my only help. I put my arms around her. Her big dark eyes shone like stars in her little white face as she looked up at me. 'Marjie darling, mamma's own little woman, Auntie is very sick and the doctor must come and see her right away. Little sister and baby are sick too, and mamma can't leave them. Will you run to Auntie Em's and ring her door bell real hard, and tell her this, and ask her to send for the doctor ?' I can see the frightened look now that came into her eyes. Her lips that were always so red, grew pale and I felt her form tremble in my arms. 'Oh, mamma !' The whisper was full of horror. My heart almost burst. I covered her little face with kisses. 'It is only a few steps, my darling. Mamma will stand at the door and watch you.' 'It's so dark, mamma.' 'I know, darling ; but you don't want Auntie and little sister and baby to die, you know, and they may if the

doctor doesn't come.' That was enough. ' I'll
go, mamma.' I helped her dress. She trembled
like a leaf all the time, and when I opened the
outside door for her to pass out, and she saw how
dark it was, she drew back and clung to me.
Then I said, scarce thinking : ' God will take
care of you, darling.' She let go of my dress,
and ran like a flash. I saw her once, as she
passed under a gas-light, turn and look over her
shoulder, as if to assure herself that I was watching her, then she fluttered on again, and out of
sight. I turned to run up stairs again, for a moment, when right towards me came Deborah — a
wild light in her eyes. ' Quick, quick !' she cried.
' I've found the wreck and I hear the boys calling
to me to come to them. I've seen Hersey, and Jo,
and Isaac. They were clinging to the mast, and
they called to me to get a boat and come.' I took
her arm and turned her around. ' This is the
way, Debbie. We will get the boat.' I led her
back up stairs, but she stopped at the door of the
room and would not go in. I heard Lillis and
Hope both moaning, and I knew Marjie would
soon be back, and I must be at the door to meet
her. ' Deborah,' I said, speaking as sternly as I
could, ' lie down on that bed and stay until I come
to you. The boat is a long way off, and I must
go for it, for I can go more quickly than you.'
She lay down on the bed immediately, only say-

ing: 'Be quick, then, or they will sink.' I hurried into my own room and bent over my children. Lillis looked up at me, but there was no reason in her look. Hope knew me and said: 'Oh, mamma, my head aches drefful.' I hastily wrung out cloths in cold water and bound them around their heads; then, kissing them both and telling Hope I would be right back, I hurried down to the door just as Marjorie came flying up the street. In another moment she was in my arms, her face perfectly deathly and her heart beating almost to suffocation. 'Mamma's own brave little woman!' I kept saying until she gradually grew calm. 'Auntie Em came to the door, and the doctor was there because little Lloyd is sick, and they wanted me to stay and come home with the doctor, but I thought you would want me to help you, so I ran right back.' What could I do but simply shower kisses on my brave darling's face? Then we went up stairs, and while I talked with and soothed Deborah, Marjie kept the cloths wet on her little sisters' heads. At 4 o'clock the doctor came. I took him first to Deborah, for she was getting to be uncontrollable. He looked at her in complete astonishment, then turned to me with the blunt question: 'Hasn't this lady ever had scarlet fever?' My heart gave one leap, then seemed to stand still. 'No, she never has,' I answered, steadily. He shook his head; then he took out

his case, drew from it a powder and said : 'Half
a glass of water, please.' I brought it to him.
He put the powder into it, mixed it, and gave it to
Deborah ; then, after watching her a few moments
and seeing that she was growing quieter, he rose
from his chair. 'Let me see the other patients,
please.' I led him into my own room. He looked at
Marjie rather curiously, as she was laying the wet
cloth on Lillis' head. 'You have a young assist-
ant. Don't let her get over-tired.' Then he sat
down beside Hope. After mixing her medicine
he went around to Lillis. I thought he looked at
me rather strangely, as he at last rose to leave the
room. He went once more into Debbie's room
and stayed quite a little while, watching her. She
was breathing very slowly and heavily ; then he
turned to go down the stairs, but at the top I
stopped him. 'You have not told me the trouble,
doctor. 'The trouble ?' 'Yes. What is their
sickness ?' He looked away from me, and down
the stairs. 'Well, er — fever.' 'What kind of
fever ?' 'What kind of fever ?' 'Yes.' 'Well,
er — don't you know ?' 'Is it scarlet ?' He looked
at me. 'Yes, my poor woman.' Still I remained
calm, for I felt so. 'Are they dangerously sick ?'
Again he looked away from me down the stairs.
'Your sister is.' 'And the others ?' 'The little
one you call Lillis is.' 'They will die ?' He
actually started, but when he put his hand out to

touch my wrist I smiled and drew it away. 'I
know what I am saying. You must tell me the
worst. It is your duty. I can bear it.' 'I cannot
tell you if they will die, of course, but they are
very sick, indeed. I will come again, this afternoon. Your sister, Mrs. Brayton, wished me to
tell you that she didn't know whether she could
come over or not, to-day, as her little boy is sick
with the same disease, though not dangerously so.'
I nodded my head. 'Shall I send some one to help
you?' 'No, thank you. I shall get along very
well.' At the foot of the stairs he turned. 'Be
careful of Marjorie,' he said; then he went out and
shut the door and I went back to my sick ones. I
shall not linger over the days that followed —
how I passed from one bed to the other and did all
that I could do to keep them with me. Marjorie,
— ah, my angel Majorie.! I can not speak of her
yet. At the end of the sixth day as I was leaving
Deborah's bedside, I was surprised to hear her say,
quite calmly, 'Charlotte.' I went back to her.
'Yes, Debbie.' The red had all faded from her
cheek and her eyes were large and languid.
'Charlotte, I think I am dying.' 'Oh Debbie!'
It was all that I could say. 'I am, Charlotte, for
I have seen Hersey, and he says he is coming
for me very soon. I would like to see mother
before I go.' I didn't say a word. I only held
fast to one of her hands with both of mine and put

my head beside hers on the pillow. She was my dearest and best sister and she was leaving me. I could not tell whether her mind wandered or not, for, although her face looked perfectly calm, she kept talking about our childhood days at home. 'They were happy days, Charley,' she murmured. 'Give my love to all the girls and tell mother I was not afraid to die — I am all ready to go.' She lay perfectly still for a moment, with her eyes closed. I heard her murmur several times: 'The child Hope,' and she smiled each time; then suddenly she opened her eyes wide and looked up to the ceiling. She caught her breath quickly as if in pleased surprise, put up both arms and said, 'I see them; father, Hersey, Jo and Isaac. Mother, do you hear?' Then her arms dropped and all was still. I closed her eyes and leaned my hot head for a moment on her cold forehead. I only gave one sob. 'Good-bye, Debbie.' 'Mamma.' I raised my head. Marjie was standing by my side. 'Auntie has gone to Heaven, Margie,' I said, and the child never cried, only looked on the still form with eyes full of wonder and awe. 'She will see papa, won't she mamma?' 'She has seen him, darling; she said so.' The child never questioned. 'Run down to Auntie Em's, darling,' I said. 'And tell her.' I went into my room. Hope was lying very quiet, but Lillis was turning restlessly on her pillow and singing snatches of school songs. I sat down beside

her and smoothed back the hair from her forehead.
Such pretty golden hair. The doctor and Emeline
came in together. The doctor looked at Hope and
then turned to me very quickly. 'What is it,
doctor?' I asked. 'She is better, isn't she? She
has not talked for some little time.' He laid his
hand tenderly on her head. 'She will never know
sickness again,' he said. I hardly know what followed. I remember of springing to the other side
of the bed and snatching the little cold form up in
my arms. Dead! My baby dead, and died out of
my arms! I wouldn't believe it. I was well nigh
crazy. Then I remembered what Deborah had
said while she was dying. 'The child Hope.'
Had they gone together then? I walked the floor
with my baby in my arms. I shook off the hands
that would have stopped me. 'Let me alone,' I
cried. 'Don't dare to touch me. My baby, my
baby, my baby.' The doctor caught my arm and
pointed to the bed. Lillis was sitting up in it,
her golden hair streaming down her shoulders,
her blue eyes wide open with terror. 'Mamma,
mamma, come to Lillis,' she cried. I started
towards her with Hope still in my arms, but the
doctor stopped me. 'Let me have her,' he said,
and I obeyed without a word. Oh, the long night
that followed! I remember that Marjie kept close
by my side while I held Lillis in my arms, and
every now and then I kissed the patient little face.

I knew they had telegraphed to mother and Hannah and they would expect them the next night. What use is there in my telling it all over?   All that night's and the next day's watching?   When the light faded from the sky, it faded from my Lillis' eyes as well, and my watching was over.   *   *

*   The minister came that night, and wished to talk with me.   I knew quite well what he would say — I hadn't forgotten his sermon.   I went down stairs to see him.   He said just what I thought he would say.   My heart swelled almost to bursting but I never opened my lips.   What could that man tell me of sorrow, with my three dear dead ones lying up stairs?   He grew impatient after a while and asked me if my heart was so hard and my eyes so blinded with wicked tears that I could not feel God's loving kindness and see His will through it all.   I simply said : 'Come with me, if you please.' Surprised, he followed me up the stairs.   I took him into Deborah's room first.   I drew the cloth down from her face.   'You see what is lying here? The sister I loved best.'   He said not a word, and I put the cloth back in its place.   I took him next into my room, taking Marjie whom I met in the hall, with us.   The two little forms lay stretched side by side, the same white sheet covering them both.   I drew it down and looked on my darlings' faces with eyes that felt hard and dry.   The golden curls and the brown curls touched as they rested on

the same pillow; the sweet faces looked soft and white and cold; the little dimpled hands were crossed alike on the pretty white night-dresses. Could that man tell me what sorrow was? I would never hear my darlings' voices again; I would never feel their sweet kisses on my lips, their soft cheeks against mine, and their dimpled arms around my neck. Could he ask me if my heart felt tender toward the One who had sent this misery upon me? Ah, those were the wicked thoughts I had that night, and I almost laughed as he turned his head away from the sight of the lovely faces on the pillow. What was it to him? He could go back home and take his fair and beautifully dressed children on his knee and listen to their talk and laughter, and feel their kisses and their soft breath on his cheek. He turned to leave the room. 'One moment, please,' I said. I stooped down and wrapped my arms about Marjie. 'This is all I have left to live for. If she is taken from me, I will take my life in my own hands and do with it as I please.' He gave me a look of reproach and horror, and murmuring, 'God have mercy upon you,' left the room.

CHAPTER XXI.

Mother and Hannah came late that same night. I had never seen mother cry as she did when she looked at Deborah and my two babies. She went first into one room and then into the other, sobbing as though her heart would break. Two days later we took them down home with us and laid them away in the old family burial lot, and the day after, Marjie and I went back to New Bedford. I was eager to get to work again, for there were heavy bills to pay and I had no one but myself to depend on to pay them. I clung to Marjie as though I could not bear her out of my sight. I lay awake nights to listen to her breathing. I was wild with anxiety lest something should happen to her. I worked night and day and spent my money freely in buying for her delicacies that she had never known the taste of before, and I sat and watched her eagerly while she ate them; it did my heart good to see her. I bought some beautiful white lace to make her a dress and a wide sash of crimson. I had her come to the shop every night after school and stay until 6 o'clock — the hour when I was free. Oh, I killed her with kindness, my one little white lamb. At the end of a week she was

stricken down with the dreadful fever. The doctor
— though he couldn't tell he was sending a knife
straight through my heart — said that she ought to
have been taking more simple nourishment, and
exercising more in the open air. Who can tell how
I felt when I heard him say that? He did all that
he possibly could do for her, for he loved her very
much. I did not leave her for one moment during
the week she was sick. She didn't seem to suffer
much, but she wanted me to sing to her continually.
The last night, after the doctor had gone, I closed
the bed-room door and knelt down beside the bed.
The doctor had told me with tears in his eyes, that
the end was not far off, and it seemed to me to be
very near indeed, as I knelt there, looking at her.
Her face was like marble, not one spot of color.
The long lashes rested on the soft cheeks, the pale,
dry lips were slightly parted, the little hands lay
quietly on her breast. I put my face down close to
her's, and said: 'Marjie, Marjie darling!' There
was no answer. I spoke three or four times, but if
she had been already dead she could not have been
more quiet. Then I threw myself down on the
floor and placing one of my hands on both of hers,
I prayed to God as I never had prayed before, and
as, thank Heaven! I never have prayed since. I
asked Him for the sake of His own beloved Son, to
spare my darling to me — the only one I had left
to live for. I prayed, I entreated, and then — God

forgive me! — I commanded Him to leave me my child. I promised, by the great love I bore her and by my hope for Eternity, that if He would do this, I would bring her up to love, fear, and serve Him all her life, and I would do the same myself. But if He took her from me I would never love Him and never serve Him. When I finished I kept my eyes on Marjie's face to watch for the change that my faith told me would come. It came. The great black eyes opened and looked at me. I sprang to my feet and bent over her — full of joy and thankfulness. ' Oh, thank God! thank God! He *is* good.' I cried. Then I said, Marjie darling, it's mamma; don't you know mamma?' She smiled and put up her little hand to stroke my cheek, but it fell again and all at once her eyes rolled up until I could see nothing but the whites. A dreadful look of pain passed across her face and she threw up both little hands in agony. But scarcely had I put my arms around her before it passed away and the most beautiful look I ever saw on anyone's face rested on hers. ' Little sis —' That was all, then her head sank heavily back against my shoulder and I was left alone. I know God has forgiven me for what I then did. I stood up and cursed Him, and swore I would never try to live a good life. Let me pass over the fearful days that followed. When I once more went back to the shop my old acquaintances scarcely knew me. I worked every minute to get money to pay to pay my bills, and, at the end of six months, I did not owe one cent. Then I commenced to associate with my shop-mates. I was still young — only twenty-seven — and I did not look that. I wore my hair in heavy curls down my back. I put red paint on my cheeks, which, with my naturally white skin made my complexion quite dazzling. I dressed in gay colors, went to parties and dances, and when I went home in the early morning, would take morphine tablets to put me to sleep. I never allowed myself to think — it would have driven me crazy. The same minister came to see me, but I said things to him that drove him from the house in horror, and he never entered it again. Emeline tried to talk with me, but I wouldn't listen to her, and in a little while she let me alone. At the end of two years word came to us that mother was dead. I washed the paint off my cheeks, made myself a black dress, and went down home to the funeral. Thankful and Mercy were both married, and to sailors. Hannah took Warren to live with her — the old home was sold, and the money divided among the children; then I went back to New Bedford and plunged once more into the gay life. Three more years passed. Thankful went on a voyage with her husband, and they never returned from it. I laughed when the news of the lost vessel reached us, and I said to Emeline : 'God seems to have a special grudge against this family. Wonder whose turn will come next!' Alas! it was Emeline who next went from us. She had always been the fragile one, and quick consumption claimed her at last for its prey. Her husband married again at the end of the year, and the family were as strangers to me. Three years more passed, and at the end of those three years Hannah and I were the only ones left out of that large, and, at one time, happy family. Hannah had a number of children and not any too much money. I was now thirty-five years old. I had had a number of offers of marriage, but I had refused them all. At last I met Mr. Hood. He was a poor book-keeper in one of the mill offices, and a good christian man. How he ever came to care for me I could never see, but he did. He met me at the home of a mutual friend where I used to call occasionally when I felt tired of my gay life. He asked me to marry him and I said' no'— although I cared a great deal for him, or would have done so had I allowed myself to, but I thought : 'If I care for him and marry him, he will only be one more to be taken from me, and I will not do it.' So I said 'no,' and went on. One night I went home from work tired almost to death. I opened the drawers that had not been opened for eight years, and looked at all the little clothes lying there. In the last one I opened

was the white lace dress, half finished, and the
crimson sash that I had bought for Marjorie. As
I looked at them, all at once my heart commenced
to swell, the tears rushed to my eyes. I laid my
head down on the dress and sobbed until all my
strength was gone and I fell asleep. Then I
dreamed the dream that saved my soul from everlasting death, and this was it: I dreamed that I was
dead and on my journey to my future home. I
thought that the three days when I was lying dead
my home were the three days that it took me to perform the journey. I passed through many scenes—
somewhat similar to those described by Elizabeth
Stuart Phelps in ' Beyond the Gates.' On the last
day of my journey I saw many people whom I
knew and whom I thought had died a little before
or on the same day that I did. They looked at
me and I looked at them, but we did not speak.
I could not help noticing the different expression
on the different faces. Our minister was there—
the one who had talked to me. He walked with
a firm, decided step, and his face wore an expression of proud triumph. He looked neither to the
right nor to the left, but kept straight on. Poor
Hester Norton kept as close to him as she could,
as though she was sure that he would get into
Heaven and she might slip in with him.' She was
a poor old woman, who had known what it was to
lose one dear one after another, but who had never

been heard to make a moan, or murmur against God's justice. But she had kept by herself, seldom going out anywhere — even to church. I could not help pitying her, as she hurried along, pale and breathless, trying in vain to keep up with the minister. At length her strength seemed to be giving out, and I heard her say sonething to him. He scarcely turned his head to look at her, as he said, sternly : ' I have no time to talk with you, now. You had many opportunities, while on earth, to listen to me, but you never availed yourself of them, and now it is too late. I must hurry on to meet my judge.' And in a few moments he was out of sight. The poor old woman sank down and covered her face with her hands. I put out my hand, as I passed her, and helped her to rise. She staggered for a moment, and I passed my arm about her. She thanked me, with tears in her eyes, and I stood there for a moment, holding her. Just then a man who had been walking back of us passed us. I could not see his face, for he kept his head turned, but, as he passed, he put out his hand and lightly touched, first Hester, and then myself, on the head ; then he passed on. I cannot begin to tell the effect his touch had upon me. In a second I felt as well and strong as though I had not taken one step and I felt Hester's bowed form straighten up in my arms. ' I can walk very well, now, dear,' she said, and so she did ;—walked just as firmly and upright as I did, and soon we were ahead of the others, and at every step we took, so far from growing tired, we seemed to grow stronger and stronger.   We caught up with the minister and as we passed him, we saw that the face he turned toward us was very white, and wore an expression of great exhaustion and pain.   He seemed about to speak to us but then stopped as though his pride would not allow him to ask assistance of one to whom he had refused his, but Hester stopped and said: .' Is there anything we can do for you?'   His pride gave way to his suffering then, aud he said with a moan, ' Oh it seems as though my head is burning up, and my eyes ache so I can scarcely see.   If there was only some water near.'   Hester left my side, saying :   ' I will look for some.'   We saw her go towards a large rock ; when she reached it she looked around it, then we saw her stoop, and in another moment she came toward us with a glass cup filled with water in her hand.   First she held the cup to the minister's lips, and though he drank long and eagerly, yet the water did not seem to diminish.   We neither of us seemed to wonder at this, but took it as a matter of course.   After he had satisfied his great thirst, Hester made him lie down on the grass, and sitting beside him, drew his head down in her lap, and bathed it with the water.   Almost immediately his eyes closed; the look of pain entirely passed away, and he slept.

It was then that I noticed the same man who had passed us when Hester was so tired, walking slowly along, a little way from where we had stopped. I know he had been watching us, but he turned his head so quickly, when I looked up, that, as before, I could not see his face. The minister slept so long that the rest of the travelers had caught up with us, by the time we were ready to move on. He said his head and eyes felt perfectly strong and well, but that he was still a little weak. I was about to offer the assistance of my arm although he had refused to recognize me in the least, during our whole journey, as one being too wicked for a righteous man to speak to, but Hester spoke before me. Almost against his will, it seemed, he accepted her support, and thus leaning on her and deriving his strength from her, he passed on, to stand before the Judgment Bar. It seemed as though a twilight atmosphere settled upon and around us, as we walked on. It was such a stillness as we used to feel on earth on some beautiful spring evening — just between daylight and dark, when the birds had all gone to their nests, and not a sound was heard. It filled us all with a deep calm, yet it seemed as though we scarcely dared to breathe — such a deep solemnity was all about us. Strange to say, the minister seemed the quietest of any, and as we approached nearer and nearer towards what we all felt to be the Judgment Hall, he

leaned more and more heavily upon Hester's arm.
All at once such a blinding light burst upon us
that it was too much for our eyes to bear, and we
all, with one accord, fell prostrate on the ground
and hid our faces. Then we heard a voice, stern,
yet full of a strange sweetness, say: 'Arise and
come forward.' We did as had been commanded
us, and, as we lifted our heads, the scene that
John describes in 'Revelations,' was before us.
The figure that sat on the throne was more beautiful than I can tell. It was clothed in a robe of
rich crimson and gold, and on the noble head was
a crown sparkling with the most precious stones.
The face was fair, the eyes a deep blue, and the
long, soft beard was of a beautiful golden-brown.
I noticed with surprise that while all of us found
it almost impossible to look up to this glorious
being, so dazzling was the light about him, Hester looked at him calmly and steadily, and her's
were the oldest eyes among us. One after another
was called up to take his place before the throne
and receive his sentence, and I noticed, as each
one turned away, their faces expressed either great
joy or deep woe. I thought when the minister
went forward he would be assigned a place among
the many standing about the throne, but what was
my surprise to see him turn, with his form bent, in
an agony of shame and humiliation, and pass slowly
out of sight. The words of condemnation that had

been spoken were spoken with deep sternness and I
trembled at the thought of what I must hear when
it came my turn to receive sentence. Hester went
next. As she knelt before the throne, He who sat
in the chair leaned over, and with His own royal
hands, raised her from the ground, and in the
sweetest voice I had ever heard or dreamed of,
said: 'Thou good and faithful servant. Enter
now into the joy of thy Lord.' He cast over her a
robe of snowy whiteness, that one standing near,
gave to Him, and on her head he put a plain gold
crown. Taking His own crown off, He took from
it a pearl of great size and beauty, and placed it in
Hester's. 'Stand at my right hand, for thou art
one of my well-beloved,' He said. It was now my
turn to go forward, and I did so, my knees trembling under me so that I could scarcely walk. I
did not dare to look into His face as I bowed myself
before Him, when, wonder of wonders, I felt myself raised so firmly, yet so tenderly, that I burst
into tears of joy and wonder, and cried: 'Lord,
have mercy upon me a sinner.' 'My poor, wandering child,' he said, in a voice like music, 'Come
with me.' Like a flash, the scene changed. The
great white throne had disappeared, and all the
beautiful dazzling forms. I found myself walking
slowly along through the same twilight atmosphere
that I had walked through but a short time before,
only now, as I walked, I could hear the low, sweet

call of the birds; I could hear the gentle babbling of brooks, and could smell the fragrant rose, lily and heliotrope. I lifted my eyes timidly to Him who walked beside me, and instead of the robe of crimson and gold, I saw he had on one of white. There was no crown upon His head, but oh, the sweetness of the beautiful face. The sternness of the Judge was lost in the love and pity of the Father. I could not forbear nestling close to Him, and timidly resting my head upon His arm. He gazed down upon me with eyes full of love, but He gently put me away from Him. 'Sometime, my daughter, but not now. Thou hast not proven thyself worthy. I can never express the feeling of sorrowful humiliation that I felt when I heard those words, but my heart took courage at the word 'sometime.' I realized, all at once, that He who walked beside me and He who had given Hester and I strength on our journey, were one and the same. By and by we came to a small hill, or knoll. The grass on this knoll was of the softest green, and felt like velvet to my feet. Dotted all over it were lilies of the valley and heliotrope — their fragrance filled all the air around. Before us there spread a level plain, and as I first looked at this, not a thing seemed to be on it, but presently I saw figures moving here and there. By and by I could recognize some of them as my fellow-travellers, and as I spoke the name of each one, my companion told me what the future of that one was to be. The first one I mentioned was Leta Randolph. When on earth she had been one of the most active members in the church. She had been the organist, and had also been the teacher of a large class of little girls. She used to talk beautifully in prayer-meeting, almost always bringing tears to the eyes of those who listened to her. She was the daughter of wealthy parents and very beautiful. Her beauty had always been heightened by costly and becoming garments, but she always gave liberally to the poor. I was thus surprised to see her moving among some people who looked very poor and some very wretched. I noticed two or three cripples among them, and the expressions of their faces was sullen and fretful. Leta passed among them dressed in a simple dark dress. She seemed to be speaking to each one soothingly, but nearly all turned away their heads — some with careless indifference, others fretfully and angrily. I could see that Leta was greatly troubled, and every once in a while she would bow her head on her hands in prayer. I turned to my companion and He answered the question in my eyes. ' She whom you see working among those poor people is one who, while on earth, only labored for the praise of the world. Everything she did, instead of doing it all to the glory of Him who reigns in heaven, she

did to her own. The praise and admiration of the
world was very dear to her, and to win it and
keep it, she worked hard and long. The world
did not see this, but He who reads the heart like
an open book, saw it and was displeased. The
people you see with her, are the children grown
to women, whom she taught while on earth. You
see the result of her teaching — not one conversion
among them. God does not bless such labors.
While in the world she labored for the praise of the
world and received it. There, she is to go on with
her work, unseen by any mortal eyes, and not
until she has performed the work entirely, will
she be allowed to receive her reward — that of
beholding the Father and living with Him in
His kingdom — one of His well-beloved. She
knows this, and she knows that her work will
be much harder here than while on earth, for
there will be none to praise her, and the hearts she
is wrestling with now, have grown hard and bitter
with the trials and disappointments of life. But if
she proves faithful, her reward will be great.' I
ventured to ask : ' Will it take her long to perform
this work?' ' Many long and weary years,' he
replied. ' But the last of them will be made lighter,
and sweeter, by seeing some of her people giving
their hearts to the Saviour.'

CHAPTER XXII.

The next name I mentioned was that of Laura Barton. She had been, while on earth, one of the most earnest workers in the Baptist Church. Everyone knew that she tried to live a good life, but even her own pastor was forced to admit that she made her religion a bug-bear to herself, and to everyone else. Her doctrine was: 'Heaven and eternal happiness to all those who come forward, acknowledge themselves as great sinners before the world, repent of their sins and be baptized; or, hell and everlasting punishment to all those who refuse to do this.' No denomination on earth was right except her own; all others were in danger of hell's fire. And she believed in the literal burning lake. No wonder she frightened timid ones with the force of her argument, and made the Saviour appear to them nothing more than a stern condemning judge; one who took pleasure in the punishment of the wicked. I saw that she was walking with her head bent down over the Holy Bible, which she held in her hands, and there was an expression of much doubt and perplexity on her face. Occasionally she would raise her eyes towards the sky and her lips would move in prayer,

then she would again cast them down upon her book.
She turned the leaves hurriedly and seemed to be
searching anxiously, first one passage of scripture
and then another, but all the time I looked, the expression of her face never changed. As I looked
into my companion's face I noticed that it wore an
expression of deep pity, and his voice was sad as
he said: 'Yonder walks a poor, misguided child.'
'She was one of the most zealous workers in her
church,' I ventured to say. He looked at me
reprovingly. 'I know all things, child. She
sinned most, wherein she wished to be most faithful. Such was her anxiety to lead, and to be
thought to lead, a true christian life, that she carried her ambition too far. She put herself before
God. She said 'I,' when she ought to have said
'He.' When she spoke to you in the prayer-
room, she said: 'I *am* a Christian;' meaning, 'I
am Christ-like,' when she ought to have said: 'I
am *trying* to be a christian.' She proved herself
hard and unforgiving towards those who often went
astray, when the Saviour himself forgave. She
preached hell and hell's-fire to all those who did
not believe as she did, when the Saviour says:
'Come unto me, *all* ye who are weary and heavy-
laden, and I will give you rest.' '*Whosoever* will,
let him come.' He also says: 'Repent and be
baptized.' Baptized with the Holy Spirit. Bap-
tism by water is right; and blessed are they who

do truly repent and are baptized both by the Holy Spirit and by the water as well. It is a sign — an outward form, but that is all. It is not the *form* that saves; it is the *spirit*.' ' I say : 'More blessed is he that comes to the Saviour with the prayer : ' God have mercy on me, a sinner,' faltering on his lips, if there is deep repentance in his heart, than the most cultured divine that ever preached from earthly pulpit, if he puts his own doctrines before those of his God. And again, I say, *I know all things*. Every heart is open to me, and I see it as it is. I shall not judge as the world judges. Many things that are wrong there, shall be made right, here. Those who are first, there, shall be last, here. Those who are meeting with deep injustice there, to them shall most heavenly justice be accorded, and they will be more than repaid. They have only to be faithful for a little while, and then come home to their reward. The poor child walking there will surely pass from her state of doubt and perplexity into the land of light, *some day*, but first she must read aright the Book that is to lead her there.' ' But *is* there no hell, a burning lake of fire ? ' He smiled down into my anxious eyes. ' There is a place of punishment for all those who refuse to believe in the Saviour and those who blaspheme His name, and it is truly a hell — a place of torment — but there is no burning lake of fire. I will show it to you

presently.' 'Why! there is Mr. Kenyon!' I exclaimed. 'And what has he on his back?' Mr.
Kenyon was the wealthiest man in New Bedford.
He was a member of the Episcopal Church and a
good man. He had given his money towards the
building of churches and reform houses. He had
always contributed largely towards the Missionary
funds. He had helped many poor families. I had
always said that if there was a heaven, Mr. Kenyon
would certainly go to it; and here he was among
the outcasts — outcasts for a time — moving slowly
and wearily along, his back bent beneath a heavy
load. Even as I spoke, he turned, and I saw,
written upon the bag, in flaming letters, 'Gold!'
I saw that his pockets were weighed down with
the same precious metal, and that at every step he
took he stumbled upon it so that he could scarcely
get one step ahead. His road to heaven was
blocked by the very gold that he had worked so
hard for, and had enjoyed working for. I saw
him hold out whole handfuls of it to different ones,
as they passed, but each one refused it scornfully.
As Laura Barton passed him, he tried to force the
gold upon her, but she rejected it with impatient
words that I heard plainly. 'No, no; keep your
gold. We do not need it here. It will not buy
the only thing we crave for — light, light, light!'
and she passed on. I looked to my companion.
'Was he not a sincere christian?' I asked. 'He

meant to be, but he loved his gold *first*. After
listening to the minister whom he helped so liberally to pay, he would go home and look over his
bank books, and the first thing he would ask for
in his prayers — his *heart* prayers, which only I
heard — was that his money might not be taken
from him.   He said that he wanted it for the good
that he might do with it; but I read his heart
aright.'   'But,' I said, 'he did do good — much
good — with his money.'   'And received his
reward on earth,' was the answer, sternly
spoken.   'The *heart* must be right, my child.
The Father must be first with all his children.
That poor man will one day see the Father, but
he must first rid himself of the gold.'   'But how
can he do that ?   No one will .take it.'   I
was sorry, the moment I had asked the foolish
question, and did not need the rebuke that came, to
make me hang my head.   'With Me, all things
are possible.'   *   *   *   There was a woman moving along, her form bent over as though she were
picking up something from the ground.   I watched
her quite a while in silence, but not once did she
raise herself.   At last she turned to come towards
us, still picking as she came and not once lifting
her eyes, and I saw that it was Margaret Huntley
— a woman who had always been considered a
good woman, but who had always been a little
inclined to gossip about her neighbors.   Not that

anyone had ever heard her say anything that could possibly hurt anyone. In fact, I had never heard her say anything outright about anyone, only *hint*, and ask if anyone had heard so and so about this one and that one, and immediately after, I have heard her speak highly of the very one about whom she had been asking questions, when someone else had been saying hateful things about her. I had always admired her and seen nothing evil about her. Why was she in this painful position? It seemed to me that her task was the hardest of any. My companion spoke and his voice was stern. 'Yonder woman is picking up the seeds she has sown by the wayside. She will have much to do for the seeds were scattered and have taken root and spread greatly.' I did not understand and He explained in the simple language He had used during our whole conversation. 'She never said anything outright about anyone, for she had too much respect for her reputation, but she committed the greater sin of the two — that of implying wrong. By her gentle hints and seemingly innocent questions, she would raise doubts and surmises in the hearts of her companions, inducing them to think and speak wrongly of absent ones. When the flame had fairly started, so far from extinguishing it, she but fanned it into fuller blaze, by loud protestations of the absent one's innocence. That was so people would think well of her — as one who never would believe ill of anyone but always spoke well of everybody. But she is the one at whose door lies the sin. She sowed the seed, and not until they are all gathered shall she see the Kingdom of Heaven. It will be a long and weary work. But look yonder, and see the last figure you are destined to see, now, although there are many, many more working their way to Heaven.' I looked in the direction He pointed, and saw coming towards us, the familiar form of our minister. When he reached a certain spot, which I noticed was hard and most uncomfortable looking, he cast himself down on his knees and bowing his head on his clasped hands, remained motionless as though in prayer. Soon I saw his bowed form writhe as though in agony, but although I watched him for some little time — now kneeling motionless, and now writhing and twisting — yet he never once raised his head. The sight was so painful I turned my eyes away. ' He sees, passing before him, forms of those he might have saved, but did not.' I understood full well, what the low, sternly spoken words meant, and asked no questions. I wondered if the minister saw me, as I had been, in my wretched, hopeless condition, and if the sight added any to his agony. Wrongly though he had judged me, yet I for-gave him fully, as I witnessed his terrible suffer-ing, and pitied him from the bottom of my soul. ' Only the prayers of those whom he condemned, but who are even now repenting and trying to live good lives, can save him. His was the most unpardonable sin of all, for he was an acknowledged representative of God, and preached the Word falsely.' As He spoke the last word, the scene faded from my eyes, and in its place appeared a sight that seemed to freeze the blood within my veins. I cannot describe it. No one on earth could. It was the place of torment. A dark, murky, chilly place, where the sun never shone by day, nor the moon and stars by night, but over which seemed to hang a thick, heavy, black substance—like a pall. Wretched creatures, murderers, skeptics, blasphemers, were all huddled together, and their groans were something terrible to hear. Most of them were in the same position that the minister had been in—writhing and twisting in an agony of remorse. Too late! Never would their conscience be lightened. Never would the darkness be dispersed by the light of God's countenance shining upon it. They had not repented before death, and their punishment would be everlasting. 'Had they murmured but one prayer in their hearts to me, even at the eleventh hour, then might they one day have been of my Kingdom, but they died blaspheming me, and their punishment will be everlasting.' And this was the most dreadful punishment that could have been thought of. Not even the literal lake of fire

could have been worse. The agony of remorse!
I asked, though my teeth fairly chattered in my
head as I spoke, 'Do their friends — those who
loved them, and who always lived good lives —
know they are here?' 'No, and they never will.
When they reach the place of eternal happiness
all tears shall be wiped from their eyes. Everything that could make them sad, while on earth,
shall be forgotten there, and they shall be at rest.'
Only one more question I asked. 'Have you no
love for these miserable creatures?' 'No. They
rejected it when I begged them to take it, and now
it is too late. I dwell with the redeemed, and with
them misery is unknown. Come! we will look on
them.' My eyes closed for a second, and then
opened on a sight — the very thought of which
fills me with an uncontrollable longing to see once
more. Oh, such a beautiful country! All light,
and joy and music. A country of green hills,
pleasant valleys, running brooks, beautiful flowers,
singing birds, happy, loving men and women,
laughing, playing children, and over all a light
that would soothe tired eyes and banish head-ache
forevermore — the light of the Father's tender presence. I stood and drew deep breaths of delight.
I could not speak — I could only look. There
were whole families grouped together, yet all
seemed to love one another with equal love.
There walked a girl and the man who had been

her affianced husband when on earth, but who had died the week before their marriage would have taken place, walking along, side by side and arm in arm, looking into each other's face and laughing at each other's talk. There was a mother and son walking the same way together, only his arm was about her, and her face, which had been such a pale and sad one on earth, was lifted constantly to his, and was now full of a rest and peace indescribable. In them I recognized two who had been very dear to each other on earth, but the son had died, and, because he had not been a professing christian — though a most worthy young man — the people had doubted much about his being saved. Only the mother had felt sure that she would one day meet her boy again in Heaven. Laura Barton had been the loudest in the expression of her doubts, and he was where she had been so sure of going. As I saw that mother's face, I felt like bowing down and worshipping Him whose Love and Justice are so great. * * * But there was one whom I knew well — my fellow-traveler, Hester Norton. Her form was straight, her eye bright, her step quick and sure. She moved about, smiling and saying cheerful words to all. Young girls and young men gathered about her to listen to her words of sweet wisdom. Little children climbed upon her knee. Her life seemed full of work — yet, it was such sweet, joyful work — work that never tired. * * * But there was a group, the sight of which made my heart beat fast. All the dear ones of my childhood's home — grouped together and talking and laughing. My tears were falling fast, but they did not keep me from seeing the two I had loved best — Deborah and Jo — walk away from the others, arm in arm ; and they did not keep me from seeing how firmly and easily Jo walked, and the fairness and the smoothness of his beautiful skin and the bright blue of his eyes ; and they did not keep me from seeing mother's happy, contented look as she watched them move away. I *could* not call them back — I did not try to — I only watched them silently for a long while, with my tears falling fast, and wished that I were with them. * * * But then I saw a woman bending over a baby she held in her arms, and the sight made my mother's heart leap in my bosom. I looked hurriedly around for *my* little ones, and then I felt a hand laid lightly on my arm and I looked up. Oh, the look on the Master's face as He watched His people ! I would have given my life then for one such look for me. He pointed, and I followed his gaze. Oh, most gracious God ! There were my darlings coming towards me, hand in hand — Marjorie, Lillis and Hope — Marjie was in the middle and held a hand of each. It seemed as though all the children had been having a frolic of some kind, and they had crowned Marjie queen, for on her dark curls rested a wreath of the most beautiful roses, and a garland of them was thrown around one shoulder and fastened at her side. Her dress was like all the others — snowy white and of a thin material. They all three panted a little, as children do, when they have been running, and when they reached a mossy bank, that was all studded with violets and the fragrant arbutus, they threw themselves down upon it and sat there, with their arms around each other. When the other children caught sight of them, they ran with a shout to join them, and forming a ring, they danced around them, singing and laughing. I watched them with strained eyes and hands tightly clasped. 'Oh, my darlings,' I kept moaning. 'Let me go to them. Let me go.' In a little while the children drew near the group, standing about Hester, and I noticed that as they passed the woman leaning over her baby, Marjie looked back at her over her shoulder—as I thought, wistfully. My heart almost burst. I threw myself down at the Master's feet and raised my clasped hands. 'She wants me. My Marjie wants her mamma. Let me go for only one moment?' He stooped down and raised me with infinite tenderness. 'Stay here, my child,' was all he said. In another moment He was among them. And then, such a burst of Heavenly music! I could hear the grand tones of the church organ, the sweet, plaintive

notes of the harp, and a chorus of glorious voices.
Then the music ceased and I saw them all kneeling
with bowed heads, and He standing among them
with lifted hand. Then they all rose and clustered
around Him, and He had a word for all. All at
once it seemed as if the vast multitude separated,
and then I saw Him standing with Marjie in His
arms and the other children clinging to Him.
Marjie's little white face was pressed against His,
and her arm was about His neck. I thought my
heart would break. 'Marjie,' I called. 'Here is
mamma, Marjie darling. Here I am up here.
Oh, come to me, my darling. Have you forgotten mamma, Marjie?' But she did not hear
my human voice, and I sank down in despair.
Then He stood beside me once more. 'Your darlings are safe — forevermore. They are of my
dearly-beloved. Would you be with them?' 'Oh,
yes, yes, my dear Lord and Master!' I cried.

'There is only one way.'

I looked up through my streaming tears. 'Repent.' 'I do, I do; oh, have mercy, Lord.'
'When you return to earth, acknowledge Me before the world and keep My commandments. Live
a good, true, upright life; work for the Master in
every way you can. Be much in prayer; help on
the work of God and do it all in His name and to
His glory, and yours shall be the Kingdom of
Heaven.' 'I will, I will!' I cried; and such

was my anxiety to be gone and commence this work, that I might some day be with my darlings, that I tried to run — stumbled and fell. He raised me gently. ' So you will fall at every attempt you make to go ahead in your own strength,' He said, with gentle reproof. As I looked up into His face, I saw it was overspread with a look of sadness. ' You promise me, my child ? ' ' Yes, Father.' ' And you will do this — for what ? ' ' That I may one day be with my darlings.' I blurted this answer out and then could have pulled my tongue out by the roots for wounding the great, unselfish heart. Before I could stammer out my regret He stood, changed, before me. On His head was a crown of sharp thorns that pierced the tender flesh so that great drops of blood trickled down His face and stained His white robe. He held His hands out before me and I saw the cruel nail prints. I saw the wound in His side and the prints in His feet, and as I looked into His face and saw the look of pain and anguish upon it, such a wave of love and pity filled my heart, as to almost overflow it. I knelt down and tried to dry the blood on His feet with my dress, sobbing as I did so. Then, when I thought I could bear no more, a shadow fell across Him and I saw it take the form of a cross. Even as I looked He stood, nailed to it before me, and I heard His dear voice. ' For *thy* sake, my child.' I gave a great cry.

'For *Thy* dear sake, oh Lord.' All thoughts of earthly dear ones vanished. Then, and ever after, it has been my Saviour first. * * * The cry I gave woke me. I was lying on the floor. The room was dark, but the light from a lamp outside, shining in, showed me the open drawers before me, and the tumbled clothes. I still held Marjie's dress close to me. I bowed my face upon it, and then and there made a vow in my heart to love and serve my Master as long as life should last, and to trust Him through everything. It was something more than a dream I had had — it was a warning. I had full faith in it. I believe things will be just as they were shown to me. I believe Heaven is just such a place as I saw it in my vision. My earnest desire is, and has been ever since that night, to live just as near right as I know how. I saw the wisdom and love of my Heavenly Father in taking my darlings from me when they were pure and sinless — fit for the Kingdom of Heaven. Had they lived, what might their lives not have been? To which of the other places I looked upon, might they not have gone to? But now I know that they are safe. 'Safe in the arms of Jesus.'"

CHAPTER XXIII.

That same evening finds our girls in their room, each one in a state of some little excitement. Jess tries in vain to braid her heavy hair smoothly, but it will wrap and twist itself around the small fingers — all she can do — and at last her small stock of patience gives out, and she throws herself down in a chair with something that sounds very much like, "Gosh take the old thing, anyway."

Garnet looks over to her with a displeased frown, but at sight of the little face looking so miserable, from out the heavy mass of dark hair falling around it, the frown changes to an encouraging smile, and she leaves her own work to help her sister. "Let me do your hair for you, Jess," she says. Then, as she lifts the great coils, "Dear me, you poor child; I don't wonder you can't do anything with such a mess. I've a good mind to cut some of it off — you'd never miss it."

"Do if you dare," muttered Jessie, who never combs it without, herself, threatening to cut it every bit off.

"Jess won't have so much hair when she gets older," says Vera, giving her own golden crown a parting pat. "I used to have as much as she has, but it has come out dreadfully."

"Hh! Hear old Granny," said Jessie. "How old are you anyway, Vera?" "Five years older than you, Miss," answered Vera, calmly.

"I don't think there is much danger of Jessie's ever being bald," gasped poor Garnet, who was being forced up on her tip-toes in her endeavors to get Jessie's hair all combed up smoothly on the top of her head. "I never saw such a mop."

"Ow-w-w! Well, for conscience sake, don't pull every hair of it out by the roots," cried Jessie, making up a most hideous face, and raising both hands to her head. "Ow-w-w! Drop that comb, Net Dare. Don't you touch my head again. Do you suppose my scalp is made of sheet-iron? Oh, you've killed me!"

"Seems to me you're a pretty lively corpse. That's all the thanks one gets for trying to help," said Garnet, obeying orders and going back to her own work. "You're chief virtue isn't gratitude; that's one sure thing, Jessie."

"Well, for pity's sake, isn't it enough to make an angel lose patience to have one's head tortured in that way?" said Jessie, sorry, but still agrieved. "And I'm no angel."

"Amen," said Garnet, emphatically.

"Let me try being lady's-maid," said Allie, looking calm and sweet, in her pretty, cream dress, with her smooth brown hair and fair face.

"Well, thank you," said Jessie. "But never mind about trying to get it on top of my head, Al. I've suffered enough for one night. Just braid it in one braid, and I'll wear it down my back in a pig-tail."

"You'll look about ten years old," said Garnet, beginning to brush her own curls vigorously.

"Don't care if I look five," retorted Jessie, smartly. "I shan't see anyone I care anything about, and I'm going in for comfort."

At last they were ready to go down stairs. "My sake! but my heart is going forty miles an hour," said Jessie, as they went down the stairs. "I feel as nervous as though I was going to be hung."

"Nothing to feel nervous about," said Vera. "It's only a little fun. There are the boys — they have just knocked."

Fred entered, with his merry face drawn down to its utmost length, and with an expression partly of fear and partly of solemnity upon it. Bowing very gravely to the girls, he walked with slow and solemn steps over to the lounge and sat down in one corner of it, with his shoulders drawn up, and his hands clasped between his knees.

"What's the matter with the silly thing, any way?" asked Jessie, scornfully. "Anybody would think he had come to a funeral."

"I pray that it may not be so," said Fred, in hollow tones. "But I fear — I fear." And his teeth chattered, and his eyes rolled wildly.

Just then the professor's step was heard outside.

"Hide me; hide me!" gasped Fred, rolling off the lounge and beginning to crawl under it.

"That's no go, Fred," said Erfort. "There won't be room under there for the whole of you. He'll be sure to see —"

But he was interrupted by gasps and gurglings from under the lounge, and Fred's feet were seen to be in a state of violent agitation. They were the only part of him to be seen.

"What's the matter?" asked Erfort. "Got stuck?"

Something that sounded like "Ga, ga, gla," was the answer.

"Shall I pull you out?"

"Ges."

Erfort stooped and took hold of the feet, and, after a few grunts and groans from Fred, drew him out. They all burst into a merry laugh at the sight he presented. Covered with dust from head to foot! It was in his eyes, his ears, his mouth, his hair. It clung to his neat evening suit. His white collars and cuffs were powdered with it. The laugh grew louder as he sat up on the floor, with an expression of intense disgust on his handsome face. Erfort took an umbrella that stood in the corner, and, standing the length of it away from Fred, offered him the handle of it.

"You'll excuse my not coming any nearer, dear chappie," he said. "But really —"

"Good evening, all," said a voice behind them, and Professor Wild came into the room.

Fred grasped the umbrella and scrambled to his feet. To say that he glared at the professor is a mild way of putting it; then, with one reproachful look into Vera's laughing eyes, he hurried from the room. Erfort excused himself and followed him.

"Serves him right for getting you into that scrape last night," whispered Jessie to Vera.

"You seem to have commenced the evening very pleasantly," said the professor, taking the chair Garnet offered him. "Was Mr. Travers performing for the amusement of the company?"

Although he smiled as he said this, Vera did not like the tone of his voice, and she did not answer, although he had looked at her as he asked the question.

"Fred is splendid company," replies the staunch Jessie; and she wonders why Vera gives her such a grateful look.

"Oh, I do not doubt it," the professor hastens to say. "He is your cousin, isn't he?" There is a slight slur on the last words.

"Yes. But that isn't the reason I said he was splendid company," flashes Jessie, and Garnet, almost trembling at what may come next, hastens to interpose.

"You don't know with what pleasure we have all looked forward to this evening, Professor Wild.

We expect, before the close of it, to be much en-lightened as to our various virtues, qualifications, etc."

" She's scared half out of her wits," says Jessie to Vera, sotto voce. Aloud she asks, suddenly, " Can you mesmerize, professor ? "

" Yes," replies the professor, much to the girls' surprise. " Why do you ask ? "

" Oh, I thought you looked as though you did,' was the rather alarming answer. " Will you try to mesmerize me ? "

" With pleasure."

He rises from his chair, as he speaks, and ap-proaches Jessie in her rocker. Garnet gives a little gasp, but does not speak. She knows it will do no good. Vera's white hands clasp each other tightly. She tries to laugh, but cannot. Allie says, faintly : "Oh, Jess !" but Jessie herself sits up straight in her chair and looks up steadily into the professor's eyes. He stands before her, tall and gaunt looking. Vera cannot bear the looks of his face ; it is pale, and, it seems to her, cruel looking. She wishes Jessie had not said anything. " The child is as nervous as a little witch," she thought. " But she has too much spirit to let him see it."

" Look steadily into my eyes," the professor says gravely, and the big black eyes look into his.

Then his great hand begins to move slowly to and fro before the little, brilliant face. Slowly, but surely the brilliancy dies out — drawn out by something in the man's gaze. The big black eyes look up just as steadily into his, but there is a startled, frightened look in them now, and the little face is as pale as death.

Garnet cannot bear it. She rushes forward and seizes the professor's arm, just as Jessie, with a little gasp, throws up both hands and bursts into a violent fit of sobbing. In the midst of it, the boys walk in.

" Rehearsing from ' William?'" asks Fred.

And no wonder he asks it, for the scene is tragic enough to warrant such a question.

The professor stands with one arm, which Garnet grasps with both hands, uplifted. Allie is kneeling on the floor beside Jessie, who is lying in Vera's arms, sobbing as though her heart would break.

Erfort walks straight up to the group, and in doing so, " breaks up the effect," as Fred said, afterward.

" What's the matter ? " he demanded.

Garnet lets go of the arm she held, Allie struggles to her feet, and Jessie sobs out, half angry, half laughing.

" Oh nothing, only I've been making a simpleton of myself — for a change."

Then they all laugh, Jessie dries her tears and sits up in her chair ; but she won't look at the professor, who is eyeing her in a half scornful, half amused and wholly triumphant manner. Fred comes forward and stands looking at her, with his hands in his pockets.

" Been getting mesmerized ? " he asks, elegantly.

His voice expresses the liveliest sympathy, but Jessie doesn't appreciate it.

" Shut up," is the answer that slightly staggers him.

But he understands his little cousin well enough by this time to know that " her bark is worse than her bite." " No; but have you, Jess ? " he asks.

"Yes, I have; if that's any comfort to you. Don't you want to try it?"

" Yes I do."

The professor comes forward, very obligingly. I think he is very glad for the chance. Fred looks at him defiantly.

" Shall I sit or stand ? " he asks.

" Either. You choose," is the answer.

" Then I'll stand."

Once more the large hand begins its mesmeric movement. The boyish handsome face and the pale, cruel-looking one, are close together. The dark blue eyes look bravely into the unmatched ones. The girls almost hold their breath and watch. Erfort looks on with disgust and disapproval written plainly on his face. By and by all see that the color is leaving Fred's face just as it had left Jessie's. The blue eyes commence to move unsteadily and look dim. There is a startled, uncertain, strange look on his face. The professor is getting excited. His subject is coming under his control just as he would best like to have him. The perspiration stands out on his face. Without once removing his eyes from Fred's, he throws back his coat and lets it slip to the floor, then he passes his hands more and more rapidly before Fred's eyes.

All expression is gone now from Fred's face. The eyes are dull and dreamy looking — he appears as though half asleep. The professor sees that his time has come.

"What is your name?" he asks.

The pale lips move once or twice and then the answer comes, stammeringly, but clearly:

"F-f-red."

"Where do you live?"

"B-b-oston."

"What is your business — your work?"

"C-c-lerk."

"What kind of a clerk?"

"Invoice and shipping clerk." The answer came unhesitatingly, now.

"On what street do you live?"

"Tremont street."

"How many in your family?"

" Four."

" Who are they ? "

" Father, mother, sister and myself."

" Are you engaged to be married ? "

" No."

" Do you care for anyone ? "

" Yes."

" Who is it ? "

But before Fred can answer, Erfort steps quickly forward and takes hold of the moving hand.

" That will do, professor," he says, gravely. " You are going too far."

Fred had certainly commenced to speak the word 'Vera,' but, as the hand stopped moving before his face, his voice stopped and the dreamy look commenced to leave his eyes. The professor saw this and clapped his hands softly, once or twice, close to Fred's face, then shook him slightly. Fred at once gave a slight shiver, yawned, stretched out his arms, as though just awaking, closed his eyes, and then opened them suddenly, and looked around the room with a wondering, surprised look.

It didn't take him long to realize what had been taking place. Thoroughly ashamed and confused, he excused himself and went out on the piazza. Vera happened to look at Garnet. Her face almost frightened her. There was scarcely a particle of color in it. She looked intensely eager.

"She believes that man has power to do with people as he pleases. She won't believe that it is simply the influence of a strong mind over a weaker one. Merely a matter of will-power. I'll prove it to her — it is my duty."

Thus Vera talked with herself. Aloud, she said:

"Will you try *me*, professor?"

Fairly elated with his former successes, the professor hastily says:

"Certainly, Miss Earle."

She brings her chair forward to the light and sits facing him. He looks down into the fair, proud face, and, as he reads the determination written upon it, he presses his lips closely together, and his eyes look angry.

Vera sees this, and laughs to herself. "Mesmerize *me*, if you can," her eyes say plainly.

The professor begins. Fred sees them through the window and comes in quietly. Two or three minutes pass without a sound being heard in the room. The professor begins to get nervous. He stoops down until his face is so close to Vera's that she can feel his breath, but still she looks into his eyes calmly and fearlessly; the mocking smile still rests on her lips, but she has to bring all the will-power she possesses to bear against his. Once or twice she feels a dreamy sensation stealing over her, but the sudden, eager look that springs into the professor's eyes brings her to herself and she is determined she *will not* yield.

Five minutes pass — it seems an hour. The professor loses sufficient control of himself to allow a look of impatient rage to appear on his face. Vera sees it and she laughs aloud. That ends it. The professor rises to his feet with a muttered exclamation.

"Simply a question of will-power, professor," says Vera, gayly, fully repaid for her little "inconvenience" by seeing Garnet look thoroughly disappointed — not to say disgusted.

"You were determined *not* to. You wouldn't put your mind on what I was doing," said the professor, trying to conceal his chagrin by speaking pleasantly.

"Ah, you confirm what I say," said Vera. "Confess now; there is no secret about it. Simply the influence of a strong mind over a weaker one."

Her will certainly proved itself stronger than his, for she forced the truth from him.

"That is the whole secret," he said; and no one but Vera heard the soft sigh that expressed Garnet's deep disappointment.

And it was the only way in which it was ever expressed.

"Well," remarked Jessie, who had been listening and watching with her big eyes growing bigger every minute. "All I can say is, that it makes 'he of the weaker mind,' feel decidedly queer, and when he comes to himself, decidedly silly. Hey Fred?"

But Fred is feeling "too full for utterance." He can't see the joke. To make a simpleton of himself twice in the same evening! And for *her* to laugh at him in the way she was laughing! It was too bad. Surely the fates were against him that night. "And all on account of that long-shanks!" he said to himself, spitefully; and was boy enough to make up a hideous face at the professor's back. Erfort caught him at it and nearly betrayed him with a laugh.

"Well now," says Jessie, settling herself comfortably back in her chair, "if success and defeat have not taken all your strength away, professor, will you examine our heads and tell us what our various pianos signify?"

She has quite regained her usual cheerful spirits and is all ready and eager for more fun.

If the professor has no other virtue, he certainly has an over-abundance of that commonly called obligingness. He is at their command at once.

"Who will be first?" he asks.

"Oh, take Vera first," says Jessie, unselfishly. "She's the strong-minded one."

"I shall have to ask you to undo your hair," says the professor.

Vera, blushing, takes out the pins and the beautiful golden mass falls over her shoulders, down to her waist. The professor looks at it admiringly.

"You have beautiful hair," he says, in a perfectly gentlemanly manner, but Fred glares at him savagely.

"I must tell you at the start," says the professor, standing with a hand touching lightly each side of Vera's head, "that there is no sham about phrenology. What I will tell you will be the truth, and nothing but the truth." This is what he told Vera, word for word: — "Mental power predominates. You have great respect for old age and religion. You are stubborn, not easily driven. You would make a splendid teacher, elocutionist, or actress. You are rather skeptical, and cautious; would advise you to get over that. You are a good entertainer and have great imitative powers. The conjugal organ is not very fully developed. I would not advise you to marry very early in life, as you are very liable to grow tired of your husband. (here Fred looks murderous). If you undertake to do a thing you will accomplish it, if it is a possible thing. You can make many acquaintances, but few friends. Anyone coming in contact with you, or having the benefit of your society, could not help feeling great affection for you. If one appealed to your benevolence, you might be easily led, but if one attempted to drive you, they would find it hard work. You can write more easily between the hours of midnight and morning — your thoughts come faster."

All looked deeply interested as the professor ceased, and Vera commenced, with Garnet's help, to do up her hair.

"There is no nonsense about that," said Erfort, heartily, and the professor smiled in a pleased way.

Jessie's turn came next. He told her what she longed to hear, that she had rare elocutionary powers, and if she persevered there was no reason why she would not, one day be a first-class elocutionist. The child's eyes shone like stars as she rose from the chair to give place to Allie.

He told Allie but little more than he had told her the night before, but she was pleased. Then came Garnet.

Vera was decidedly nervous, now. What would the professor say! This is what he said:

"Your organ of discretion is very largely developed. You would be a safe person to trust a great secret with, for you would allow all manner of evil things to be said about you before you would betray a friend's confidence. You are of a dreamy, though deep nature. Not being able to hold personal intercourse with great men, you do the next best thing — read their thoughts, through their works. Such a man as Emerson is your ideal. You are one who can suffer in silence. People call you indifferent because you do not carry your heart on your sleeve. You will always be a great thinker, but you will never do anything remarkable to make yourself known outside your own circle of acquaintances. You are too easily discouraged. You cannot sympathize with the ordinary man and woman of to-day — they weary you. You want something higher, nobler, loftier, but you will never reach the standard of living that you would be glad to reach, for, instead of working, you will only think, and dream and read, and long. But even this will bring you much pleasure — a pleasure such as only deep natures like your's can enjoy. There is one thing that I must warn you against. Do not encourage any inclination you may have to believe in the supernatural. Let such things as spiritualism, mesmerism, palmistry and all other nonsense alone. To such a person as you, indulgence in these beliefs would prove fatal. It would bring you great unhappiness, and I tell you candidly, there is no truth in them. Take a leaf from your friend's book and be more matter-of-fact and less romantic."

The professor bowed towards Vera, when he gave this bit of advice. Garnet was indignant at being called romantic (what really romantic person is not?) but she was used to keeping her indignation to herself—as a general thing—and said nothing.

Erfort and Fred took the chair in turn, but space will not allow me to give the result of the examinations.

It was a pleasant evening, in spite of the rather unfavorable beginning, and when the professor left them they all thanked him heartily for his kindness.

Garnet made them all laugh by asking him, gravely, what was the commercial value of her skull. He told them he had parts of more than one human head in bottles of alcohol in his office at home. Jessie made believe faint away at this, and after they had gone to their room she made Vera and Garnet barricade the door, for fear, as she said, that the professor would come in there and murder her in her sleep, for she was sure he had discovered, that night, that she had a remarkable head, and he would do his best to come into possession of it.

CHAPTER XXIV

"Say girls" said Jessie the next morning after prayers, "guess what I'm going to do."

"Have mercy upon us, Jessica," said Vera, "and don't make us guess this hot morning, but tell us at once."

"Well then, lazy-bones, I'm going down to 'Macy's' and look at that lovely amber set I saw there the other day."

"You'll only come back and have another crying spell because you can't have it," said Garnet. "I wouldn't go."

"Well, I will go; and I shan't come home and cry because I can't buy it either, I've got too much to be thankful for. But dear me! wouldn't I love to have it though. Wouldn't that pin look lovely in my hair? Yellow and black. Oh — h!" and Jessie sighed as she stood before the glass and put her hat on.

"You'll come with me, won't you, Allie? I shall want some one to tear me away."

"Of course I'll go. Will you go down to the Tower afterwards and watch the bathers?"

"Yes, I believe it is your turn to treat on soda to day, isn't it?"

"Jessie," said Garnet, "I wish you would bring me home a bag of that pop-corn that the little boys carry around down there; I think it is so nice."

"All right; I will, hand over the five cents."

"The idea! Can't you trust me until you get back?"

"No sir. You always forget when you owe me, and it hurts my feelings to remind you of it."

"It doesn't hurt them to ask me for it now, though. Well, here it is; and don't you eat up all the pop-corn before you get home."

Jessie made up a face, and waltzed out, followed by Allie.

"What shall we do all this forenoon, Net?" asked Vera. "I feel too lazy to move."

"So do I. I wish Jess could have that amber set — she wants it so badly. Poor little thing."

"Yes, I know. But oh Net, just think of poor little Robin."

"I know it, Vera. I am so glad we came down here this summer, and I am so glad that we have met with Charlotte Hood. I think I shall be a different girl when I go home. If I am not, I shall deserve to be punished."

"So shall I, Net. We have so much to be thankful for. Oh, I don't see how that woman has lived through all these years."

"She has had someone to help her, Vera," said Garnet, reverently. "And we can have the same One, if we will."

Garnet's face flushed as she said this, and so did Vera's as she heard it. They did not say much, but each understood the other.

"Let us take Him, will you, Net?"

Garnet put out her hand and clasped Vera's.

"Yes, Vera."

That was all; but that was all that was needed. Had Charlotte Hood lived and suffered in vain?

"I was thinking last night before I went to sleep, Net," said Vera — after a moment or two — "if there were no cure for little Robin."

Garnet started, then was all eager interest. "There must be, Vera. But —" and she looked very grave. "It would cost a great deal, and she is so poor."

"I know it, and we are not rich, by any means, and, most unromantically and unfortunately, have no rich relatives, but there must and will be some way in which we can help her."

"We might tell the folks of it at home — the girls, and all our acquaintances. I wonder how much it would cost."

"We will find out. Mrs. Hood is proud, but she isn't foolish, and if her little boy can only be made well — Oh, Net, what happiness for her and for us! I tell you what let's do. Let us bring it up before the Literary Society at our first meeting when we get home. Let us take the money we will make next winter, and instead of buying our new piano, let us give it towards making Robin a well boy. What do you say, Net?"

No need for Net to say anything. Her eyes are answer enough.

"We'll tell the girls when they come back from the beach, and the boys, this afternoon. They must know of some good doctor in Boston who would undertake the case."

When Jessie and Allie returned, about 12 o'clock, they found Vera and Garnet still in their room — their eyes very bright, and their cheeks very red. Jessie looked at them sharply, as she threw Net's bag of pop-corn into her lap.

"You girls look as though you were being roasted alive. Why don't you go out and get a breath of fresh air? But the sun *is* hot! Where is the 'Gloria water?' My nose is burnt to a crisp. Ah, thank you, Al. I'll bathe the injured member. Oh, Al and I have had such fun! I didn't buy the amber set, Net, so I am not bankrupt, but I did want it so I ached. There were as many as two hundred in bathing, this morning, wasn't there Al? and the band played beautifully. Oh, you ought to have seen the old fattie trying to learn to swim. I thought I should die! Two or three young men held him up, and you ought to have seen him kicking his fat legs around! More than half the time he was all under water — all we could see was his bald head bobbing up and down, and then all of a sudden he would pop up and splash about and almost knock the young men off their feet. And then, to cap all, I declare if he didn't try to dive off the raft. Ha, ha, ha! Oh, my sakes — I almost had a fit. I guess the inhabitants of the briny deep thought there was an earthquake when he struck the water. Ha, ha, ha!" and Jessie, who had been sitting on the foot-board, swinging her feet, leaned back to laugh, lost her balance and fell—heels over head, on to the bed, where she lay, laughing immoderately. The others laughed in sympathy, and then Allie said:

"You girls have been planning something, while Jess and I have been out. What is it?"

Vera told her. Jessie stopped laughing and sat up on the bed to listen, her eyes growing brighter and brighter, until by the time Vera stopped, they were like two stars. She clasped her hands, gave one very deep, long sigh and then sat very still, and all that the girls could get her to say was: "Let me alone. I'm thinking."

She went off by herself in the afternoon, and no one knew where she went, or what she was doing. The boys came at the usual time, and they all sat waiting for her on the piazza. Just as they were beginning to grow anxious, she appeared around the corner of the house, walking very slowly, and with a very clouded, troubled little face.

Fred was rash enough to say: "Well, what a forlorn-looking little thunder cloud!"

"Look out for the lightning," said Garnet, laughing.

"Would the lightning strike a cousin?" asked Fred, in a wheedling tone.

"No. It never strikes twice in the same place," said Jessie, but her smile was very weary.

Fred laughed. I know, and you have struck me pretty hard, eh? But I forgive you. Now, shall we start?"

"Yes," said Garnet. "We are a few minutes late."

Of course the girls had told Erfort and Fred about their plan, and they had been at once as eager to help as the girls could wish.

On their way to Mrs. Hood's they talked of nothing else, but no one, except Erfort, noticed how little Jessie had to say.

"Of course it will cost a big sum," said Fred; "but we will manage somehow to pay it. I will cheerfully promise to try and stop smoking cigars, and I won't go to the theatre more than three times during the winter. *That* money will go into the box with as much more as I can conscientiously give."

Fred felt amply repaid by the look Vera gave him.

"Well," remarked Erfort, "I know of a doctor who is just the one we want. I will see him. If any one can help Robin, he can. I expect his charges will be high, but I will do all that I can to help pay them."

He did not tell what he would do, but all felt that it would be no little thing.

"Net and I are going to give one-tenth of every month's salary," said Vera. "That will be just $4.80 apiece."

Jessie turned at this and looked at Vera and Garnet. "Are you, really?" she asked slowly.

"Yes," answered Vera. "And *then* we won't begin to pay the debt we owe Mrs. Hood."

Jessie looked puzzled for a moment, then understanding, she looked away with flushed cheeks. Allie walked between Vera and Garnet, and as she took an arm of each, gave it a loving little squeeze. Erfort looked pleased, and Fred broke down in the middle of "Comrades," that he had commenced to softly whistle.

"Father gives me $1.00 a week," said Allie. "I don't know what in the world I have always done with it, but I shall know after this."

All waited, but Jessie never spoke, and even Fred refrained from asking her what they all wanted to know.

When they reached Mrs. Hood's, all was very still. They went to the open door and listened. They heard the same pitiful moaning, and the same loving, caressing voice that they had heard on their first visit, and they stood and looked at each other with tearful eyes. Jessie sobbed outright, and so hard, that Garnet put her arms about her and tried to soothe her. Then Mrs. Hood stood before them in the doorway.

For the first time, they saw the calmness of that face broken up. It was quivering with untold suffering, and the blue eyes were full of tears. She put out her hands to them in a beseeching way.

"Oh, my boy is suffering so. It is terrible. Will you be displeased with me if I ask you not to come in? To-morrow, perhaps, but not to-day. Oh, it breaks my heart to see him."

Then she turned and went hurriedly back into the room, and our young people — knowing that the greatest kindness they could do her, although they longed to help her, would be to go away — turned their steps homeward.

Jessie stopped sobbing, after a little while, and walked quietly along with her arm drawn through Garnet's.

"Let's not go back to the cottage, said Vera, "let us walk along the beach."

They turned and went down to the beach. Everything was so bright, so gay, so beautiful! Children's voices came merrily up from the shore where they were playing. They thought of that other childish voice that so seldom uttered anything but moans, and their hearts were very sad. They sat down on the sand, silent and thoughtful. All at once Jessie startled them by saying vehemently:

"I want to tell you all what a mean little wretch I have been. I have been trying, all this afternoon, to make up my mind to give up one paltry winter's pleasure, for the sake of adding my mite towards helping that little angel who is suffering so terribly. Don't you hate me for it? I hate myself. Here I have lived seventeen happy, painless years, while that poor boy has had scarcely as many pain-less months, and now it has actually been a trial for me to relinquish one little pleasure for the sake of seeing him well and happy. Oh, I am such a miserable little sinner."

Down went the little dark head into Vera's lap and the sobbing commenced again. Vera smoothed the head tenderly.

"Don't cry, Jasmine," she said. "We are all miserable sinners. Tell us what your paltry pleas-ure is. We may not call it so."

"Why, it was only this. I have been trying to make up my mind to give the twenty-five dollars I have saved for my elocution this winter, towards the doctor's bill. Isn't that sinful and selfish and everything else that is bad? But I'll give it cheer-fully and freely, and only wish it were twice as much."

All were silent for a moment. Every one was touched, but perhaps Garnet was the only one who understood thoroughly, what Jessie was giving up. Her elocution was everything to her. She had placed great dependence on the following winter's course, and now to give it up for another year —

Garnet almost reverenced her little sister at that moment, and from that time she loved her and respected her as she never had done before and had almost been afraid she never would do.

After a little while they were more cheerful. It was impossible to see so much light-hearted carelessness around them and not catch the infection. At the end of an hour they were laughing and talking as usual, though not for one moment forgetting the suffering ones.

"Are you going to tell Professor Wild of your plan?" asked Erfort.

"A lot of good it would do to tell him," said Fred. scornfully. "I bet he's a stingy beggar. I don't like that man, He looks like a wife murderer."

They fairly shouted at this, and Fred looked slightly aggrieved.

"What are you laughing at? Didn't you ever hear of a wife-murderer?"

You'll have to christen him over again," said Erfort, "and call him "Blue Beard.'

"He may be one for all I know," said Fred lying back on the sand and pulling his cap over his eyes.

"We'll give him the benefit of the doubt anyway," said Erfort. "We won't exactly ask him to contribute, because he may think we'll skip over the line with it, but we'll tell him the story — or the principle part of it, and then he can do as he pleases about it."

"And that will be nothing, I'm thinking," muttered skeptical Fred. "We'll try anyway."

And they did, that very evening, sitting out on the piazza. Professor Wild listened, leaning back in his chair with his hands in his pockets. When Erfort finished, he said:

"I'm going home to-morrow. I can't tell how sorry I am to leave you all."

Then he stopped, and Fred, confident that he had judged the professor rightly, put out his foot and gave, or intended to give Erfort a suggestive kick, but instead, kicked his chair. He made no slight noise, and what was worse, the professor turned his head and looked down with a curious smile, just in time to catch sight of the hastily withdrawn foot.

"Confound the man," said Fred to himself. "He's always catching me."

The professor drew one hand out of his pocket and held it towards Erfort.

"There is a little towards helping on the good work," he said. "And here — taking a card from his card case — "is my address. If you need more money than you can raise, I hope you will not forget me. I'm not a rich man, but I will do what I can."

Although no one, not even Erfort himself, knew how large or how small the bill was that the professor had given, yet they thanked him heartily for his good will and kindness in giving even a little. Their gratitude pleased him, but very soon after, he said good-night and good-bye, and left them, and they have never seen him since, but you may be sure they will never forget him.

The girls crowded eagerly around Erfort.

" What did he give? Do let us see."

Erfort smoothed out the crumpled bill — ten dollars.

" Oh, isn't he splendid ! " " Isn't he kind ! " " I never will judge a man by his face again ! " " That serves me right for calling him ' Uriah Heep.' " " He's just as good as he can be ! "

Such were the very feminine expressions that were uttered by our girls, but Fred did not " die easily."

" Better see if it's a counterfeit, Er," he suggested, warily.

" It's a good one," assured Erfort.

Still Fred did not give up. " He's got an ugly temper, anyway. He proved that last night. Wasn't he as mad as a hatter because he couldn't mesmerize Vera ? "

" No one is perfect," said Vera, ashamed of her own ungenerous thoughts and feelings toward the professor. " And it seems to me that *you* are not in a very *angelic* temper this evening, Mr. Travers."

That almost broke Fred's heart. As soon as the others were talking, he drew Vera one side and asked her to go rowing with him. She wanted to go but said it was too late.

" No, it isn't," urged Fred. " It's only 8 o'clock, and we'll get back here by ten. Do come. People stay up all night down here."

"Why, what a story," said Vera.

" Well, pretty near, anyway," replied Fred, un-blushingly. " Won't you come, please ? "

Of course Vera went. Garnet, promising to sleep with one ear opened, was to unlock the bed-room door and let her in.

It was a beautiful moonlight night, and it was perfectly lovely on the water. They rowed around on the lake a little while, and then began to cast wistful looks across the channel to the ocean. A beautiful yacht that was going to take part in the race, the next day, lay at anchor, her lights twink-ling like so many eyes.

" Let us cross," said Fred, at last, unable to resist the temptation.

Vera longed, but hardly dared. At last she con-sented.

" But I must be back at 10 o'clock."

" Oh, we will — sure," said Fred, commencing to row with all his might.

He had on Vera's long cape, for he had worn only his tennis jacket, and as Vera had been row-ing, she had insisted on his putting her cape on. Both forgot all about the cape, and everything else, now, in their anxiety to cross the channel. But the tide was out, and only a narrow strip of water connected the little lake — (which is called " Sunset Lake ") with the ocean. There was barely room for the boat to pass through. It went from one side to the other, and, at last, stuck fast in the sand.

" Oh, mercy, what shall we do ! " cried Vera.

Fred grew excited. He was determined to accomplish what he had undertaken. He passed one oar to Vera, and stood up in the boat.

" There, you take that and push just as hard as you can with it, on that side," he said, " and I'll push on this."

Vera obeyed, but glancing up at Fred, she commenced to laugh until she could hardly stand. His bicycle cap was on the back of his head and twisted around so that the visor covered one ear. The moon shone on his face and showed clearly the determination, amounting almost to fierceness, upon it. To crown all, the long cape hung from his shoulders and made him appear seven feet tall. He was pushing on his oar with all his might. "Washington crossing the Delware," thought Vera, and was just going to speak her thought aloud, when, all at once, the boat gave way, under the force of Fred's oar, and the next thing Vera knew she was lying on her back on the bottom of the boat, with her hand over the side, still clinging weakly, but desperately, to her sinking oar.

"Hang on to that oar," shouted Fred, forgetting everything but the danger. And Vera, frightened at his voice, gave the oar a desperate wrench and drew it into the boat. The next minute they drifted into the ocean.

I shall not tell what Fred said as he lay at her feet, wrapped in her cape, and she rowed him up and down the silvery path that the moon made on the water, but she looked across at the twinkling eyes of the beautiful yacht, and she said "that she had known him only two weeks, and she was sure that he did not know his own mind. Of course, she couldn't know hers in that short time. No, she was not displeased, but she could not promise anything."

There must have been something more encouraging in her looks than in her words, for Fred did not appear a bit cast down. He fervently assured her that he loved her just as much at the end of two weeks as though he had known her two years. But Vera stopped him and ordered him back to his own end of the boat. It was late and they must go home. She would row and he must steer.

Fred obeyed; but when he felt for the rope, there was no rope there. "We've lost the rudder!" he exclaimed.

"Dear, dear!" said Vera. "What shall we do?"

"Oh, we'll find it. It must have stuck in the sand,"

And so it had. They saw it gleaming white on the spot where they had had their brief excitement. They had no difficulty in getting back, for the tide was going in and they drifted across with it.

Vera crept softly up the stairs, after bidding Fred a little longer " Good-Night " than usual. It was 10.30, but she trusted to Garnet's " keeping one ear open." She took hold of the knob and turned it softly, then listened. Not a sound. She tried again, a little louder. No sound. She dropped softly down on her knees. " Net," she whispered through the keyhole. No answer. " Net," a little louder, this time. Still no answer. " Net." It was spoken aloud, this time, and accompanied by a gentle rattle of the door-knob. Still not a sound.

Then Vera grew desperate. She put her mouth close to the key-hole, and repeated aloud, and in order : " Net ! Allie ! Jess ! Jess ! Allie ! Net ! " accompanying each call with a vigorous rattling of the knob, regardless of all consequences.

All at once she heard a bed squeak, as though some one turned in it suddenly, and a loud sigh (very suggestive) seemed breathed right into her ear. Horrors ! It came from the professor's room, and seemed to be given as a gentle hint that he was awake and could hear her.

Vera scrambled to her feet. What should she do. She must not call again. Oh, those heartless girls! How could they sleep so soundly! Just then she happened to think of a room at the left of theirs. It was not occupied, but would be the next day. She went in and closed the door, but did not lock it. There were no clothes on the bed, but there were pillows, without, however, any cases. "Good thing it is a warm night," thought Vera. "I'll just wrap my cape around me and I'll be all right. I won't close the door tight — the girls may waken before me."

It seemed to Vera, that she had but just fallen asleep, when she felt something come down upon her — soft, but by no means light. Then she felt two arms about her neck, and then a little wet face pressed against hers, and then two soft lips, kissing hers, and then the dearest voice murmur, "Oh, you darling; you darling;" and then the voice cried out: "Girls, girls, she's in here. Come, quick!"

Vera has just time to open her eyes and see that Garnet was doing her best to smother her, and that she (Garnet) had on her sailor hat and red shawl. The sailor hat was on the back of her head, and bent out of all shape, and no wonder. Then two more figures burst into the room and threw themselves on the bed, and poor Vera was in a fair way of meeting death by strangulation.

Well, the explanations were given in due season, intermingled with many hugs, kisses and expres-

sions of deepest regret on the girls' part, and of
assurances of forgiveness on Vera's. Not one of
them had heard Vera when she had come the night
before. Garnet had been the first to waken that
morning, and not finding Vera beside her, had
been dreadfully frightened, fearing that she and
Fred had been drowned. She had dsessed as
rapidly as her trembling hands would allow her,
not calling the girls, feeling that they would be but
little help, but determining to go down to the
"Wesley House" and call for Erfort. But before
she had left the room she had knelt beside her bed
and prayed to God to go with her and help her,
and then she had cried and the girls had heard her
and she had had to tell them, and they were almost
wild, just as she had known they would be. The
professor had gone to breakfast, for his door was
open, but as she had passed the room where
Vera was, she had happened to glance in (" not
happened." Garnet corrected herself. " God *told*
her to look in,") and then she had caught sight of
Vera's cape, and she had known it, and then —

"I know the rest," interrupted Vera. "No need
of telling me the rest of it."

Then there was another spell of hugging and
kissing, and then Garnet's nature asserted itself.
" Let's celebrate the joyful event by getting our
breakfast at the restaurant."

" Spoken wisely and well," quoth Jessie, and
they went to prepare for it amidst much rejoicing.

CHAPTER XXV

That afternoon, a trifle earlier than usual, our young people walked to Mrs. Hood's, but they were again met at the door by Mrs. Hood, who told them that little Robin was no better. She was very calm, outwardly, but they saw that she was putting a great restraint upon herself. She looked very pale and very tired: they knew that she must be terribly worried, not only about her boy, but about her work. Erfort surprised them all by asking:

"Are you alone here with him night and day, Mrs. Hood?"

"Yes," she answered.

"Then I will come up after supper, and stay with you all night."

They saw how her eyes filled with tears and how her lips trembled so that she could not speak. Vera spoke next.

"And won't you please let me stay until Mr. Richards comes?"

Well, the end of it was, that during the next week — the last one they spent at Cottage City — the young people took turns staying at the cottage with Mrs. Hood. Vera would go down one morning and stay the forenoon, Garnet would take her place in the afternoon. Allie would go down the next morning, Jessie in the afternoon. Fred and Erfort divided the nights between them.

So that night that Professor Wild had said good-bye to them on the piazza, was the last night, except the very last one of all, that they all spent together. Anyway, more lodgers had come — the little parlor was taken — no more cocoa drinkings took place — and the evenings were spent either on the piazza, or down on the beach, or at the concert, but there was always one of their number missing.

Did those young people have the least idea when they started for the beautiful little summer resort happy, light-hearted, careless and gay — that their last week there would be spent in a sick room, watching such agony that their young eyes had never beheld before, and that they had never dreamed could be borne, and that, by one so young, so frail, as little Robin? But the lessons they learned by that bed-side, will last them through their lives.

First it would be Vera's fair face framed in a halo of golden hair, with the proud lines all smoothed away, bending over the white, suffering child's face; then Garnet's, with its rich coloring, and the head covered with its dark curls; then Allie's pale, tranquil one; then Jessie's, with some of the brilliancy and the sparkle gone, but with the loveliest, tenderest light in the glorious eyes. Then, at night when the lamp was burning, and the pain was almost unendurable, Robin would feel his little tortured body lifted by arms that were young and strong, and his eyes would open, sometimes on a fair, handsome face, with blue eyes and clustering brown curls, and sometimes on a dark, grave one, with a noble brow and tender, dark eyes. He would know then all, and would almost break their hearts, by trying to smile up in their faces and thanking them in a weak little voice, but the smile would change to a spasm of pain and the voice to a moan.

So the days and nights passed, until the last one came, and found Robin lying on his bed, white as a snow-drift, but, for the time, free from pain. They were all there with him, sitting in their accustomed places — for the last time. The night before, Erfort had spoken to Mrs. Hood about their plan, and he had been more surprised than he could tell, when she had sunk down in the kitchen rocker, buried her face in her hands, and sobbed as though her heart would break.

But it was all settled now, and as she sat in their midst this afternoon, it seemed as though she could scarcely take her eyes from their faces. They had been speaking about it, just a little, and Jessie expressed the wish of all, when she said in her old, impulsive fashion:

"Now, Mrs. Hood, *please* don't spoil it all by saying you will accept our little gift on one condition : — That you will pay it back to us some day. It will take all the good away if you do. Let our first effort to do a little good, be as successful as it can possibly be. Besides, you will not owe us anything ; we are only paying our debt."

And then Jessie had stopped, her face all one rich color.

Mrs. Hood had looked a little surprised at first, but only for a minute, then she had understood and her heart was so full that she could only kiss each one silently and then sit back in her chair and they had heard her say softly : "For *thy* dear sake, Lord."

And now they were waiting to hear the last chapter that had been written, from the book of her life. She told it in a very few words. It seemed as though her heart was so full that she could not bear to talk much.

"After that night, when I had my dream I was very sick with brain fever. Was it any wonder ? And when, after many weeks, I rose from the bed, I was a different woman. Mr. Hood was very kind to me, and at the end of a year I married him. I united with the Baptist Church, and I tried, earnestly and faithfully, to lead a true, christian life. I felt that I owed my Saviour for all those wasted years. It was sweet to trust Him ; it took all care from me. I slipped back many times, but His hand was always held down to me, and all I had to do was to reach up and take it. It is true that "if we reach up as high as we can, God will reach down all the rest of the way." For the first time I realized what blessing there was in:

> " The peace that suffers and is strong,
>   Trusts where it cannot see,
> Deems not the trial way too long,
>   And leaves the rest with Thee."

I am still trusting in Jesus. He grows more and more precious to me every day. I know what it is to try to live without Him, and I know what it is to live with Him. I do not care how happy any-one may seem to be, there is no real happiness out of Christ. I truly know what it means to say that *Jesus satisfies*. I thank God for the feeling of rest and peace that is daily growing deeper and deeper in my heart. The thought of Jesus and His saving love is very precious to me. It is something that will go with me through the remainder of this life — strengthening and upholding me — and it will go with me into the life beyond, even through the 'Valley of the Shadows.' Oh, I know — we all know our short-comings. We all know that our hasty tempers often get the better of us, that too often there are angry thoughts and feelings in our hearts, that too often we weakly yield to temptation — but God knows it all. He knows the cause of everything, and He knows the hard heart-struggles to overcome. We cannot deceive Him. We may deceive the whole world, but He knows whether we are sincere or not, and He alone will judge us. To Him alone will we be responsible. Isn't it a comforting thought that He who knows us as we are will be the One to judge us. If we can only carry some little gift to Him — something to prove that we have tried to do His will — that we have tried to work for Him, won't it be blessed to hear Him say: 'Well done, thou good and faithful servant?' Isn't that a happiness worth striving for? Love Him, trust Him, be faithful in the few things, and He will make you ruler over many. * * * One more little girl was given to me, but scarcely could she say the word 'Mamma,' before she went to live with her little sisters in Heaven. I could bow my head over *her* little face, as it lay on its white satin pillow, and say, from my heart, 'Thy will be done.' Two months before Robin was born, Mr. Hood died. He took a severe cold and it resulted in quick consumption. I shall never forget how he looked at me as I sat beside him the night before he passed away. I had my head resting on the pillow beside his, and he stroked my hair and said: 'I shall not be afraid to leave you now, Lottie, for I know you will come to me some day. What a happy

reunion there will be!'   Oh, it *will* be a happy
reunion — a glorious time.   Robin was born, I gave
him all the love that a hungry, lonely mother's
heart could realize, and as he grew and I saw my
brother Jo living again in him, I loved him more
and more.   I called him Robin Johial.   One summer when he was about four years old, I took him
to the Cape on a visit to Hannah, and it was then
that he received his terrible injury.   We went on
board a vessel belonging to Hannah's brother-in-
law.   Robin fell down the cabin stairs, and — you
know the rest.   Oh, it was hard, and I could not
help asking, 'Lord, how long?'   But sometime I
shall know why such troubles have been sent to me.

" Sometime, when all life's lessons have been learned,
    And sun and stars forevermore have set,
The things which our weak judgments here have spurned,
    The things o'er which we grieved with lashes wet
Will flash before us out of life's dark night
    As stars shine most in deeper tints of blue ;
And we shall see how all God's plans are right ;
    And how what seemed reproof, was love most true.

"And we shall see how, while we frown and sigh,
    God's plans go on as best for you and me ;
How, when we called, he heeded not our cry,
    Because his wisdom to the end could see.
And even as wise parents disallow
    Too much of sweet to craving babyhood,
So God, perhaps, is keeping from us now,
    Life's sweetest things because it seemeth good.

"And if, sometimes, commingled with life's wine,
  We find the wormwood and repel and shrink,
Be sure a wiser hand than yours or mine
  Pours out this portion for our lips to drink;
And if some friend we love is lying low,
  Where human kisses cannot reach his face,
Oh, do not blame the loving Father so,
  But wear your sorrow with obedient grace.

"And you shall shortly know that lengthened breath
  Is not the sweetest gift God sends his friend,
And that, sometime, the sable pall of death
  Conceals the fairest boon his love can send.
If we could push ajar the gates of life,
  And stand within, and all God's workings see,
We could interpret all this doubt and strife,
  And for each mystery could find a key.

"But not to-day.   Then be content, poor heart!
  God's plans, like lillies, pure and white unfold,
We must not tear the close shut leaves apart,
  Time will reveal the calyxes of gold;
And if, through patient toil, we reach the land,
  Where tired feet, with sandals loosed, may rest,
When we shall clearly see and understand,
  I think that we will say, 'God knew the best.'"

Mrs. Hood paused, and Jessie said:
  "Oh, Mrs. Hood, how *can* you endure it?"
Mrs. Hood smiled.   "*He* knows, Jessie, and I
am so glad that He does know and that he pities
us even as a father pitieth his children.   I do not

like to think of God as being a stern, condemning
judge, but as a loving, pitying, merciful Father —
One to whom we can go in our trouble and distress,
go to Him just as we are in all our sin, and ask
Him to help us and forgive us. I know there is
danger of our taking advantage of His willingness
to forgive, but we ought not to do that, and if we
think of all His tender love for us, and all His
patient goodness, we will not do it. But it is blessed
to me to have the assurance of His great love, and
His forgiveness *is* the assurance."

"Mrs. Hood," said Erfort, "do you really think
that Heaven is like the place you dreamed of?"

"I am *sure* it is. I love to think of its being so."

"When do you think it is too late to repent?"
asked Vera.

"Not until the breath leaves your body. But it
always seems to me that such a repentance is an
insult to God. It is dreadful for one to give his
whole life to the world, and only a few paltry, miserable minutes — and those his last — to God."

"But you don't think such persons go straight
to Heaven?" said Fred.

"No, I do not. It doesn't seem to me that they
ought to. Not that I begrudge them the happiness, but they ought to do their part of the great
work while on earth. I may be wrong. I dare
say most ministers would pronounce such theory
heretical, but I am jealous for God. I want to see

Him worshipped and served by every one for whom He gave His dear life."

There was little more talk after that. Jessie asked the same old question :

"Do you think dancing and the theatre are wrong ?"

And Mrs. Hood shamed her — although unintentionally — by smiling brightly and saying :

"Every one must answer that question according to his own conscience. I can only answer for myself. I have never had the least desire to indulge in such pleasures since I entered the christian life. But I *do* think, when a person feels in his heart that he ought not to do such things and *does* them, then he commits a sin, but if he truly thinks there is no harm in them, then there can be no harm in his doing them. But we have no right to judge *any* one."

"And haven't you danced or gone to the theatre since — since you had that dream ?" asked Jessie, with big eyes.

Mrs. Hood smiled. "No, not once."

Jessie drew a long breath. "My ! But you have been good."

Mrs. Hood could not help laughing. "Not at all Jessie. Don't you know I said I have never had the least *desire* to go ? Then there has never been any virtue in my staying away, for I have never been tempted. There is no virtue where there is no temptation."

After a few moments more our young people rose to go. It was a hard parting, but they all looked eagerly forward to the glad, happy meeting in the fall. At last they were on their way to the cottage. They talked a little while at the gate, then the boys left them, but they came again, after supper, and spent the evening with the girls, on the piazza.

The next morning at 8.30, the trunks were standing in the room, packed, locked, and strapped, and the girls stood, pulling on their gloves and looking around the dear room with dim eyes. What happy hours they had spent there!

A knock sounded on the door — a timid, uncertain knock, and all smiled as they called together: "Come in!" The door opened and there stood 'Mother,' with the pretty blue morning cap on, that the girls had given her the night before, tears in her dim blue eyes, and her hands full of books. 'Grandpa' appeared in the background, the girls' present, a black silk handkerchief, clasped in his shaking hand.

"My dear children," said 'Mother,' and her voice trembled more than they had ever heard it before, "I can't tell ye how sorry me and Mr. Atherton are to lose ye. We shall miss hearing ye laughing and singing, and running up and down the stairs, but we shall never forget ye and will pray for ye every night. Here is something for ye to remember us by," and she put into the hands of each a neat black testament.

The girls opened them and saw their names written in a trembling, shaking hand, and under the name was written in each: "From Grandpa and Grandma Atherton."

'Mother' put her hand out and commenced to force 'Grandpa' gently out of the room, but the girls ran forward, and, putting their arms around first 'Mother's' and then 'Grandpa's' neck, thanked them and kissed them until 'Mother's' new cap fell off and 'Grandpa's' spectacles were slipped down on the extreme end of his nose.

Then the man came for the trunks, last good-byes were said, and the girls ran down the stairs, through the little parlor, down the walk, and out through the gate, where they stopped and looked up to the balcony. 'Mother' and 'Grandpa' stood there, his left hand clasping her's, as it rested on his arm, her right shading her dim blue eyes, as she looked after the girls.

And so they passed from their sight, and the next time their eyes will look upon them will be in a better world than this, where none ever grow old, and where friends never part from friends.

CHAPTER XXVI

It has been accorded authors the privilege of adding any number of years to their heroes' and heroines' lives, that they find most convenient. I will take advantage of the privilege and add the number of five years to the lives of my young people, and even they will pardon me, I think, when they can see what pleasure I can give my readers by doing so.

I want you to come with me to a house on S— street, in the city of Pawtucket, R. I. We have reached the house, rung the bell, and been conducted up the stairs by a young man whom we have certainly seen before. He stops on the first landing and looks back at us. The light from the upper hall-lamp shines full upon him. We give an exclamation of delight. We know that fair, handsome face, with its dark blue eyes and curly brown hair, although the "faint apology" of five years ago on the upper lip, has grown into a handsome drooping mustache, with just enough curl in the ends to make it "too lovely for anything;" so his wife says.

Fred Travers? Yes, of course it is he. He is in evening dress and wears a red pink in his buttonhole. We ask him no questions, but follow where he leads, which is to a room on the right of the hall, into which he bows us and closes the door upon us.

But we are not in the least dismayed for there are plenty of other ladies there, all doing what we proceed to do, *i. e.*, take our wraps off, shake out our trains, go up to one of the mirrors, pat and smooth and gently pull out our curled bangs, fasten the roses and lilies among the lace on our bosoms, and then stand one side to make room for those who are just entering, and talk and laugh and ask each other "if our train hangs right," and, "*will* you please fasten that hateful little lock to my back hair? it *won't* stay where it belongs," and, "*will* you please tell me if you think my flowers are pinned too high up on the shoulder? Do you think they would look better at the left side?" To all these questions we receive the flattering answers: "Your train hangs perfectly lovely." "That lock looks too cute for anything — don't touch it." "Your flowers look just right — they are lovely." Answers which our vain hearts had expected to receive and which would have been disappointed if they had *not* received.

But as we look around we do not see one face that is familiar to us. All bright, fair, girlish and sweet, but not one familiar one. At last the door opens and a voice says: "Now, ladies; Prepare!"

There are little flutters of excitement. Bright eyes grow brighter; pink cheeks deepen into red, as one by one each in turn take the arm of an usher and disappear from the room. There are quite a number in the room, and there are only two ushers, so it takes some little time. At last, as all leave the room but you and I, a door that we have not noticed before, opens, and — surely that is no stranger who comes toward us! See if you recognize her. A tall, slender figure; a fair face; large gray eyes; a crown of golden hair. She has on a beautiful dress of pearl-gray lansdowne. It is fastened at the front with a huge bunch of bright red carnations. Who is she?

Now we look at another figure that follows the pearl-gray one. A little figure in a pale yellow satin, with the scarlet salvia twined in a wreath and resting on the dark curls. A little face, richly colored, and large black eyes. Who is she?

Still another figure. A quiet figure in a pale blue cashmere, with lilies of the valley nestling in the smooth brown braids. A pale, tranquil face with dark blue eyes. Who is she?

One more figure. It is dressed in a gown of dove-color silk, soft and shimmering. The face is pale and spiritual looking; the eyes large and blue with a wonderful light in them. The hair, once a light brown, now silvery white. The hair is all that is strange to us. Who is she?

We wait a few moments for one who has not come and whom we long to see. We miss the brilliant little face, and the ringing, girlish voice, but we wait in vain.

Listen.

"Oh, Vera, you look for all the world like a bride yourself."

"And why shouldn't I? My wedding dress is only three years old."

(So Vera is married then? Why yes; didn't I say that Fred's wife says — you know what, about his mustache). "Don't you wish it were you, Allie, who was going to be the centre of attraction to-night?"

"Oh no, Net. Father couldn't get along without his housekeeper."

"And Net won't get married until she meets with a second Emerson. What was it the professor said, Net?"

"Stop your nonsense. We will shock Mrs. Hood."

"Not at all, my dears. I am too happy to-night to be shocked."

The door opens. Vera starts forward.

"Oh, Fred, your pink is falling out. Let me fix it."

Fred stands obediently still, but there is an anxious look on his face, which cannot be brought there by a drooping flower.

"Vera, *do* you suppose Marjorie will be frightened?" he asks.

Who is Marjorie? We see Mrs. Hood's tremulous smile at the sound of the name.

"No, of course not, Fred. She is too much like her papa, to be easily frightened."

The proud, paternal look on Fred's face, tells us plainly who "papa" is, So they have a little girl! Will wonders never cease?

"Mr. Vincent has come, and they are all going through with a final rehearsal in the other room, so you had better be escorted to the parlors now," says Fred.

No one notices us, so lets you and I go too.

What pretty rooms! There is an arch of smilax and white flowers. It looks as though it were intended for some one to stand under. What is Vera seating herself at the piano for? A hush settles upon the room. Even the fans are motionless. The first chords are struck. We look up. Here comes a form we have certainly never seen before. A tall, slender, but strong young form. The face is fair and beautiful as a picture, the eyes large, blue and thoughtful. The hair lies upon the broad, white forehead in loose, golden curls. He looks like a young prince, in his evening suit, with the one white rose bud in the button-hole. His eyes scan the faces before him quickly and eagerly. They rest upon one face and a tender light creeps

into them. We follow his glance and we see that
it is the face that is framed in silvery-white hair
that his eyes rest upon. Do you know who he is?

After him walks a tiny figure that makes everyone smile. It walks along in such a sedate, dignified manner. The little form is covered with a
dress of white silk. Lovely golden curls cluster
in the dimpled, white neck. The large gray eyes
shine like two stars out of the small pink and white
face. The tiny hands grasp a large bouquet of
orange-blossoms. A wee maid of honor! Is she
frightened? Not a bit. Two-year-old Marjorie is
a brave little lady.

Next comes — well, did you ever, in all your
life, see a more charming bride! A lovely white
silk dress, covered, but not hidden, by a beautiful
bridal veil. A small head with a wreath of orange-
blossoms resting on the heavy, dark braids. Eyes
that we know full well by the way they flash and
shine. But what makes the small face look so
pale? Where is all its brilliant color? We hear
Garnet whisper to Allie: "The poor child is
frightened half out of her wits." Isn't the speech
characteristic? We know the one who walks beside her, and on whose arm she is so trustingly
leaning. The dark face is scarcely changed.
The eyes are just as tender and dreamy as when
we first saw them five years ago. He is one with
whom we can safely trust our little girl, for

every look the dark eyes give her are full of a deep, abiding love.

Really, I am so confused that all the words I hear, are : " Erfort Merlin Richards, Jessie Isabel Dare, I pronounce you man and wife." But then, they are the most important ones after all.

Will you please excuse me if I omit the congratulations and the supper, and the talking and laughing, and everything else ? They are only a very small consideration anyway. And at what better time could I leave my young people than at this most joyful of all joyful occasions, when they are all together, and oh, so happy ! In as few words as I can possibly cut it down to, let me tell how the noble plan was carried on and out.

Erfort was true to his promise, and held an interview with Dr. C. —, one of Boston's leading physicians. His price was almost startling — $500. But our young people were determined. Mrs. Hood and Robin were taken to Boston. They had a private room in the great hospital. Two years passed slowly by, and one day, at the end of the two years, our girls started for Boston, Vera carrying the same "bank" that she had carried to Cottage City, but now it was a bank in earnest, for it contained the big sum of $500. I wish you could have seen them as they drew near Boston. It would be hard to tell which pair of eyes was the brightest. They had worked hard and denied themselves, but they were going to their reward.

The boys met them at the station. Considering that Fred and Vera were to be married the following week, we must not be surprised at his taking such complete possession of her the moment she stepped from the train. They all took the car for the hospital. Upon reaching there, they were shown into a small room and the door closed. Soon the door opened again and on the threshold stood — well, the happiest mother that day in Boston, for she was leaning on the arm of her boy, and that boy was as tall, as well, and as strong as any boy of his age in that city. Was it any wonder that the girls stood and stared, and couldn't speak one word? Although only twelve years old, Robin looked almost a man to them.

Well, of course there was a vast amount of hugging and kissing, and then the door opened again and the great doctor stood before them. But what a kind face he had, and in what a fatherly manner he put his arm across Robin's shoulders!

Jessie stepped forward with the roll of bills in her hand. She had prepared a very neat, dignified speech on her way up in the train, but she couldn't think of a single word of it now, and she just stood, looking up in his face with her big eyes, and the bills held out to him.

He took them and counted them. $500, he said.

Then he stopped and looked down on her with a smile.

Of course Mrs. Hood had told him the whole story, but even she was not prepared for what he then did. He counted out just half the amount and handed it back to Jessie.

" There is *my* part towards the good work. I cannot let you young people — and especially a little girl like you — get ahead of me."

Everyone was stupefied, but they all felt like applauding Jessie, when, without a word, she walked straight up to Mrs. Hood and pushed the money into her hands.

You can guess the rest. During the next three years matters progressed rapidly. Dr. C. — proved himself a good man, indeed. His wife was, in every sense of the word, his " help-meet." Mrs. Hood found employment as a seamstress among their friends, or that is, the doctor and his wife found it for her — Robin was sent to the public school, and for the first time since her child-hood days, Charlotte Hood's life was comparatively free from worry, and care and trouble.

Nothing to do but Jessie must have Robin for " best-man " at her wedding, and you may be sure Robin was only too glad to oblige her.

Mr. and Mrs. Richard's home, as well as Mr. and Mrs. Travers', is very near to Mrs. Hood's, and if you should call at either of the three houses and the lady of the house should not be at home, just go to the other two houses and you will find her at one of them.

I suppose, before many years, the plate on Mrs. Hood's door will bear the name: " Dr. R. J. Hood," and who can doubt that, with such a physician as Dr. C — to help, advise and teach him, Robin will be one of the leading physicians of Boston, some day. He has made np his mind to make all diseases of the spine his special study. If he were to live to be one hundred years old, he could never forget the pain he suffered — child though he was; and he will do all in his power to alleviate the sufferings of all who are afflicted, even as he was.

With such a mother to love and cheer, such a friend as Dr. C — to help and advise, and, above all, such a Father in Heaven to guide, strengthen and protect, who can doubt his success ?

THE END.

THE END